THE GERRY MULLIGAN 1950S QUARTETS

OXFORD STUDIES IN RECORDED JAZZ

Series Editor JEREMY BARHAM

Louis Armstrong's Hot Five and Hot Seven Recordings
Brian Harker

The Studio Recordings of the Miles Davis Quintet, 1963–68
Keith Waters

Benny Goodman's Famous 1938 Carnegie Hall Jazz Concert
Catherine Tackley

Keith Jarrett's The Köln Concert
Peter Elsdon

Thelonious Monk Quartet with John Coltrane at Carnegie Hall
Gabriel Solis

Pat Metheny: The ECM Years, 1975–1984
Mervyn Cooke

The Recordings of Andy Kirk and His Clouds of Joy
George Burrows

Dave Brubeck's Time Out
Stephen A. Crist

The Gerry Mulligan 1950s Quartets
Alyn Shipton

THE GERRY MULLIGAN 1950S QUARTETS

ALYN SHIPTON

Oxford University Press is a department of the University of Oxford. It furthers the University's objective of excellence in research, scholarship, and education by publishing worldwide. Oxford is a registered trade mark of Oxford University Press in the UK and certain other countries.

Published in the United States of America by Oxford University Press
198 Madison Avenue, New York, NY 10016, United States of America.

Library of Congress Cataloging-in-Publication Data
Names: Shipton, Alyn, author.
Title: The Gerry Mulligan 1950s quartets / Alyn Shipton.
Description: [01.] | New York, NY : Oxford University Press, 2023. |
Series: Oxford studies in recorded jazz | Includes bibliographical references and index.
Identifiers: LCCN 2022058189 (print) | LCCN 2022058190 (ebook) |
ISBN 9780197579763 (paperback) | ISBN 9780197579756 (hardcover) |
ISBN 9780197579787 (epub) | ISBN 9780197579794
Subjects: LCSH: Mulligan, Gerry. | Mulligan, Gerry—Discography. | Gerry Mulligan Quartet. | Jazz musicians—United States—Biography. | Composers—United States—Biography. | Saxophonists—United States—Biography. | Jazz—1951-1960—History and criticism. | Jazz—1961-1970—History and criticism. | LCGFT: Biographies.
Classification: LCC ML419.M79 S55 2023 (print) | LCC ML419.M79 (ebook) |
DDC 788.7/165092 [B]—dc23/eng/20221212
LC record available at https://lccn.loc.gov/2022058189
LC ebook record available at https://lccn.loc.gov/2022058190

DOI: 10.1093/oso/9780197579756.001.0001

Paperback printed by CPI Group (UK) Ltd, Croydon CR0 4YY
Hardback printed by Bridgeport National Bindery, Inc., United States of America

SERIES PREFACE

The Oxford Studies in Recorded Jazz series offers detailed historical, cultural, and technical analysis of jazz recordings across a broad spectrum of styles, periods, performing media, and nationalities. Each volume, authored by a leading scholar in the field, addresses either a single jazz album or a set of related recordings by one artist/group, placing the recordings fully in their historical and musical context, and thereby enriching our understanding of their cultural and creative significance.

With access to the latest scholarship and with an innovative and balanced approach to its subject matter, the series offers fresh perspectives on both well-known and neglected jazz repertoire. It sets out to renew musical debate in jazz scholarship, and to develop the subtle critical languages and vocabularies necessary to do full justice to the complex expressive, structural, and cultural dimensions of recorded jazz performance.

Jeremy Barham
University of Surrey
Series Editor

PREFACE

THE FIRST GERRY Mulligan "pianoless" quartet was formed in California in 1952 and it marked a significant departure from what had been the standard instrumentation of jazz ensembles since the dawn of the music, in which a chordal instrument generally supplied a group's harmonic basis. There had been other isolated experiments in playing without chords, but Mulligan's group defined a method in which trumpet (later trombone or alto saxophone), baritone saxophone, bass, and drums supplied all the necessary ingredients for a harmonically satisfying performance. Yet although there have been (to date) three biographical surveys of Mulligan's work,[1] this period of what was arguably his greatest innovation and lasting influence has not been covered in the detail it deserves. Elsewhere, in many of the more general studies of postwar jazz, the quartet is often given brief and inappropriate labels such as "West Coast cool."

Each book in this series sets out to place a set of "recordings fully in their historical and musical context, . . . thereby enriching our understanding of their cultural and creative significance."[2] As a biographer

1 Horricks, Raymond: *Gerry Mulligan's Ark* (London, Apollo, 1986); Klinkowitz, Jerome: *Listen: Gerry Mulligan—An Aural Narrative in Jazz* (New York, Schirmer, 1991); and Josephson, Sanford: *Jeru's Journey* (Milwaukee, Hal Leonard, 2015). A fourth biography, Mulligan, Gerry and Poston, Ken: *Being Gerry Mulligan: My Life in Music* (Lanham, MD, Backbeat, 2023), had not appeared at the time of writing, although I have referred to some of its source material from the Library of Congress collection, and this is credited in footnotes.

2 Barham, Jeremy: "Series Preface" (Oxford Studies in Recorded Jazz).

and oral historian, I have attempted to look at Mulligan's 1950s quartets (and his related larger ensembles) through the prism of interviews with many of the participants, ranging from musicians to record producers and observers, and also to see how contemporary commentators in the press of the time reacted to the music. A comprehensive sweep through newspaper and magazine reports has also helped to establish a detailed chronology for the development of the quartet. I have also attempted to outline key events in Mulligan's life that affected and influenced the course of his music.

At the same time, in keeping with other books in the series, I have included numerous music examples. These begin by tracing Mulligan's background as a big band arranger, and show how he transferred those skills via smaller groups (notably the Miles Davis nonet of 1949–1950) into what became the quartet. He often revisited earlier repertoire and compositions in the process, but developed his writing and playing in equal measure as he progressed through the 1950s, culminating in his 1962 quartet, ten years on from the original band.

The musical template of the quartet and its approach—often described as contrapuntal—is explored in detail, both in terms of how it offered a considerable degree of harmonic freedom, and how it served as a starting point for significant aspects of Mulligan's larger groups, notably the Sextet of the mid-1950s, and the Concert Jazz Band, launched in 1960.

I have been fascinated by Mulligan's playing, writing, and bandleading since my schooldays. In November 1995, I was in New York, conducting a series of interviews with musicians for the BBC, and it had been arranged for me to meet Gerry Mulligan when he returned from a Caribbean cruise on the SS *Norway*, on which he had been playing with his quartet. Sadly, that meeting did not take place as we learned that he was not at all well, and after playing his last concert on November 9, he headed straight home. I was fortunate enough subsequently to speak with members of his band including pianists Ted Rosenthal and Bill Mays, who had both played with him on that cruise. Sadly, Mulligan did not recover and died on January 20, 1996. A little later, I was privileged to be asked to write the liner note for his *Final Recordings* (Telarc CD 83517) but during the process of listening to all that material I was downhearted that the fates had prevented me from meeting and talking to a musician I had admired for so long.

In 2002 I was commissioned to make a four-part series for BBC Radio 3 that explored Mulligan's music, and this gave me the opportunity to meet with fellow musicians and associates from all periods of his career. I was particularly grateful for the participation of his widow

Franca Mulligan, who opened doors for me in the Mulligan world, and also consented to be interviewed herself. Fortunately, as we worked on the programs, my producer Felix Carey (and his colleague from the BBC World Service, Oliver Jones) gave me time to have extended conversations with most of those interviewees, going way beyond what we needed for the broadcasts. Some of the material in this book was included in the series, but many of the interview segments appear here for the first time.

My fellow critic and broadcaster Charles Fox (who died in 1991) knew of my interest in Mulligan and kindly gave me a transcript of a long conversation he had with him at the time of his visit to Scotland in 1988. This has been an invaluable guide through the music, and also ensures that his voice is represented here along with those of his colleagues. Gordon Jack was fortunate enough to talk to Mulligan, and to several of the members of the 1950s quartet. On a number of subjects, his interviews dovetail with mine. He also had a conversation with Arlyne Mulligan, Gerry's wife from 1953 until they divorced in 1959, which gives a most helpful additional perspective.

Although he is also mentioned in the acknowledgments, I would especially like to single out bassist Bill Crow for his help, not only in interviews, on both sides of the Atlantic, but in being a willing and informative correspondent on many matters of detail, as well as kindly providing pictures from his collection.

I hope that as well as presenting a clear chronological account of Mulligan's work from the mid-1940s until 1962, and investigating some of his music in detail, this book will be accessible to non-specialist readers who wish to know more about this remarkable musician. Nonetheless I also hope that specialists will benefit from the transcriptions and examples, which are largely the work of my long-term colleague in the Buck Clayton Legacy Band, Adrian Fry, who undertook the music setting. We have adopted the convention of using concert pitch throughout, in the hope that this makes the harmonies more accessible and easier for a reader to assimilate or play over on the piano. The scores (with a couple of minor exceptions) follow the standard system of instrumental layout, with reeds at the top, then as we move down, trumpets, trombones, and other lower brass. The rhythm section is shown at the bottom.

For much of the 1950s, Mulligan's bands were racially mixed, as was Miles Davis's nonet of 1949–1950 for which Mulligan arranged and in which he played baritone saxophone. In this book the issue of race appears from time to time—for example, in Chico Hamilton's comments about the collaboration with Lee Konitz in 1953. But it is not a major theme, because the guiding force behind Mulligan's work was always the music itself. For a musician who won twenty-nine consecutive *Down Beat* polls as best baritone saxophonist, he was modest about his achievements and seldom felt he attained his own high standards. For example, discussing George Russell's score for *All about Rosie* that his Concert Jazz Band recorded, he said, "It's a very tough thing to play . . . they went through those saxophone parts like they were nothing. . . . I struggled with them but they gave the impression there was nothing to it."[3] And above all, he said in several interviews that "I hired guys because I liked the way they played."[4]

Alyn Shipton
Oxford, UK
June 2022

3 Gerry Mulligan interviewed by Charles Fox, Glasgow Jazz Festival, July 1988.
4 Jack, Gordon: *Fifties Jazz Talk* (Lanham, MD, Scarecrow Press, 2004) p. 148.

CONTENTS

1 Antecedents *1*

2 The First Quartet *41*

3 The Second Quartet *89*

4 The Quartet with Art Farmer *143*

5 The Aftermath and Legacy *187*

ACKNOWLEDGMENTS *221*

DISCOGRAPHY 1952–1962 *225*

BIBLIOGRAPHY *239*

INDEX *241*

CHAPTER 1

ANTECEDENTS

GERALD JOSEPH MULLIGAN was born in Queens Village, Long Island, on April 6, 1927, but because his father, George, was a management engineer, working on the earth-moving equipment and steam-powered machinery used in giant construction projects, he was not to stay there for long. The family was frequently on the move during Gerry's early life. With his three brothers and his mother Louise, he spent time following George's career, taking them by turns to Marion, Ohio; New Jersey; Chicago; and Kalamazoo, Michigan. In Marion, his mother hired an African American nanny to help care for the young Gerry, and he recalled that much of his introduction to music came from the player-piano in Lily's house, which had piano-rolls by stride and rag-time players such as Fats Waller. Lily and her husband often hosted Black musicians as they came through Marion, as the town's hotels catered for a white clientele, so the young Mulligan frequently encountered players

The Gerry Mulligan 1950s Quartets. Alyn Shipton, Oxford University Press. © Alyn Shipton 2023.
DOI: 10.1093/oso/9780197579756.003.0001

from African American touring groups, and saw a very different kind of community from that which his parents inhabited.[1]

As he got a little older, he recalled his first experience of hearing a twelve-piece jazz big band, playing live between the movies he was taken to see in the opulent surroundings of the city's Palace Theatre (a building that looked—inside and out—like an annex to the Alhambra in Spain that had somehow escaped from Granada and landed intact in North America). The exhilarating sound of this group playing in the theater's orchestra pit was a childhood memory that stayed with him.

During the three years he subsequently spent at a Catholic school in downtown Kalamazoo (presumably St. Augustine's, as Mulligan vividly remembered the railroad tracks adjacent to the schoolyard), he began seriously learning the clarinet, having already had some piano lessons, as well as a brief period trying out the trumpet. Barely into his teens, he started writing his first arrangement for the school's motley collection of fellow young instrumentalists who took music lessons. He picked Rodgers and Hart's "Lover," having been drawn, he said, to its chromatic progression.[2] However, because the teachers (aside from his male clarinet instructor) were nuns, they took exception to the title on the sheet music, and confiscated the parts, so he never heard it performed.

Yet the urge to arrange had begun, and when the family moved to a more long-term home in Philadelphia, giving the young Mulligan his final years of schooling at the West Philadelphia Catholic High School for Boys, he continued to try his hand at writing music, alongside developing his playing skills. In due course he migrated to alto saxophone, and eventually, via the tenor, to the baritone. "More than anything," he recalled, "it was the register itself that attracted me. In the same way, if a young person is attracted to the stringed instruments and chooses the cello over the violin—it might be cumbersome, awkward to carry around and a pain in the neck on buses—but if you like playing in that register you're stuck with it."[3]

Before he left his high school, without graduating, in 1943, he had already started sending arrangements to Johnny Warrington, the bandleader who broadcast on the local WCAU radio station. Some of these charts were accepted and played. When he did leave school, after starting

1 "Early Childhood" and "Later Childhood" in the *Gerry Mulligan Autobiography* at Library of Congress [www.loc.gov/item/ihas.100010952/; accessed April 20, 2021].

2 Ibid. He is presumably thinking of measures 13–15 that descend Gm7/G♭7/Fm7.

3 Gerry Mulligan interviewed by Charles Fox, Glasgow Jazz Festival, July 1988.

out by selling more of his work to Warrington, he landed a job as staff arranger for the touring big band led by Tommy Tucker. This ensemble had enjoyed a big hit a couple of years before, with "I Don't Want to Set the World on Fire," and it had a sizable national following, in the wake of its popular *Pot O' Gold* radio show, which was networked in several areas. At this point in World War II, swing was still the most popular form of musical entertainment in the United States, and despite the AFM recording ban of 1942–1944, which would radically change the musical landscape in the longer term, bands like those of Warrington and Tucker were typical of this style.

Around the time of his seventeenth birthday in 1944, Mulligan went on the road with Tucker's band, initially on a string of one-nighters, and then for a two-month stay in Chicago. Because Mulligan did not play in the orchestra (unless another saxophonist was unwell), once he had finished writing and copying the parts for new arrangements during the daytime, he was free to hear the other music on offer in Chicago at night. "It had," he recalled, "five theaters with playing bands at that time. And it was like being a kid in a candy store. I went from one theater to another . . . there were a lot of arrangers who were evolving approaches to writing for the bands, putting such creative energy into it, and the attitude in the bands was an enthusiasm for the music. This was a tremendous motivating force for me as a musician."[4]

In most overviews of Mulligan's life and music, the period after he left Tucker, and returned to Philadelphia, before he joined Gene Krupa as an arranger and occasional saxophonist in February 1946,[5] tends to be passed over quite briskly. Yet there is a strong argument for exploring the year or so that he spent with the young bandleader Elliot Lawrence as a rather more significant formative experience than has hitherto been recognized.

Lawrence, born in 1925, was a child prodigy at the piano, and he not only overcame an attack of polio in infancy that threatened the use of his hands, but, by age twelve, had formed a band of teenagers that included the young Buddy DeFranco on clarinet. His parents ran a radio talent show on which he appeared more than once. He went to the University of Pennsylvania to study music at age sixteen, and there he started showing

4 Ibid.

5 Klinkowitz, Jerome: *Listen: Gerry Mulligan* (New York, Schirmer, 1991) p. 14 dates this as April, but as most interview and oral history accounts say that Mulligan and Red Rodney left Lawrence together, and because Rodney was in Krupa's trumpet section by February 20, 1946, the earlier date is used here.

entrepreneurial promise by organizing those students who belonged to the Reserve Officers' Training Corps into a band that played for the opening of football games. That way, in the months before they were sent off for active service in World War II, his sports-mad reservists got to see the games for nothing, and gave him a ready-made band to write for and direct. He graduated after three years rather than the usual four, carrying off the university arts prize in the process. Then, instead of being drafted (for which he was rejected, owing to chronic asthma), he was offered the job of leading the in-house band at the aforementioned Philadelphia radio station WCAU.

Superficially, this might have looked like nepotism. His father, Stanley Broza, had actually founded the station before selling out his interest to CBS, and although Lawrence had switched his last names from Lawrence Broza to Broza Lawrence, most people in the Philadelphia musical world knew of the connection. Yet Lawrence was very much his own man, taking on the job when the incumbent, Johnny Warrington, decided to retire. Lawrence was just coming up to twenty years old when he started at WCAU, at the beginning of 1945. His style was more jazz-orientated than that of his predecessor, and as critic George T. Simon, who lauded the group's broadcasts in the March 1945 edition of *Metronome*, wrote: "He continued his swinging ways, despite the fact that studio bands are supposed to be strictly commercial. It paid off, though, because soon people started noticing his band much more than they did other studio groups."[6] A press report notes that in June 1945 he would be launching "a new series of modern jazz programs."[7] It was clear from this and other newspaper coverage that it was Lawrence's prodigious musical talent that had secured the job. A typical piece from a New Jersey paper in mid-1945 ran:

> Elliot Lawrence "the young man at a piano" and his 20-piece Columbia Broadcasting Station orchestra will come to the Ringside at the Long Branch Stadium, Saturday July 7, at 9 o'clock. . . . Highlighting the arrangements are the brilliant piano interpretations of Elliot Lawrence. Among Elliot's outstanding arrangements is the one he made on "Rumanian Rhapsody" for Benny Goodman, which B.G. featured on *Seven Lively Arts*. He has collaborated with Raymond Scott in creating

6 Simon, George T.: *Elliot Lawrence Plays Gerry Mulligan Arrangements*, Fantasy F 3-206 (July 1955) [liner note].

7 "Elliot Lawrence Orchestra," *Madison State Journal*, June 15, 1945.

new acoustical effects for radio music. . . . The band's theme "Heart to Heart" is an excerpt from the symphonic tone poem composed by Lawrence, which was awarded the Thornton Oakley prize for creative composition, and premiered by the Philadelphia Orchestra.[8]

From the moment Lawrence took on the WCAU / CBS band, he shifted its instrumentation away slightly from the pattern of the conventional 1940s big band, adding at least one French horn, often a tuba, and usually additional woodwinds, in particular an oboe. The results were immediately obvious, and well summed up the following year by one critic who wrote:

> A plaintive French horn rising and falling in a mournful and wailing obbligato, a suddenly daring piano phrase that interrupts yet propels the melody back into the tuneful rhythm of the ensemble—that's the kind of transformation that occurs when 21-year old Elliot Lawrence and his orchestra catch hold of an old song like "In Apple Blossom Time." This youthful maestro inspires his arrangements with a classical touch, drawn from a background of old masters, and the result? New melodies faintly reminiscent of something like the combined effects of the bands of Claude Thornhill and Russ Morgan would produce.[9]

The Thornhill point is well made, as it is often assumed that Gerry Mulligan's own fascination with the tonal effects (in particular) of French horns and tubas developed a little later, when he worked with Thornhill in 1947–1948, but it is clear that it was with Lawrence that he was first able to experiment with such instrumentation. The eighteen-year old Mulligan joined Lawrence's radio band almost from its beginning, because he had been suggested as a potential arranger by Warrington, who told Lawrence, "There's this young guy who's been dying to write for me. I thought you two might get along."[10]

8 "Elliott [*sic*] Lawrence, Jack Hunter at the Stadium, Saturday, Sunday," *Red Bank Register*, July 5, 1945, p. 12.

9 "Sad French Horn and Daring Piano Catch Apple Time," *Commerce East Texan*, September 27, 1946, p. 2. Drew Techner's article on Lawrence's career for the *Mulligan International Newsletter* (June 2005) dates the arrival of these instruments to October 1946, but this press piece and recorded evidence of airshots confirm they had been present in various configurations from mid-1945 onward.

10 Myers, Mark: "Interview: Elliot Lawrence," *Jazz Wax Blog*, February 9, 2016 [www.jazzwax.com/2016/02/interview-elliot-lawrence.html; accessed April 20, 2021].

Lawrence's own accounts vary somewhat as to quite when and how he got to know Mulligan,[11] but from Mulligan's various interviews, it seems that it was indeed Warrington who brokered the introduction. Soon afterward, particularly as Mulligan was not having an easy time at his parental home, he began to stay quite frequently with the Broza family, a few miles outside Philadelphia. The two young men were close in age and at that point became fast friends through listening to music together (particularly the new sounds of bebop, which was just beginning to emerge, and which enthusiasm they shared with another teenage musician, the trumpeter Red Rodney, who joined the Lawrence brass section). There was soon an informal agreement between Mulligan and Lawrence, who recalled: "Gerry was given the jazz things—the 'hot' things—and I wrote the ballads."[12] Mulligan confirmed that during the time that the band remained predominantly a radio orchestra he was solely an arranger, but from mid-1945, he started to play quite frequently in the lineup. Often this was on tenor saxophone but sometimes on alto or baritone, depending on which other members were available, when the group began to do road dates in between its regular *Listen to Lawrence* broadcasts, which aired coast-to-coast over CBS several times a week.[13]

Mulligan said, "When he went out and tried to conquer the big band world, I played with the band for a while. In fact, it was Elliot who had the idea that I should play, and actually he got two baritone players . . . and we had a small band within the band. Too bad we didn't record more with Elliot."[14] Mulligan doesn't appear on any of Lawrence's Columbia records, although he is present (playing baritone) on a handful of airshots from June 1945. But at this point in his career, it was his arranging not his playing that was his strongest suit. His first chart for Lawrence was a successful makeover for the old Dixieland standard "Indiana," which survives in a 1946 radio transcription recording, made at around the time Mulligan left the band. From these discs, made for broadcast, Mulligan's settings of Benny Goodman's "You're Right, I'm Wrong" and Duke Ellington's "Just a Sittin' and a-Rockin'" survive as backings for the band's singer Rosalind Patton.

A radio transcription also exists of Mulligan's first attempt at arranging "How High the Moon," and for this piece, his handwritten score survives in the Elliot Lawrence archive at the University of Wyoming. Mulligan is

11 Ibid. and PhilaVideo's filmed interview: [www.youtube.com/watch?v=1ozoajOeyvk; accessed April 20, 2021].

12 Josephson, Sanford: *Jeru's Journey* (Milwaukee, Hal Leonard, 2015) p. 7.

13 Listing from *Bakersfield Californian*, August 10, 1945, p. 10.

14 Gerry Mulligan interviewed by Charles Fox, Glasgow Jazz Festival, July 1988.

FIGURE 1.1 Mulligan's chart for "How High the Moon," p. 5. Box Number 100; Folder Number 2; Elliot Lawrence papers, 1934–1990, Collection Number 09101-p, American Heritage Center, University of Wyoming. Used by permission.

playing baritone on the recording, but his name is not penciled in on the score, where most individual players are named against the part assigned to them, including some swapping between roles—for example when trombonist Herb Collins is instructed to move from third to first chair to take a high note solo lead in measures 28–32 of the first full run through the sequence. Most interesting is that in this 1945 chart, written at least a year and a half before he was to join Claude Thornhill, Mulligan is already experimenting with the use of the French horn.

In this chart it first appears on the second run through the thirty-two-measure sequence. Until this point, trombones and reeds have functioned independently, but as they come together, the horn is added (doubling the second alto) bringing another timbre to the combined sections (see Figure 1.1).[15] Although used sparingly, the French horn takes

15 Score dated July 30, 1945, in the Elliot Lawrence Papers, American Heritage Center, University of Wyoming.

FIGURE 1.2 Mulligan's chart for "How High the Moon," p. 8. Box Number 100; Folder Number 2; Elliot Lawrence papers, 1934–1990, Collection Number 09101-p, American Heritage Center, University of Wyoming. Used by permission.

the role of a fourth trombone elsewhere (see Figure 1.2). Judicious use of the instrument, either working with other brass or with reed sections, was something he would explore further, both in writing for Thornhill and in Miles Davis's 1948 nonet.

Mulligan contributed numerous arrangements to the band book, and in years to come, these were the cause of what became almost a love-hate relationship between Lawrence and Mulligan. Lawrence was not just a musical prodigy, but as the son of a media entrepreneur, he had been brought up to be tidy-minded when it came to contracts, copyright, and the publishing of sheet music. So when he paid Mulligan $50 per chart (or $150 if it was an original composition), Lawrence took care of securing the publishing rights and deposited copies at the Library of Congress. It irked him that Mulligan frequently ignored the niceties of intellectual property and sold the same charts to various other bands, including that of Gene Krupa (who also recorded "Indiana" for a transcription disc in February 1946). When Mulligan later formed his own big band he wanted the rights back, but Lawrence pointed out that he had bought them quite fairly, and thus owned the publishing.[16]

In due course, Lawrence cashed in on Mulligan's later success by recording a very fine album of Gerry's big band charts in 1955.[17] Also, even though Gerry and the band's eighteen-year-old trumpeter Red Rodney left Lawrence at the same time to join Gene Krupa, in February 1946,[18] Elliot continued for the next two years, on an ad hoc basis, to buy arrangements from Mulligan, wherever he happened to be. Meanwhile, despite Lawrence's ownership of rights in some of his work, Mulligan began his lifelong practice of continually returning to his compositions, or in some cases his arrangements of others' work, and tweaking and refining them to suit whichever band he was working with.

Around the time Mulligan joined his band, Krupa (having returned to the spotlight after a 1943 incarceration on drug charges) was pondering on his future direction, as he sensed audience tastes were changing. He told the syndicated show business columnist Jack O'Brian:

> I'm not going mushy, but the era of blatant swing is passing. Bands are putting their emphasis on sweet danceable melodies. I've changed my band around a little. Now I'm just another drummer in a very good band. Of course I'll do a few exhibitionistic drum acrobatics for the convinced jitterbugs. They pay our salaries too. But I think audiences are getting away from the purely orgiastic stuff. . . . The best jazz tunes are good music basically, with excellent chords, interesting intervals and surprising changes, like "Blue Skies."[19]

The column goes on to speculate that the next step would be to add "oboe, bassoon, flute and French horn," which was not a route that Krupa took in the end, particularly after the mixed reception of his short-lived "Band that Swings with Strings" experiment the previous year. Yet by hiring Mulligan, Krupa knew that he was bringing in an

16 Myers, Mark: "Interview: Elliot Lawrence," *Jazz Wax Blog*, February 9, 2016 [www.jazzwax.com/2016/02/interview-elliot-lawrence.html; accessed April 20, 2021].

17 *Elliot Lawrence Plays Gerry Mulligan Arrangements* (Fantasy F 3-206) [July 1955].

18 As in footnote 5, I have gone with this date although Richard Samuel Fine in his PhD thesis on Mulligan's composing and arranging career suggests he flew to California to join the band in late December 1945, but contradicting this, he later says that Mulligan joined in February 1946. Fine, Richard Samuel: *The Birth of Jeru* (PhD thesis, University of Maryland, 2010) p. 47; p. 58.

19 O'Brian, Jack: "Broadway," *Salamanca Republican Press*, August 7, 1946, p. 4.

arranger who was experienced in writing more commercial or "sweet danceable" music, through his work with Elliot Lawrence. A piece like Gerry's arrangement of "Love Is in My Heart," which Krupa recorded for transcription in February 1946, exactly fits Krupa's description of the "best jazz tunes," yet tellingly mingles muted trumpet, piano, and tenor solos with a chorus in which, after a sudden pause, the entire band plays a close-harmony version of the melody—something ideal for catching the ears of the "non-jazz" general audience. Equally Mulligan's chart for "Begin the Beguine," recorded at the same time, barely strays from the melody throughout the entire disc, the tune being initially stated by a high-register trombone, and later harmonized for the reeds in a Glenn Miller manner.

Although he had increasingly been playing baritone saxophone in Elliot Lawrence's orchestra, Mulligan joined Krupa not as an instrumentalist but as an arranger. He recalled:

> Each one of the bands I wrote for, at some point I wound up playing for. With Gene Krupa's band I was an arranger, and got called into service when somebody dropped out for some reason, or somebody was taken sick on the road. On one occasion they hired a new alto player, and after a couple of nights it didn't work out and as luck would have it I had my alto with me and so I got stuck playing in the section for the whole tour. And although I didn't really like it very much, I learned a lot because there were some very good saxophone players in the band. So I was forced to learn more about playing the saxophone than I had really thought about up until then.[20]

Mulligan also said that this was the first time he had worked with musicians so proficient that they could immediately sight-read and play anything that was put in front of them. As an arranger, this helped his writing to develop, but so too did the time he spent off-stage with Krupa.

It would be easy to typecast Krupa as a musician rooted in the early jazz and swing era, who managed to keep playing the kind of jazz he had pioneered, after it fell out of fashion, not least through the subsequent good offices of Norman Granz and Jazz at the Philharmonic. But this does not chime with a man who experimented with strings,

20 Gerry Mulligan interviewed by Charles Fox, Glasgow Jazz Festival, July 1988.

and whose own listening was extremely wide-ranging. He carried a phonograph on the road with a collection of records, and from time to time members of the band joined him in his hotel room to listen to music. Mulligan recalled how Krupa was an astute listener, encouraging his colleagues to appreciate classical composers such as Ravel and Delius, and focus on detailed sections of the music. "That's the best way to learn about something new that you don't know about," Mulligan said, "[which is] to have somebody who pushes your attention and your focus, and zeroes in on aspects of the music that, left to your own devices, you might miss."[21]

The Krupa transcription discs from early 1946 are not just a matter of Mulligan producing quite commercial and tuneful arrangements. The band's record of "Indiana" is a quite radically amended version of his Elliot Lawrence chart, and it suggests how much he had absorbed from Krupa's informal listening sessions. In the Lawrence band's 1946 recording, the reeds play a harmonized version of the theme in the first full chorus, and answering phrases come from Lawrence's solo piano.[22] For the Krupa version, Mulligan transfers the thematic phrases to the brass, and harmonized reeds provide the answers. But the unexpected and brilliantly dramatic addition to the Krupa chart comes at two beats before measure 25 of this opening chorus (see Example 1.1). The rhythm section and brass drop out and the reeds take a harmonized segment that carries the listener forward to the final four measures of the chorus. This writing, showing a classical command of harmony (accentuated by the "straight" classical timing of measures 25–27 before a swing feel returns), is a harbinger of much of Mulligan's later arranging, from its harmonic density to the clever use of a different time feel to move a piece on, yet done without the accompaniment of a rhythm section.

The early 1946 Krupa recordings also include "Birdhouse," from February 26. This takes an idea that also appears in Neal Hefti's "The Good Earth," written for Woody Herman and recorded in August 1945, which is to use phrases from Charlie Parker's compositions or solos as thematic motifs. It's not clear whether Mulligan would have heard the Herman record before writing his chart, as it appears not to have been released until early 1946, but in any event he takes the concept much further. Mulligan builds his composition on a single fragment of a

21 "Gene Krupa," in the *Gerry Mulligan Autobiography* at Library of Congress [www.loc.gov/item/ihas.100010952/; accessed April 22, 2021].

22 *The Uncollected Elliot Lawrence and His Orchestra 1946* (Hindsight 182, track 4).

EXAMPLE 1.1 Mulligan's arrangement for Gene Krupa of "Back Home Again in Indiana" (Hanley/MacDonald) measures 24–29 (transcription).

Parker theme, but particularly in the channel of "Birdhouse," he repeatedly transposes the motif for the saxophone section, and from time to time provides answering phrases, also drawn from Parker themes, for the brass. In his May 1946 arrangement for Krupa of "How High the Moon," he rethinks the piece radically from his earlier Lawrence chart. This number's chord sequence was the source of Parker's contrafact "Ornithology," and on Krupa's record Mulligan quotes Parker's theme in full for an entire reed section chorus. Owing to arrangements such as these, and the fluent solos of Red Rodney and Charles Kennedy, the 1946–1947 Krupa orchestra became known as his "bebop band."

Fortunately, a short film of this edition of the band exists, made for RKO in Hollywood in June 1946, under the title *Follow That Music*. We not only see the tall, thin, but unmistakable, figure of Mulligan in the reed section (playing alto saxophone) but, after some fine vocals from Carolyn Grey and an interlude during which the musicians try to break into the New York scene by working as waiters, the young Red Rodney takes a rapid-fire bebop trumpet solo in the closing number. Mulligan, again playing alto, is also clearly visible in this band's other screen appearance, in two scenes from the full-length movie *Beat the Band*, released in February 1947, but also shot for RKO in mid-1946, during the band's West Coast stay. The picture's star, Frances Langford, sings "I'm in Love" in a hotel boiler room, with Mulligan and the reeds standing to the left of the screen behind an array of metal plumbing, before Krupa plays a very creative solo (beautifully photographed) on various other pipes and fittings of the heating system. Later (on a proper bandstand, with Mulligan just visible over his shoulder), Krupa performs "Shadow Rhapsody," in which, partway through, the stage lights are dimmed and a spotlight projects his giant silhouette onto a screen during an extended cymbal and tom-tom solo.

Movies apart, the most famous and long-lasting outcome of Mulligan's ten-month stay with Krupa is his composition "Disc Jockey Jump," recorded in January 1947, shortly after Mulligan had actually left Krupa's organization. In its linear theme, the piece bears a superficial similarity to Jimmy Guiffre's subsequent composition "Four Brothers," but it has two elements in place that would recur in Mulligan's later arranging work. Firstly, the theme is carried by a band-within-a-band of trumpet, trombone, alto saxophone, and tenor saxophone, a voicing that prefigured Mulligan's 1950s sextet, in which the alto was replaced by his baritone (see Example 1.2). This also looks ahead to elements of his 1960–1962 Concert Jazz Band writing, where a similar tight-knit group of soloists played together against the backing of the full band. In the immediate future, he would also experiment with a band-within-a-band while working with Miles Davis's nonet in 1948.

Secondly, the remaining brass and reed sections play a response to the theme in close harmony. In effect, the melody is the component that would be carried by trumpet or valve trombone in Mulligan's 1950s quartets, while the rest of the band plays a part that prefigures his harmonic and sometimes contrapuntal lines on baritone. If we stretch the metaphor a little by comparing this to a baroque *concerto grosso*, the soloists have the melody, the remaining brass and reeds are the *ripieno*, and the piano and bass have a *continuo* role, joining in unison to play a single bass line, just as the quartet's bassist would later do. Mulligan recalled that even Gene Krupa himself remarked, "It was like a *concerto grosso* idea, a small band out of a big band."[23]

The immediate reaction to this record, from disc jockey Fred Robbins on New York's station WOV, was that "Geney with the light brown drumsticks . . . has touched up the vocabulary of the nation's younger set . . . with this cookie, biscuit, brisk disc or drastic plastic," otherwise known as "the shellac, the lacquer or a fetching etching."[24] As the record gained momentum in the market, it was regarded as "some of Gene's ace

23 Mulligan oral history at Library of Congress, quoted in Fine, *The Birth of Jeru*, p. 61.

24 Syndicated article in *Laredo Times*, January 13, 1947, p. 10.

EXAMPLE 1.2 Opening, showing the "band within a band," of "Disc Jockey Jump" by Gerry Mulligan and Gene Krupa. Copyright © 1947 Jeruvian Music Co. and Gene Krupa Publishing Designee. Copyright renewed. All rights for Jeruvian Music Co. administered by Universal Music Corp. All rights reserved. Used by permission. Reprinted by permission of Hal Leonard Europe Ltd.

skin beating,"[25] and it featured in Columbia's panel advertisements for the rest of the year in the "Popular Records" section.[26]

As mentioned, Mulligan was no longer with Krupa for the public reception of this disc, his best-known arrangement for the band. He had again been deputizing on alto saxophone in the reed section in late 1946,

25 "In the Groove," *Amarillo Daily News* (TX), August 8, 1947, p. 23.

26 Examples include: *Portsmouth Times* (OH), September 27, 1947, p. 7; *Pottstown Mercury* (PA), October 15, 1947, p. 27; *Charleston Gazette* (VA), December 21, 1947, p. 30.

and at one performance, as the set came to an end he rounded on his fellow players and told them off, in earshot of the audience, for being "sloppy." Consequently, Krupa fired him, with immediate effect, even if he was later to express the view that he "admired" Mulligan, because "you get too much obsequiousness in this business."[27]

Some years later, Krupa was to pay Mulligan a similar compliment to that of Elliot Lawrence, by recording an album of his big band arrangements, in October 1958. On that record, "Bird House" benefits from the fine Parker-tinged alto saxophone playing of Phil Woods, and "Disc Jockey Jump" has tighter ensemble work (and a more cogent drum solo from the leader) than the 1940s record. Lamenting that Mulligan's 1950s quartet had taken him away from big band arranging, the *Oakland Tribune*'s jazz critic, Russ Wilson, wrote: "The arrangements, which were written in 1946 while Gerry was a member of the Krupa band, demonstrate his extraordinary talent for utilizing interesting tonal blends, harmonies and dynamics, while at the same time charting a firmly swinging course and leaving space for solos."[28]

By late 1946, Mulligan had already met Claude Thornhill and various members of his band, and liked their sound very much. Consequently, soon after his hasty departure from Krupa, he joined them as an arranger. "With Thornhill it was the same thing," he recalled, "I wrote for the band for quite a while before I played with them."[29]

Claude Thornhill had spent World War II in the South Pacific, first in Artie Shaw's Navy band and then leading a smaller group of his own that included the singer Dennis Day and the drummer (and actor) Jackie Cooper. His present orchestra had taken shape after his discharge at the start of 1946 and his stock-in-trade was playing ballads, the richness of their sound enhanced by the French horns and tuba that, as they had been in his immediate prewar band, were a permanent part of his lineup.[30] Mulligan made good use of them in a harmonically dense arrangement of Noël Coward's "Poor Little Rich Girl," as well as in the call-and-response between sections of his medium tempo chart for "Sometimes I'm Happy."

27 Crowther, Bruce: *Gene Krupa, His Life and Times* (Tunbridge Wells, UK, Spellmount, 1987) p. 102.

28 Wilson, Russ: "Mulligan Music Points Up Loss," *Oakland Tribune*, July 22, 1959.

29 Gerry Mulligan interviewed by Charles Fox, Glasgow Jazz Festival, July 1988.

30 Crosbie, Ian: *Claude Thornhill—The 1948 Transcription Performances*, Hep CD 17 (1994) [liner note].

The alto saxophonist Lee Konitz was in Thornhill's reed section at the time Mulligan joined and he said:

> I knew Gerry only in that context, I didn't know anything about him before. His arrangements were always a delight to play. As a saxophonist himself, he was very sympathetic to saxophone players. It was a beautiful ballad band basically. . . . I mean they were older players, most of them, but as a ballad band it was thrilling with the two French horns and a tuba, and that was the real experience of playing with that band.[31]

Before the war, Thornhill had produced many of the arrangements himself, but his fellow arranger had, for a time, been Gil Evans—Canadian-born, peripatetically raised, and whose mother lived in Stockton, California. In the late 1930s, Thornhill and Evans had both worked with the West Coast band of Skinnay Ennis, playing for the Bob Hope show and working at prestigious West Coast hotels. When Claude went out on his own, he hired Evans to join him in 1941. Their partnership was integral to the success of the band, as saxophonist Jack Dulong, who played with them a little later, recalled: "Its excellence [was] largely due to Gil Evans' writing and meticulous rehearsing. But on the stand, Claude shaped the whole mood and sound through his playing and selection of charts."[32]

When Evans stepped off the train in New York at Penn Station in early 1946 to rejoin Thornhill's band, he headed straight for 52nd Street, to hear for himself the sounds of Dizzy Gillespie and Bud Powell, which he had hitherto mainly experienced on phonograph records or broadcasts. Soon he had immersed himself as fully as possible in the sounds of the "new jazz," that had largely emerged while he was enlisted in the Army Reserve, and running a military band at Camp Lee in Virginia.[33] It was not long before he was bringing these bebop sounds into the Thornhill band, as trumpeter Ed Zandy remembered: "Some of us were skeptical at first. Gil had to teach us how to play this new conception, but eventually we got to enjoying playing things like 'Anthropology,' 'Donna Lee,' and 'Yardbird Suite.' And Claude hired guys like Bill Barber, one of the

31 Interview with Lee Konitz, July 2002.

32 Crosbie: *Claude Thornhill.*

33 Stein Crease, Stephanie: *Gil Evans, Out of the Cool* (Chicago, Chicago Review Press, 2002) p. 126.

finest tuba players in the business, alto saxist Lee Konitz . . . and little Red Rodney."[34] Yet Evans was sensitive to the aesthetic of the Thornhill band, and just as Mulligan had adapted Charlie Parker's ideas in a way that would work with both the limitations and strengths of Krupa's orchestra, Evans now did something similar. "I arranged those Parker things the way I figured Claude would like to hear them," he said.[35] A case in point is his chart for "Anthropology," where, on the second time through the chord sequence, cup-muted trumpets join a clarinet trio and a pair of alto saxophones to play Parker's theme, accompanied only by bass and drums.

Mulligan achieves a similar lightness in the thematic chorus of his own twelve-bar blues composition "Elevation," originally written for Lawrence's band, and somewhat rejigged by the time Thornhill recorded it for NBC's Thesaurus Transcription series. Here, coming after Thornhill's piano introduction, the reeds are scored in the manner of Evans's "Anthropology." Yet the second time through, we hear trombones and horns playing a countermelody below the reed section lead.[36] Again, this points to the way Mulligan would create just such a baritone countermelody in his quartet, while trumpet or trombone took the main theme. In the Thornhill band, for that recording, were trumpeter Johnny Carisi, alto saxophonist Lee Konitz, French horn player Junior Collins, tuba player Bill Barber, and Gerry himself, playing baritone and tenor saxophones. Of the nine pieces that they recorded that day, six were arranged by Gil Evans. At around the same time, all these musicians were involved in another project, which first came to widespread public attention in September 1948, when a syndicated newspaper column announced:

> Proprietor Ralph Watkins and producer Monte Kay announce that starting Thursday September 9th, the Royal Roost, otherwise known as the Metropolitan Bopera House, will feature Count Basie and his 17-piece orchestra. . . . An extra added attraction on the bill will be the very popular recording favorite, Dinah Washington. Miles Davis' bebop aggregation, featuring Max Roach on drums, will round out the entertainment.[37]

34 Crosbie: *Claude Thornhill.*

35 Ibid.

36 Recorded October 1948 and released on *Claude Thornhill—The 1948 Transcription Performances* (Hep CD 17).

37 "New York Night Club Notes," *Hanover Evening Sun*, September 18, 1948, p. 7.

The Miles Davis "aggregation" seems to have begun playing at the club the previous week, opposite Charlie Parker's Quintet, on September 2, and a broadcast recording exists of its set on Saturday the 4th. This Davis band was the nonet that went on the following year to record for Capitol, and which was eventually nicknamed "The Birth of the Cool," when its individual records were gathered together on a 12-inch LP in 1957. (There had been a previous 10-inch version with eight tracks in 1954, but this did not carry that title.) The band largely came about through the somewhat unorthodox living arrangements of Gil Evans, who kept open house at his one-room basement apartment at 15 West 55th Street in Manhattan. It seems that Mulligan, although on Thornhill's arranging staff, had briefly returned to his hometown to play some dates with Elliot Lawrence. He recalled:

> I had gone back to Philadelphia for a while, and I got a postcard from Gil saying, "What are you doing in Philadelphia? Why don't you come back to New York where things are happening?" And so I did, and at that time he had this room that was something you couldn't dignify with the name "apartment." It was a basement room with the pipes showing, behind a Chinese laundry on 55th Street and 5th Avenue. It had a back door that opened out onto a kind of courtyard, where you could see some weeds and things growing. It was a very large room and for quite a while I wound up staying there. I found furnished rooms, but it was inconvenient running back and forth and I didn't like them, so he said, "Well, come and stay here." We took turns using the piano, we took turns using the bed, and people were in and out all hours of the day and night. It was a wonderful time for us.[38]

Hence during Mulligan's second year of working for Thornhill, he was in daily contact with Evans, and being a short distance from 52nd Street, this meant he was also in regular touch with the musicians who were playing there, and who dropped in to the apartment at all hours. Gil Evans himself recalled:

> I left the door open for two years. I left it open literally, so people just came down there. It was just one room, but I had everything in there I needed. I had a piano, a record player, and one of the early recorders that made the acetate recordings—a great big disc machine that Claude Thornhill gave to me. So I had all that there, plus a wild

38 Gerry Mulligan interviewed by Charles Fox, Glasgow Jazz Festival, July 1988.

> interest. We'd get together and compare notes and chords, and sounds, and that's how I got together with Miles Davis. The thing that Miles Davis and I had in common was the appreciation of a certain kind of sound. That's the thing that kept us together. So we figured out a way to get that sound of Claude Thornhill with a small combination, with just six horns that would cover the whole harmonic range.[39]

It helped that the band assembled for the Royal Roost (and therefore for their first broadcast) included Collins, Barber, Konitz, and Mulligan, and that Gil Evans arranged two of the pieces they played, since this meant that several current or recent members of Thornhill's orchestra were involved, and stood a better than average chance of getting "that sound of Claude Thornhill." But overall, the nonet was the result of long hours of discussion and experiment in Evans's apartment, and while the Thornhill aesthetic was present, so too was the state-of-the-art sound of bebop. Some of the other musicians involved in the new group, pianist John Lewis and drummer Max Roach, had worked with Miles Davis and Charlie Parker on 52nd Street (indeed Davis and Roach broadcast as members of Parker's Quintet from the Royal Roost on September 4, 1948, the same night as the nonet.)

Lewis and Roach frequently dropped in on the Evans ménage after their evening gigs. Indeed, on the night of the Davis nonet's second Royal Roost broadcast, September 18, 1948, Davis, Lewis, and Roach had spent the day recording with Parker for Savoy, in the session that produced the celebrated "Parker's Mood." (Owing to the yearlong AFM recording ban of the time, which prevented members from making commercial recordings until mid-December 1948, this Savoy session was undertaken under a cloak of secrecy.)

Trumpeter and arranger John Carisi was a regular at Evans's apartment as well, and a thought-provoking contributor to the discussions, even though his arrangement for the nonet, "Israel," would not be recorded until April 1949. Hanging out after hours and spontaneously trying out new ideas might have led nowhere, but as Gerry Mulligan recalled, what their informal gatherings needed (including some forays into rehearsal studios) was a catalyst:

> Left to our own devices Gil and the Johns (Lewis and Carisi) would probably have procrastinated and maybe never have gotten the

39 Gil Evans interviewed by Charles Fox, 1978.

> rehearsals together. But Miles was the prime mover. There's another fact I think is far more important, which is thinking of Miles as the lead voice. This affected the way we all wrote for him. Stylistically, Miles was the perfect choice. It's hard to imagine other trumpet players having the same effect on the ensemble, for instance, if we'd had a player who had a more conventional open trumpet sound, I don't think it would have had the same effect and impact as an ensemble sound.[40]

The first full-length piece to be played by the band during their initial broadcast from the Royal Roost on September 4, 1948, was John Lewis's arrangement of Denzil Best's composition "Move." It is by no means as neat and tidy as the studio version cut on January 21, 1949, in which Lewis's chart tops and tails what is in effect a quintet performance by Miles, Konitz, and the rhythm section. (Indeed a similar quintet, though with Curley Russell on bass, made the 1948 Christmas Day broadcast from the Royal Roost during a later residency there, so the two horns had functioned together in a working band between the nonet's inaugural broadcast and its first studio date.) When it was suggested to Lewis that his arrangement worked as a sort of aural picture frame for the quintet, he disagreed, saying that the details of the fully scored elements of the arrangement were far more important:

> What I was doing was finding a way to use that instrumentation. In jazz it was a little unusual instrumentation, with the tuba and French horn, especially with the tuba, and I tried to create the piece a little bit in a polyphonic way. You'll hear a couple of melodies going on at the same time.[41]

In the first main eight-measure sequence, trumpet and alto carry the melody exactly as they would in a standard bebop quintet, but Lewis then adds a countermelody for horn and trombone, with (mainly) unison punctuations from tuba and baritone saxophone. (See Example 1.3.) The end result is clear, decisive, and has an immediately distinctive sound. Listeners to the Royal Roost Broadcast would—despite the slightly chaotic opening, and a less-than-top-notch first solo from trombonist

40 Gerry Mulligan interviewed by Charles Fox, Glasgow Jazz Festival, July 1988.

41 Interview with John Lewis, January 3, 2000.

EXAMPLE 1.3 "Move" (Denzil Best) arranged by John Lewis, first section (transcription).

Mike Zwerin—nonetheless have immediately recognized the band's individuality.

When it came to Mulligan's own arrangements (half of the dozen pieces on the eventual 12-inch LP are his work, three of them also being his compositions), he drew on a similar template to Lewis's for some pieces, but on others he also added additional layers of complexity and used the instrumental voices in more challenging combinations. Nonetheless, he was at a crossroads between the density of his big band writing and the spartan simplicity of the quartet he would go on to form in August 1952. His nonet chart for George Wallington's "Godchild," which he also arranged for a recording by Claude Thornhill's full band at around the same time, shows him taking the former approach, while his own piece "Jeru"—although having an unorthodox compositional form[42]—is an example of the latter, having originally also been written for Thornhill, but subsequently being progressively pared down, first for the Davis nonet and then for the Mulligan Quartet with Chet Baker in April 1953.

In his survey of the "Birth of the Cool" recordings, Frank Tirro suggests that "Godchild," as played at the Royal Roost, is the epitome of "cool." Listing elements to back up this definition, he draws attention to nine aspects of the piece: Roach's restrained drumming; the voicing of the arrangement (in particular the doubling of baritone saxophone and tuba); the overall moderate volume; the exploitation of the coloristic timbres of the instruments; the "quiet passive roll" [*sic*] of the rhythm section; the parallel voicings in measures 71–76; the unassuming relaxation in Mulligan's baritone solo; Konitz's vibratoless tone and use of eighth notes in the upper partials of the chords; and finally, the ending which harks back to the opening figures.[43] Interestingly, writing in 1950, Barry Ulanov observed that, starting with the Capitol nonet discs, Lee Konitz "defined the cool sound" of the alto.[44] Yet there is relatively little further literary or press coverage of Mulligan or any of his associates in the Davis

42 The basic theme is in 4/4 time and covers 16 measures. The next 12 measures are of unequal length and time signatures: 4/4; 3/4; 2/4; 3/4 × 4; 6/4; 4/4 × 4. The following scored section is 9 measures long, then 8 measures introduce a 24-measure trumpet solo, which concludes with a recap of the introductory underscoring. The next nine measures are: 3/4 × 4; 2/4 × 1; 4/4 × 4. This is followed by 3/4 × 4; 2/4 × 1, ushering in a 20-measure baritone solo in 4/4. The next 8 measures, in 4/4, are repeated, before the pattern of the second 12 measures returns, and the piece finishes on a 13-measure final section in 4/4.

43 Tirro, Frank: *The Birth of the Cool of Miles Davis and His Associates* (Hillsdale, NY, Pendragon Press, 2009) pp. 75–76.

44 Ulanov, Barry: *A History of Jazz in America* (London, Hutchinson, 1950) p. 326.

recordings that uses the word "cool" much before 1954. In his pieces for *Metronome* in 1950, Ulanov applied the adjective to Stan Getz, rather than the members of Davis's nonet. More significant, perhaps, is that when directly compared, it is clear that this arrangement of "Godchild"[45] is directly scaled down from the full band Thornhill version, recorded in October 1948. It is a perfect example of the nonet "trying to get that sound of Claude Thornhill with a small combination," as Gil Evans put it. Despite a slightly shorter introduction and an extended coda, the ensemble voicings are similar throughout, as is the overall structure of the piece, and although they are shorter in the larger setting, the solos from Konitz and Mulligan display a similar character.

The fully scored sections of the Thornhill chart are thematically and harmonically almost identical to the Davis version, and thus the overall durations of both studio recordings are similar (the Roost recording being a little more opened up for solos, and therefore almost two minutes longer). In the Capitol nonet version, Mulligan clearly uses the piano to replicate the harmonies of the six horns, exactly matching them rhythmically and tonally, to retain a sense of clarity in the aforementioned fast-moving segment from measure 71 (see Example 1.4).

"Jeru" was not played—or at any rate recorded—at the Royal Roost, but it was Mulligan's own composition. The nonet's thematic sections are lightly orchestrated with, initially, the tuba moving in a contrary direction to the other horns, and then four measures in which alto and trumpet carry the melody in unison, with baritone, horn, trombone, and tuba playing a gently harmonized countermelody, before the head returns. The feeling is one of space, and this continues as the other horns play a simple descending countermelody behind the opening of Miles Davis's solo. His level tone, triplet ornaments, and mid-range improvised line all point forward to the way Chet Baker would address this music in the later Mulligan quartet.

There are similar moments in Mulligan's other pieces for the nonet that look very clearly toward his future direction as both a composer and arranger. Most notably, his "Venus De Milo" has the kind of spare, open theme that Mulligan would later explore with his quartet, and Davis's vibratoless, open-horn solo prefigures Chet Baker's sound in that group, especially in the way that it complements Mulligan's own baritone solo. Overall, "Godchild" and "Jeru" show very clearly where he had come from and where he was going. "Jeru," as Frank Tirro demonstrates in his

45 Ulanov, Barry: "The Sound: Stan Getz That Is and That's Cool Jazz," *Metronome*, June 1950.

EXAMPLE 1.4 "Godchild" (George Wallington) arranged by Gerry Mulligan; January 21, 1949, recording by Miles Davis, measures 71ff. (transcription).

book on the Davis nonet,[46] was developed from the original chart that Mulligan wrote for Thornhill, but unlike the relatively similar treatment of "Godchild" by both big band and nonet, it is a piece whose unusual structure and strong melodic content allowed its composer to chip away at it, and reveal an ever-simplified version of its contours, without sacrificing its harmonic originality. The nonet parts (except for trumpet and piano) can be seen in the Gerry Mulligan Collection at the Library of

46 Tirro: *The Birth of the Cool of Miles Davis and His Associates*, pp. 99–107.

EXAMPLE 1.4 Continued

Congress,[47] and they display Mulligan's clear vision for the piece as he refined it from his more conventional big band arrangement.

The relative lack of press attention given to the band's September 1948 appearances at the Royal Roost means that, compared to the debuts of some other groups of the period, we are short of eyewitness accounts,

47 https://www.loc.gov/collections/gerry-mulligan/about-this-collection/.

but one critic and writer who did hear the nonet there was writer, and erstwhile Prestige producer, Ira Gitler:

> I happened to run into Miles on Broadway, and he said, "I've got this new band, you're gonna have to come down and hear it." So I did and I was knocked out by it. A lot of people thought it was effete. When the records came out, I know a lot of hard-core beboppers, and I certainly was one of those, would say to me, "I dunno, this is . . ." and without saying "effete" that's what they meant. But I said, "I think the textures and the arrangements are beautiful, and the playing is great!" But maybe it wasn't hard enough for them?[48]

It may not have been "hard" enough for those who admired the Parker Quintet or the contemporaneous Gillespie Big Band, but when (following the end of the AFM recording ban) the titles recorded in January 1949 were released, there was no question of marketing them as "cool." Capitol saw the Davis nonet as a bebop band, pure and simple. It marketed "Budo" and "Move," coupled on one of the first two 78s to appear, as part of a determined assault on the bop market, but this did not find favor with the anonymous United Press Agency columnist who wrote:

> Capitol Records is the first of the disc companies to go all out for bebop, announcing that, "the feeling here is that this new music has moved in to stay." The company admits that this new form has yet to catch the public's fancy, though it has been plugged by "hot tick" artists for four to five years. In a special release of eight singles, ten of the sides are bebop originals, full of noise and discordances, while the others are variations on standard tunes. Devotees of Bop rant that the conventionalists are trying to hold them back—seemingly out of entrenched jealousy. But it is only necessary to listen to Capitol's eight new releases by such performers as Tadd Dameron, Miles Davis, Lennie Tristano, Dave Barbour and others, to realize that it is the form itself that prevents its popularity with the masses. Unless a popular tune can carry a melody, something that can be carried in the head by the listener, the music just can't be appreciated by the non-expert. And that is bop's trouble. There's no tune, no melody and very little harmony.[49]

48 Interview with Ira Gitler, March 25, 2002.

49 "Popular Music Record Review," (NY UP), *Oxnard Press Courier*, April 23, 1949, p. 2.

Even when journalists did like what they heard, by following the guidance from Capitol, they felt quite certain how to pigeonhole the music. So, for example, one of the more positive reviews read:

> "Budo" is one of Capitol's first steps in the trek down the bebop trail, a frantic uptempo original performed by Miles Davis and band. A bevy of top boy instrumentalists turn in a series of exciting solos to spark the inventive arrangement. Flip is "Move," another fast-moving instrumental, a strictly bop affair, with the Davis trumpet highlighting a brilliant performance.[50]

Of the relatively modest number of reviews that greeted the two 78s released from the first session, only one critic, Robert West, noted what would become the defining "cool" characteristics of the Davis nonet, when he wrote: "'Jeru' . . . is smooth and could easily have been ruined by sloppy ensemble work, but [is] exceptional."[51] The band was back in the studio for further sessions on April 22, 1949, and March 9, 1950.

Despite the relative absence of the word "cool" in press coverage of the nonet, until the time that the full 12-inch LP of recordings appeared in 1957, subsequent critical and academic writing on the band has tended to follow the lead of Amiri Baraka in his 1963 book *Blues People*, arguing that "Cool jazz developed almost completely as a white form of jazz, although the ubiquitous Miles Davis is the salient exception."[52] The Marxist historian Frank Kofsky adds: "Cool jazz manifested a severance from its Black roots, and its repotting, so to speak, in the world of more 'dignified' contemporary Europeanized music. Usually this entailed making the music more melodic."[53] As was often his wont, Stanley Crouch went further, saying, "This style had little to do with the blues and almost nothing to do with swing," and that Davis was making "a failed attempt to marry jazz to European devices."[54]

Such observations might usefully be contrasted with Davis's unarguable observation in his autobiography that the nonet's music did indeed

50 *Amarillo Globe / Times* (TX) March 13, 1949, p. 41.

51 West, Robert: "Paramount Reissues; Other Jazz Documents," *Kent Stater* (OH) May 17, 1949, p. 2

52 Baraka, Amiri: *Blues People: The Negro Experience in White America and the Music That Developed From It* (New York, William Morrow, 1963) p. 218.

53 Kofsky, Frank: *Black Nationalism and the Revolution in Music* (New York, Pathfinder Press, 1970) p. 31.

54 Crouch, Stanley: "Play The Right Thing," *New Republic*, February 12, 1990, p. 31.

come from “Black musical roots,” and that you could “hear everything and hum it also.”[55] He goes on to suggest the band’s work mainly derived from things that Duke Ellington and Fletcher Henderson had already done, and which Evans and Mulligan developed further. Yet apart from the paradox of whether or not the music’s Black roots had been severed, the critical accounts cited and others in the same vein mostly overlook Davis’s observation elsewhere in his life story:

> This whole idea started out as an experiment, a collaborative experiment. Then a lot of Black musicians came down on my case about their not having work and here I was hiring white guys in my band. So I just told them that if a guy could play as well as Lee Konitz played—that’s who they were mad about most because there were a lot of black alto players around—I would hire him every time, and I wouldn’t give a damn if he was green with red breath. I’m hiring a motherfucker to play, not for what color he is.[56]

Mulligan himself concurred, saying:

> You know, there was never any of the dissonance created by the racial attitudes in those years that I experienced. This is not to say that they didn’t exist. What was going on in the real world outside might have been different, but the thing that was going on in jazz was quite unique. Jazz was in the forefront of having blacks and whites work together in bands. The black arrangers were arranging for white bands, and the white arrangers were arranging for black bands. These were things that created a different atmosphere.[57]

Whatever the later and wider developments elsewhere in jazz that stemmed from the nonet’s musical exploration, in terms of Mulligan’s work, Davis’s concept of the “collaborative experiment” is important, and just as the nonet brought Black and white musicians together, this was frequently to be the case in Mulligan’s 1950s quartet, that started life in 1952 as an interracial group.

55 Davis, Miles (with Troupe, Quincy): *Miles: The Autobiography* (London, Macmillan, 1990) p. 109. The Baraka and Kofsky sources are quoted along with this in Krenshaw, Kimberley; Gotanda, Neil; and Peller, Gary: *Critical Race Theory* (New York, New Press, 1995) p. 328.

56 Davis: *Miles*, p. 107.

57 Mulligan oral history at Library of Congress, quoted in Fine, *The Birth of Jeru*, p. 110.

Between the later two nonet recording dates in 1949 and 1950, in his day-to-day professional life, Mulligan left Thornhill and worked for a while with a small group alongside his Davis colleague Kai Winding (the trombonist who replaced Zwerin for the nonet's first studio sessions), and tenorist Brew Moore. That band recorded three times between May and August 1949, after which Mulligan returned for a while to Philadelphia to play again with Elliot Lawrence. The "band-within-a-band" was re-formed, and from late 1949 until mid-1950 the "Gerry Mulligan Quintet with Elliot Lawrence's Orchestra" with tenorist Phil Urso joining Gerry, backed by the band's rhythm section, made a number of appearances.

During this period, Mulligan transferred much of his energy from arranging to playing. But there was an underlying reason for this, on account of his having been introduced to heroin in late 1948 or early 1949, by some of his New York colleagues. He later reflected very honestly on this period in a remarkably frank 1959 interview, when he said:

> The junk seemed to help us get through a bad time. A few months after that first shot I was hooked both physically and mentally. Within a year it had become a tremendous problem. I had been doing some arrangements, but the junk had such a sedative effect on me I just couldn't finish anything I sat down to write.[58]

In April 1949, Kai Winding's sextet, with Mulligan and Max Roach, recorded a version of "Godchild"[59] with George Wallington himself, the composer of the piece, on piano. The head arrangement is reduced to Wallington's basic bebop theme, and all the subtlety and interplay of Mulligan's arrangements for the Davis nonet, or the Thornhill orchestra, are absent. There's a sparkling solo from Winding, and Brew Moore's half chorus is brisk and to the point in his post–Lester Young style. (In similar vein, he had played the opening solo on the 1948 Thornhill record of the piece.) By contrast, Mulligan's sixteen measures sound as if the sedative effect of the heroin has affected his playing, and alongside the crisp timing of the other soloists he strays into the slurred patterns of intoxication. Compared to the precision of his slightly earlier recordings, this is a worrying sign, although his ensemble work on two other tracks recorded at the same time, "Bop City" and "Sleepy Bop," is still comparatively disciplined and tidy.

58 Abramson, Martin: "Big Beat Comes Back," *Dover Daily Reporter* (OH), November 20, 1959.

59 Originally issued on 78 as "Wallington's Godchild" (Roost 500).

By August, his soloing on the same band's "Broadway" is back under control, and this was in no small measure due to a woman called Gail Madden, who, according to one press report, "believed she could help addicts with the power of suggestion, made him her responsibility for a while and got him back to work."[60] Soon Mulligan and Madden were an "item," and according to a press report they were eventually married in March 1951.[61] (There is some doubt about the veracity of this, as Mulligan's subsequent wife Arlyne averred that he had never legally married Madden.)[62] Although Gail Madden did not successfully persuade him to quit his narcotic habit, she put considerable effort into trying to help him keep working, and contributed some of her original ideas to his music. She had previously been involved with the composer and arranger Bob Graettinger. Through knowing him and various other jazz players, whom she had also tried to wean off drugs or drink, she knew her way around the contemporary music scene. The bassist Bob Whitlock met her a little later, in California, and said: "Gail was nothing if not flamboyant. . . . I also found her to be intelligent, resourceful, rebellious, bold, opinionated, and altogether fascinating."[63]

Around the time of the final Miles Davis nonet recording of March 9, 1950, it appears that the Davis band reconvened for a live performance at Birdland, the club that Morris Levy had recently opened as a home for bebop in late 1949 at 1678 Broadway, the former premises of the swing era venue known as the Ubangi. Although, when the author spoke to him in 2002, Lee Konitz remembered no additional live nonet sessions other than the 1948 Royal Roost appearances, an eyewitness account places him there (albeit that he was busy doubling with the Lennie Tristano band the same night, which might have clouded his memory). Konitz's name was noted, along with a full set of colleagues from the Capitol recordings, save for the pianist, who on that occasion was Bud Powell.[64] It is probable that Davis convened this session shortly before the final studio date to refocus the performers' minds on the music, since it had been almost a year since they last played together. The front line for the

60 Abramson: "Big Beat Comes Back."

61 Cutting citing the marriage from *Downbeat* reproduced in Myers, Mark: "Interview: Elliot Lawrence," *Jazz Wax Blog*, February 9, 2016 [www.jazzwax.com/2016/02/interview-elliot-lawrence.html; accessed April 20, 2021].

62 Interview with Arlyne Mulligan by Gordon Jack, transcript supplied courtesy of Gordon Jack.

63 Jack, Gordon: *Fifties Jazz Talk* (Lanham, MD, Scarecrow Press, 2004) p. 157.

64 Pullman, Peter: *Wail: The Life of Bud Powell* (New York, Peter Pullman, LLC, 2012) p. 138.

final Capitol date was almost identical to the Birdland lineup, with Davis, Konitz, Mulligan, Barber, and J. J. Johnson, with French horn player Sandy Siegelstein replaced by Gunther Schuller, while in the rhythm section John Lewis returned on piano, along with bassist Al McKibbon and drummer Max Roach, who had both played at Birdland.

Following this reunion, Mulligan split his time between working with Elliot Lawrence; leading the quintet drawn from that band with saxophonist/pianist Phil Urso; and playing on record sessions; as well as appearing for a few nights at the Apollo Theatre in a big band fronted by Stan Getz. By 1951, he led his own band quite frequently at Club 43 in the Woodside area of Queens, sharing saxophone duties with Urso, as well as starting to write again, and producing arrangements for a larger band that he planned to form. One outgrowth of the Club 43 booking was Mulligan's first serious experimentation with a "pianoless" rhythm section. He wrote:

> I was first made aware of the possibilities of a pianoless rhythm section by Gail Madden, a person who possesses a most refreshing and revolutionary conception of the rhythm section and its function. I agreed with her wholeheartedly as to the misuse of the piano with the rhythm section. To have an instrument with the tremendous capabilities of the piano reduced to the role of a crutch for the solo horn was unthinkable. Gail organized and rehearsed a pianoless rhythm section consisting of drums, bass and maracas, which she played herself in a swinging musical way. . . . I used this rhythm section successfully on many dates in Long Island and New Jersey.[65]

Some of the musicians involved, such as drummer Al Levitt and the expatriate British bassist Peter Ind, recalled these experiments. Ind, who was studying with Lennie Tristano, remembered the "serious rehearsals" that took place "when Gerry was rehearsing his pianoless quartet . . . which was unsuccessful in New York."[66] Nonetheless, even if it did not immediately win commercial success, Mulligan was adamant that this quartet (himself, Levitt, and Ind plus a trumpeter such as Don Ferrara or Don Joseph) had been "a deliberate policy" and that "I had a band in rehearsal that really didn't need a piano . . . it was an experiment and we tried some gigs."[67]

65 Mulligan, Gerry: *The Gerry Mulligan Quartet*, Pacific Jazz PLP 1 (1952) [liner note].

66 Ind, Peter: *Jazz Visions* (London, Equinox, 2006) p. 31.

67 Gerry Mulligan interviewed by Charles Fox, Glasgow Jazz Festival, July 1988.

This quartet configuration would be the foundation for Mulligan's main work in the 1950s, and is the principal subject of the following chapters, but before that on September 21, 1951, he made his first recordings as a leader for the Prestige label. For those records, he both brought in the arrangements he had been working on (for a basic nine-piece lineup, but with Gail Madden added to the instrumentation on maracas) and he also made the experimental recording of a small-group piece that was intended to last an entire side of one of the first LP records. This was "Mulligan's Too," an eighteen-minute track, using a duo front line with tenorist Allen Eager, but giving Mulligan space for a solo lasting thirty-five choruses, and which remains his longest ever on record.

His relationship with Bob Weinstock, the founder of Prestige, and its principal producer, goes back a little earlier. Weinstock owned a record store close to the Royal Roost where the Miles Davis Nonet had played. He was—and remained to the end of his days—a traditional jazz and swing fan, but he had been alerted to the sounds of bebop by his neighbor, Kenny Clarke. As a consequence, he became a regular at the Roost. Apparently when they first met, Clarke was horrified when Weinstock told him he knew his work from the recordings he had made with Sidney Bechet, and he immediately resolved to introduce Weinstock to more contemporary sounds. Weinstock recalled:

> A lot of the musicians who played at the Royal Roost would pass my store on the way to work. It was on the second floor and I had a loudspeaker that played into the street, and people could hear the music some blocks away. I had "from Bunk to Monk," and all the reissues on bootleg labels and so on. But after meeting Kenny, I got all the latest Bird and Diz records. Kenny Dorham used to come by, and Lee Konitz, and that's how I ended up in the recording business, because finally Kenny Clarke said to me, "Man, you know so much about jazz you should own your own record company." He introduced me to all the musicians, Fats Navarro, Tadd Dameron, Monk and so on, and he said, "Everybody says they're goin' to help you out and work with you." So I got a free pass to go down to the Roost all the time and started to record the musicians from the Roost, and also Dexter Gordon, Wardell Gray and Allen Eager. And that's where I met Gerry, down in the Roost one day.[68]

68 Author's interview with Bob Weinstock, August 22, 2002.

The consequence of this first meeting was that Mulligan composed and arranged two tracks for the Stan Getz Prestige session *The Brothers*, recorded in April 1949, and featuring the tenors of Getz, Zoot Sims, Al Cohn, Allen Eager, and Brew Moore. The session was recorded in New York at Apex Studios after 4 A.M., when the Woody Herman band, in which several of the saxophonists played, had finished its evening gig. Mulligan's piece "Five Brothers" takes the Jimmy Giuffre template for "Four Brothers" and combines it with the kind of section writing he had perfected in "Disc Jockey Jump." More interesting is his head for "Four and One Moore," which is an excellent example of Mulligan's grasp of ensemble voicing. Weinstock's idea for this session was that Getz should put together a band with what he called "the children of Lester Young," and he said, "Getz went to Mulligan for the charts." (What Weinstock did not mention was that Getz failed to pay for the arrangements. Mulligan took him to the AFM, but the case foundered when it was discovered that Mulligan had not paid his union dues.)[69]

Weinstock recalled that these records sold well, not least because they garnered a lot of radio play. A particular fan was the DJ, "Symphony Sid" Torin, who not only presented live radio transmissions from the Royal Roost, but promised that Prestige's discs would get plenty of exposure on his regular record show, if they were "in my groove."

"They were indeed in his groove," said Weinstock, "and you could hear him, right across to the Mississippi River, all the way to St. Louis, up to Chicago, and then the whole way down from New York to Florida."[70]

Weinstock's connection with Mulligan continued when Prestige recorded Chubby Jackson's All Star Big Band in March 1950. The group was squeezed into the small space of New York's Cinemart Studio ("like sardines" as Weinstock remembered), and on the day it turned out that some of the charts were unplayable by the musicians who had been recruited. Consequently, for some of the tracks, Weinstock broke the group into smaller constituent parts, and featured some of his soloists more extensively than originally planned. Mulligan was featured in a lengthy solo on his own (playable) chart of "I May Be Wrong," which would later become a staple of his quartet repertoire. There's an impromptu descending brass riff on the "A" sections of his final solo chorus (in AABA format) that foreshadows the spontaneous riff-making in the

69 Jack, Gordon: "Stan and Gerry—Occasional Collaborators," *Jazz Journal*, October 2017, p. 14.

70 Author's interview with Bob Weinstock, August 22, 2002.

Concert Jazz Band of the following decade. His other chart for the session is "So What (Hoo Hah)," which has a densely written head for the reed section of Charlie Kennedy, Zoot Sims, Georgie Auld, and Mulligan himself.

Following this, the stage was set for Mulligan's label debut as leader, although it took another eighteen months to happen. It came about in part because there was a hall on West 49th Street in midtown Manhattan called Don José's where a group of musicians regularly rented the space to rehearse privately, with no audience. The players, who chipped in 50 cents apiece to cover the rent of the room, included trumpeter Jerry Lloyd, saxophonists Mulligan, Zoot Sims, Al Cohn, Brew Moore, and Lee Konitz, plus pianist George Wallington. Looking back, Bob Weinstock recalled:

> Only two people were allowed in there when they were playing. Ira Gitler and myself. We used to go there all the time, and experienced some of the best jazz I ever heard. By this time Gerry was a really good jazz player. He'd made his reputation mostly as an arranger, but he was a very good player, and at the time I ranked him only behind Serge Chaloff as the best baritone saxophonist. And at this particular time, Gerry wanted to play, simply because he loved playing. During that Don José period, I used to invite him to my house for dinner. My mother would cook, and every two or three weeks, he'd come and eat with us, sometimes along with other musicians, such as Sonny Stitt. And afterwards we'd go in my room and play records. For the store I was buying up collections, so I had tons of records there. Whatever they wanted to hear, it was likely I had it. I remember Stitt asking to hear early Bird with Jay McShann, and I whipped out the records and played them.

Mulligan's listening tastes at those sessions focused particularly on Ellington, notably where Harry Carney's baritone saxophone was featured, and he also listened intently to Ernie Caceres, who played the baritone in Eddie Condon's Dixieland circle of players. So the decision to record Mulligan's "New Stars" for Prestige largely came about through that friendship, and the personnel included several of the musicians who jammed at Don José's. "After Miles's nonet," said Weinstock, "Gerry's Tentette arrangements came about. He brought them to me first, and we did it."

As mentioned, "Mulligan's Too" from that session was a long, open-ended jam with Allen Eager and rhythm section, which would occupy an entire side of an LP. Weinstock knew by 1951 that the LP would be the medium of the future, and decided that for his own enjoyment, after recording the arrangements for the larger band, he'd ask a smaller group of the musicians to stretch out. He did the same thing on a Zoot Sims date, intending to make some publicity capital from these innovative decisions, but also giving his friends room to blow in the studio in a way that had not been possible to capture on record before. When it appeared on Prestige LP 141, "Mulligan's Too" (a title from the company's ever-ready punster Ira Gitler) was marketed under the banner of the novel "Prestige Long-playing Microgroove Non-Breakable Record," selling at the price of $3.35.[71]

Compared to this extended quintet jam, Ira Gitler remembers that, owing to the lack of suitable and affordable rehearsal space, some of the ten-piece arrangements were initially rehearsed (somewhat informally) outdoors, close to the 72nd Street Lake in Central Park. Bassist Bill Crow photographed this occasion with various musicians including Tommy Allison, Harry Bugin, Allen Eager, Jimmy Ford, Phil Leshin, and Brew Moore visible in the pictures. (See Figure 1.3.)
However, on the musicians' second appearance at the location, Crow recalls:

> They set up closer to the men's room in the park restaurant. Someone from the restaurant complained to the police, who asked if they had a permit. Of course, they didn't, so the police told them to move on.[72]

The full band arrangements on the Prestige session included one piece reworked from an Elliot Lawrence score, "Mullenium"; another that would surface again a year or two later in a West Coast group with Shorty Rogers, "Ide's Side"; and a third (also reworked from a Lawrence score) that would—like "Jeru" and "Godchild"—reappear in Mulligan's later quartet work, namely "Bweebida Bobbida." George Simon's liner notes for Lawrence's 1955 recording of Mulligan arrangements suggests that the big band chart for "Bweebida Bobbida" was written after the 1951 tentette arrangement, but Mulligan himself was adamant, when interviewed in

71 "Jazz! Jazz! Jazz!" (Prestige panel advertisement), *Kingston Daily Freeman* (NY) September 23, 1953, p. 3.

72 Message to the author from Bill Crow, March 29, 2021. Personnel from that message, and from Jack, Gordon: "Bill Crow," in *Fifties Jazz Talk* (Lanham, MD, Scarecrow Press, 2004) p. 71.

FIGURE 1.3 Rehearsal in Central Park, Gail Madden standing to the left of Mulligan. Photograph ©Bill Crow; used by permission.

1988, that "the first version of that was for Elliot Lawrence's band."[73] The Lawrence chart is dazzlingly well-written, and the trombone figures that follow Al Cohn's tenor solo evoke the tune's title, which as Mulligan recalled, "reflects some of the rhythmic phrases inside the piece."[74] (See Figure 1.4.)

Indeed, the chart for Lawrence makes much of the trombone section (including a brilliantly fluid solo by Eddie Bert) and the lower brass (complete with French horns) provide some fine backing patterns, while the five-person trumpet section gives a scintillating edge to their part in the call-and-response of the theme, and the bridging passages between solos.

The smaller forces of the Mulligan Tentette, at a more leisurely tempo, contrasts with the full-throated big band, sounding more like the comparatively restrained effect of the Davis Nonet. (See Example 1.5.) The reduced number of instruments is the main difference, but the bass line is simplified, two baritone saxophones give the ensemble comparable

73 Gerry Mulligan interviewed by Charles Fox, Glasgow Jazz Festival, July 1988.

74 Ibid.

FIGURE 1.4 First trombone part for the opening of "Bweebida Bobbida" (Gerry Mulligan), in the copyist's hand. Elliot Lawrence Papers, Box 37, "Bweebida Bubbida" [*sic*] Folder, American Heritage Center, University of Wyoming, dated 1951. Used by permission.

EXAMPLE 1.5 The opening of Mulligan's Tentette chart for "Bweebida Bobbida" (transcription).

depth to the baritone and tuba combination, and the smaller brass section points to the way Mulligan would pare this piece down further in the repertoire of his mid-1950s quartet with Bob Brookmeyer.

Toward the end of 1951, not long after making these recordings, Mulligan took a decisive step to try to quit his drug habit. As Elliot Lawrence recalled, he sold all his horns save the baritone, and asked his friends to meet him outside the Paramount Hotel in New York City. Mulligan was wearing a long robe and a skullcap, and pushing a baby carriage containing his baritone. Lawrence said, "He was with Gale Madden, his new wife. He told everyone that they were walking to California. I think they got as far as the George Washington Bridge."[75] From there, they hitchhiked, and despite the cross-continent journey being long and difficult, the couple were in Los Angeles by the start of 1952, and the stage was set for the founding of the Mulligan quartet.

75 Myers, Mark: "Interview: Elliot Lawrence," *Jazz Wax Blog*, February 9, 2016 [www.jazzwax.com/2016/02/interview-elliot-lawrence.html; accessed April 20, 2021].

CHAPTER 2

THE FIRST QUARTET

It was unique because at that time no one else even thought of it, not having a chordal instrument. Gerry was cool. He was a very sincere musician. He was honest. Honest with his music and honest with his feelings. Chet had an unusual ear. He reflected the harmonic aspect of Gerry. Gerry created the harmonic structure for the melodies that Chet would play. But it was done in a way so that the average listener wouldn't even think about it. It was just done as a natural thing.

—CHICO HAMILTON[1]

IT HAD BEEN one thing to play experimental quartet dates in 1951, out of the mainstream, around the greater New York area, but it was quite another to start recording as a leader for the nascent Pacific Jazz label in the summer of 1952, with Chet Baker, Bob Whitlock, and Chico Hamilton, while pulling in crowds every week to a Los Angeles nightclub.

When Mulligan and Gail Madden arrived in California in early 1952, he had no work, and his reputation (as the Prestige discs had yet to make any significant impression on the national jazz scene) was as an arranger, rather than a player. Some accounts (including Mulligan's own in the Library of Congress Oral History) suggest that he had even sold his baritone saxophone, but while it is clear that he borrowed a tenor for a short

1 Interview with Chico Hamilton, September 3, 2002.

The Gerry Mulligan 1950s Quartets. Alyn Shipton, Oxford University Press. © Alyn Shipton 2023.
DOI: 10.1093/oso/9780197579756.003.0002

period playing with a Western Swing band in Albuquerque on his route to California, it seems—as Elliot Lawrence recalled—that he hung on to the baritone. To keep hand to mouth, Gail Madden spoke to her former partner Bob Graettinger who had been working as a composer/arranger for Stan Kenton, and whose multi-part masterpiece "City of Glass" had been recorded by Kenton's Innovations in Modern Music Orchestra in December 1951. Could Bob effect an introduction to Stan for Gerry?

The result was that Mulligan was commissioned to write some scores for the Kenton band. They were not recorded immediately, but he was, for a short while, taken on to the Kenton staff. This was born out of financial necessity more than empathy between Mulligan and Kenton. At a time when Mulligan's most recent tentette arrangements showed a move toward the chamber jazz aesthetic of the Davis nonet, he now found himself writing for one of the largest, loudest, and most bombastic big bands of all. In early 1952, Kenton had slightly reorganized his band, and after a tour that took him from New York to Texas, he reopened at the start of March at the Municipal Auditorium in Long Beach, with his twenty-piece "Artistry in Rhythm" orchestra, which one local journalist dubbed "continuously controversial."[2] Confronted with a band of this size, Mulligan's instinct, as has been shown in the evolution of several of his charts so far, was to pare away unnecessary detail, to the extent that Bob Brookmeyer would later joke that at big band rehearsals of Gerry's music, the essential tool was an eraser. Many years after he had worked for Kenton, Mulligan reflected:

> I kind of wracked my brains trying to find things to write for that band. I didn't really feel a rapport with the band itself, although in the particular edition of the band that I wrote for, the guys were very enthusiastic to have me write for them. But there are certain limitations in an instrumentation like that, which I never could cope with. I don't really like to write extremely high trumpet parts. The band's approach to music was very vertical, whereas I always like things more horizontal, to evolve in lines and in counterpoint.[3]

The best known of his charts "Young Blood" (commissioned by Kenton, and recorded in September 1952) somehow manages to reconcile these two aspects of the arranger's art. The opening theme is a long sinuous

2 Schott, Fred: "Curtain Call," *Long Beach Independent*, March 2, 1952, p. 38.

3 Gerry Mulligan interviewed by Charles Fox, Glasgow Jazz Festival, July 1988.

line that soon invites a contrapuntal melody to sneak in alongside it, just five seconds into the track. After two restrained choruses, the high note trumpets blare out, introducing the first solo, and from that moment onward, the excitement of the piece rests on the tension between the horizontal: its overall melodic flow, and the underscoring below the solos; and the vertical: its stacked chords. The alto soloist is Lee Konitz, who had followed Mulligan and Madden to the West. Yet this upbeat, extrovert piece is something of an exception in Mulligan's work for the band. He did not look back favorably on his early months in California, later reflecting that—this track and one other called "Swing House" apart—during the time he was on Kenton's arranging staff, alongside Pete Rugolo and Bill Holman, the leader "made sure that I understood that the other guys were to do the concert stuff, and what I was writing would be the dog work, writing the dance arrangements, which was alright with me because I liked the tunes. I did the best I could with them."[4] What he may not have appreciated was that Holman, at least, understood exactly what he brought to Kenton, saying that "The things Gerry Mulligan had done with the band, gave me a glimmer of light of what could be done."[5]

Partly as a consequence of his contacts with Kenton's sidemen past and present, and partly by just turning up at open jam sessions, Mulligan gradually began to make a reputation as a player in Los Angeles, and by the summer he was a welcome addition to bassist Howard Rumsey's All Stars at the Lighthouse Club on Hermosa Beach. There is documentary evidence of him playing there at more than one of the venue's lengthy weekend sessions, alongside trumpeter Shorty Rogers, in June 1952.[6] Rogers recalled:

> The whole bunch of guys working down there included Shelly Manne, Milt Bernhardt, Art Pepper and Hampton Hawes. It was at 30 Pier Avenue, and just a few doors West of there you're on the beach. Go out and walk a few feet further on, and you're in the Pacific Ocean. So it was very much a beach place. On Sundays, which became the big marathon all-day session there, from two in the afternoon 'til two in

4 www.loc.gov/collections/gerry-mulligan/articles-and-essays/jeru-in-the-words-of-gerry-mulligan/young-blood/#young-blood-madden [accessed May 15, 2021].

5 Gioia, Ted: *West Coast Jazz* (New York, Oxford University Press, 1992) p. 159.

6 A limited edition record including tracks recorded at the Lighthouse on June 1 and June 14 and issued by the Los Angeles Jazz Institute is listed in the online Mulligan discography by Gérard Dugelay and Kenneth Hallqvist [pdalbury.files.wordpress.com/2012/09/gm-discography-2011.pdf; accessed May 16, 2021].

> the morning, the prices were very inexpensive. People would come in and have a beer for 25 cents. People would hear the music and come in off the beach at around 2:15 in their bathing suits. Sometimes I'd look up off the bandstand and see the same guy sitting there with the same beer—been there all day long.[7]

According to Mulligan himself, these twelve-hour sessions also happened on a Saturday night.[8] At least he was being paid as a player for these long gigs every weekend, and Rogers (always generous toward other musicians, and especially those whose talent he admired) inveigled him into other live appearances and the occasional broadcast. Soon Mulligan was also being paid to lead a Monday night jam session at the Haig Club, a relatively small venue at 638 South Kenmore Avenue, on the short block between Wilshire Boulevard and 6th Street, in the center of Los Angeles, which had a legal capacity of just eighty-five. Pianist and vocalist Bobby Short, who preceded Mulligan's arrival there, described the place thus:

> The Haig was totally out of its place. It was planted in the middle of a lot of very tall buildings, across the street from a very famous and grand hotel called the Ambassador, that was all very glamorous and grand. And the Ambassador, of course, had Freddy Martin's Band in the Cocoanut Grove nightclub, and big stars played there. And then there was the Haig, looking like a little Cape Cod cottage with a picket fence around it. It was a one-story building, not terribly spick and span inside, with a grand piano on a raised platform, and dim lights and a bar. And an owner, John Bennett, who I guess you'd call a snob about music. When I went to work there, he was delighted because I'd just come from New York. He wanted to have something New York–ish in his club, and also the two of us shared an enthusiasm for Broadway show tunes. And so he felt he'd done something special by bringing me there. I remember one night we were doing turnaway business there, and people were standing in the line outside to get in, and I was doing my best to entertain those people, but I sang a song that John did not like. Although the place was so crammed you couldn't get in, he said, "How dare you sing that awful song in my place?" I said, "Your customers are all very, very happy, John, and

7 Interview with Shorty Rogers, November 23, 1991.

8 Josephson, Sanford: *Jeru's Journey* (Milwaukee, Hal Leonard, 2015) p. 25.

there's a line outside waiting to get in." He said, "I don't care about that! I want just good songs!" So that's the kind of person he was.[9]

Bennett managed most aspects of the club, but his musical adviser, who booked several of the acts that appeared there, was Richard Bock, who had been working as a producer for Albert Marx's Hollywood-based jazz label, Discovery Records. He brought in some major artists, not least because, despite this being such a small club, its significance in the early 1950s was that, along with the Lighthouse, it was one of the very few Los Angeles clubs that countenanced modern jazz (despite the pioneering work of Billy Berg's with Dizzy Gillespie and Charlie Parker in the 1940s). The French horn player John Graas, a regular colleague of Shorty Rogers, wrote that, elsewhere in the area, "It was all Dixieland territory then, the club owners in Hollywood and Los Angeles wouldn't hear of anything but Dixieland."[10] At the time Mulligan began to run the Monday night jam sessions at the Haig,[11] the grand piano mentioned by Bobby Short was being played on the other six nights of the week by Erroll Garner, who was enjoying a long-term residency.

Richard Bock was something of a musical visionary, committed (initially for Discovery, but subsequently on his own account) to documenting and promoting the musical scene of Southern California, and this press report from the period catches something of his character and attitude:

> His appearance is as startling as the music he records. A lanky individual, Bock wears crumpled clothes, horn-rimmed glasses and sports a reddish mustache and beard. He looks like a reserve forward for the House of David basketball team, instead of the pied piper of a new musical trend. But Bock's eccentricities end with his beard. A serious minded businessman, he is free of the hot cat jive drivel of the bop gang. His approach to the West Coast "school" of jazz is obvious. "Each generation tries to express itself differently," he said. "It's true in literature, art, and music. We're just carrying on the tradition."[12]

9 Interview with Bobby Short, September 3, 2002.

10 Shipton, Alyn: "To the Lighthouse," *Jazz FM Magazine* (No. 11, 1992) p. 32.

11 I have gone with the general consensus that these took place on Mondays. But, the Dugulay/Hallqvist discography places all the informal recordings of Haig jam sessions on Tuesdays, and Richard Bock in his liner note to Pacific LP-1 (the quartet's first album) specifically mentions the "Tuesday night jazz concerts" that Mulligan took over.

12 Scott, Vernon: "Hollywood Scene—Strong Rhythm Combos Play New Long Haired Jazz," *Galveston Daily News*, January 6, 1956.

Mulligan is first noted as appearing at the Haig on May 27, 1952, and over the next few weeks his jam session sextets included fellow saxophonist Dave Pell; pianists Paul Smith, Donn Trenner, and Jimmy Rowles; guitarist Howard Roberts; bassists Joe Mondragon and Red Mitchell; and drummers Billy Wilson, Tommy Rundell, and Chico Hamilton. Various trumpeters, including Vern Smith and Ted Ottison, also joined these events. If nothing else, this shows that Mulligan was becoming well connected in the local jazz scene. But just as important musically as the gigs he relied on to earn a subsistence wage (and to support his continuing—although better controlled—heroin habit) were the informal sessions in which he played across the greater Los Angeles area.

Some of these jams took place in the San Fernando Valley, and Mulligan would occasionally bring musicians together for impromptu rehearsals during the daytime at a restaurant in that area called the Cottage Italia that had a small stage, on which there were jam sessions most evenings. Accounts vary of exactly when and where he first met trumpeter Chet Baker, who had been recommended to him by bassist Bob Whitlock, but there are eyewitness accounts of the two failing to hit it off, at what was to have been their first rehearsal together at the Cottage Italia. Apparently, Baker warmed up at ear-splitting volume, leading to an expletive-laden argument with the sensitive Mulligan, and no playing took place that day.[13]

Yet Baker had a talent that it was hard to ignore. Twenty-two-year-old Chesney Henry Baker had been born in Oklahoma, but spent his teenage years in Los Angeles, before playing trumpet in various US Army bands. He had left the military in 1951, but had already developed his distinctive jazz style, which was lyrical and centered in the middle range. In late May 1952 he joined the quintet led by the visiting Charlie Parker at the Tiffany Club on West 8th Street in East Hollywood, situated just two short blocks away from the Haig. Apparently at the Tiffany, which had played host in the recent past to traditional or mainstream musicians such as Muggsy Spanier, Helen Forrest, and Art Tatum, Parker encouraged Baker by staying with repertoire that the trumpeter knew well. Bird appears to have been impressed with what he heard, apparently sending word to his New York colleagues Dizzy Gillespie, Lee Morgan, and Miles Davis about the "little white cat on the coast who's gonna eat you up."[14]

13 Gavin, James: *Deep in a Dream: The Long Night of Chet Baker* (London, Chatto and Windus, 2002) p. 54.

14 Ibid. p. 53.

On June 16, bassist Harry Babasin recorded a jam session with Parker and Baker at the Trade Winds Club in Inglewood, close by Los Angeles International Airport. The session does not convey more than a few glimpses of the talent that Bird had perceived in the trumpeter, when inviting him to join the quintet. This is in part due to the presence of another saxophonist, the locally based Sonny Criss, who had a point to prove to Parker. On the uptempo pieces, Baker is almost literally elbowed out of the way by the two altoists, but on the medium-paced ballad "Irresistible You" (see Example 2.1) the trumpeter produces a spontaneous countermelody to Parker's theme statement that shows exactly the kind of melodic and harmonic invention that would become a cornerstone of the Mulligan quartet. Parker observed at the time that "Chet's playing is soft and light, and at the same time, straight and honest."[15]

The pianist on that version of "Irresistible You" was Donn Trenner, who had already appeared with Mulligan at his Monday night jams at the Haig, and he seems to have been quite a catalyst in bringing musicians together. At almost the same time that Chet Baker was playing with Charlie Parker, Mulligan (who had long since shed the strange garments of his last days in New York, and was adopting a more straight-laced appearance) began rehearsing in earnest for a more permanent band of his own. With the encouragement of Richard Bock, who captured the sessions on tape, he first recorded in a trio with bassist Red Mitchell and drummer Chico Hamilton, who had been quite regular members of the Monday night jams. Bock asked Phil Turetsky, a recording engineer who lived in a small home in the Hollywood Hills, to host the recording at his house. The setup, with a single microphone connected to Turetsky's Ampex, mirrored to some extent the acoustic environment of the Haig, where the musicians played with no amplification.

On July 9, Mulligan was back at Turetsky's again, this time with Jimmy Rowles on piano and Joe Mondragon, bass. His frontline partner was Chet Baker. This was the first time that the two of them recorded together. But the vital ingredient of what would become the Mulligan "pianoless" quartet came about later that month, after Erroll Garner finished his run as the headliner at the Haig. The grand piano that Bobby Short mentioned was put into storage, because the next main band to appear there was the trio of vibraphonist Red Norvo, who worked with just guitar and bass. Bennett offered Mulligan a small upright spinet for the

15 Tercinet, Alain: *The Complete Charlie Parker, Vol. 11*, Fremeaux, FA 1341 (2016) [liner note].

EXAMPLE 2.1 "Irresistible You" (Don Raye, Gene DePaul), showing Charlie Parker's phrasing of the theme, Chet Baker's accompaniment, and Harry Babasin's bass part. Recorded June 16, 1952 (transcription).

jam sessions, but Mulligan refused. Now was his opportunity to put into practice the idea he had tried in New York of a band with no chordal instrument. And it would also—with Bock's agreement—change Monday nights at the Haig from a somewhat random jam session to a group with regular personnel. This would be Mulligan, Baker, bassist Bob Whitlock, and drummer Chico Hamilton. Mulligan later observed:

EXAMPLE 2.1 Continued

> I didn't want to play on a little old tiny upright piano, and I'd heard and played around Los Angeles sessions with Chet Baker, and Chico Hamilton was playing with a little group that Charlie Barnet had, so it gradually jelled and we got it together, and musically it worked out very well. The thing with Chet was really incredible, because some of the things that we would do that were . . . totally improvised, not worked out ahead of time at all, were seamless in the finished quality that we wound up doing. I never played with anybody, including Brookmeyer, where we had that kind of rapport.[16]

The band rehearsed regularly before appearing in public. Some of these practice sessions were outdoors on the verandah at Baker's home in Lynwood, just east of Watts, where he and his girlfriend Charlene lived with her parents,[17] but for the most part the quartet met at Chico Hamilton's house. Hamilton said:

> Gerry tells me one day, "I'm gonna put a group together." So he comes up with Chet. I'd seen Chet when he was with Bird, and he came over

16 Gerry Mulligan interviewed by Charles Fox, Glasgow Jazz Festival, July 1988.

17 Jack, Gordon: "Bob Whitlock," in *Fifties Jazz Talk* (Lanham MD, Scarecrow Press, 2004) p. 157.

with Chet and Bob Whitlock and we met right in my house. Right in my living room. He didn't want me to use a bass drum. So I used the snare and a sock.[18] And one thing I was very proficient at, and could do exceedingly well, was brush. In fact all the good gigs I had gotten was because I could brush well. Playing for Lady, playing for Lena, all the singers. So we started off with the first rehearsal, right there. As a matter of fact the first tune we did was "Bernie's Tune." That was also the first tune we recorded for Pacific Jazz. We did that up in Phil Turetsky's living room. Not in a studio—the living room. And as you know, it became a record label. Pacific Jazz.[19]

In the quartet's recording of "Bernie's Tune," a slightly bigger drum set can be heard than just the snare drum and sock cymbal mentioned by Hamilton, but after the first rehearsals, Mulligan remained adamant that he wanted something less than the conventional full kit that the drummer had been using with Charlie Barnet. Yet Hamilton knew he needed some form of bass drum, not least because he needed to keep using his right foot, which had stayed idle during the band's practice sessions. In the end he found a solution that worked:

I told Gerry, "I want to bring in a bass drum, cos I'm losing my foot." He didn't dig that at all. So I bought a little 16-inch tom-tom, and I converted it into a bass drum. So I had the snare and the sock and this bass drum. No cymbals, just that, and man, it worked! The minute I started kicking Gerry in the ass with it, he dug it—as you can tell on all those first recordings, with the bass drum work that I did, double kicking, and things like that, making the accents with it.[20]

For Hamilton, it was not just his bespoke small bass drum that was important (although when I spoke to him fifty years later, he still owned it), but the snare. By 1952, Chico (whose full name was Foreststorn Hamilton) had the highest-profile playing career of any of the musicians in the band, having toured widely (including visiting Britain) with Lena Horne, and worked with Lionel Hampton, as well as recording with Wardell Gray and Dexter Gordon. He was from a very different

18 A hi-hat cymbal.

19 Interview with Chico Hamilton, September 5, 2002.

20 Ibid.

background from the three white players in the band, having grown up in the African American community in Los Angeles. He said:

> The snare drum was the first drum that I ever owned. I bought that drum when I was in junior high school, by shining shoes. As a kid I had a shoe shine box, and I made myself enough money to buy myself this great big 12-inch snare drum. It was a Leedy. They don't make them anymore. It was a classic. It had a dynamite sound, and resonance. You actually could hear the snares well, and *feel* it in a band. It was a good-sounding drum.[21]

If Hamilton was on the receiving end of Mulligan's strictures as to what he wanted, so too was twenty-one-year-old Bob Whitlock, just starting his career as a freelance bassist. He was sometimes forbidden to leave the rehearsals until he had proven that he had memorized his parts in the arranged ensemble sections of the music.[22] But the hard work paid off.

The sound of this quartet playing live at the Haig on the five Mondays prior to the lineup's first recording session at Turetsky's on Saturday, August 16, 1952, convinced Richard Bock that he had a commercially viable product on his hands. This seemed to be the right moment to set up his own record company to record and release the group's music. He and his business partner, the drummer (and drum shop owner) Richard Harte, borrowed the money ($2,000 each) to set up a new firm, and according to Bock: "We recorded the memorable 'Bernie's Tune' and 'Lullaby of the Leaves.' That record, released as a single in the fall of 1952, put Pacific Jazz in business. The quartet rapidly became a West Coast sensation."[23]

"Lullaby of the Leaves" had been a staple of the jazz repertoire since Art Tatum's 1941 recording. Mulligan's opening statement of the familiar theme has subtle underpinnings from Baker, and the melody switches between the horns, notably after a brief double-time episode, when Mulligan produces a fine countermelody to Baker's lead. Later that year a syndicated record review newspaper column gave it four stars as one of the year's "Commercial Best Records."[24]

21 Ibid.

22 Gavin: *Deep in a Dream*, p. 65.

23 Gordon, Robert: *Jazz West Coast* (London, Quartet, 1986) p. 73.

24 "Commercial Best Records," *Jefferson City Lincoln Clarion*, December 12, 1952.

Fine and relaxed as this piece is, the number that captured the public imagination and set a template for much of the quartet's future work was "Bernie's Tune," written by a little-known Washington, DC–based pianist, Bernie Miller, who had died in 1945. It had found its way into the collection of arrangements for Boyd Raeburn's Orchestra, which made a transcription disc during the AFM record ban in 1944, under the title "Bobby Socks," giving the piece a somewhat Kenton-esque makeover, yet it was otherwise not well known. Mulligan's record immediately grabs the listener's attention, the catchy opening theme played by the two horns in close harmony being instantly memorable, but it is the solo sequence that highlights the group's originality.

Although by 1952 some Jazz at the Philharmonic performers—notably Roy Eldridge—would ask the rhythm section to "stroll" for a chorus or two, in other words, to continue with just bass and drums as the piano dropped out, the idea of an entire medium tempo jazz performance with no explicitly stated harmonic background was highly unusual. The piece has, on the face of it, a simple chord sequence, in AABA format, in the key of D minor.

The "A" section runs:

Dm | Dm | B♭7 | B♭7 | A7 | A7 | Dm | Dm.

The "B" section contrasts with:

B♭ / Gm | Cm7 / F7 | B♭ / Gm | Cm7 / F7 | B♭ / Gm | Cm7 / F7 | B♭ | A7

But Mulligan, working closely with Bob Whitlock, adds passing chords that enrich the texture without losing the essential approachability of the piece. His solo begins as shown in Example 2.2.

The two voices of bass and baritone imply a denser harmonic sequence. Hence, the stage is set for Mulligan to continue enriching the harmonies behind Baker's solo; see Example 2.3. Here, after the final phrase of his solo, the alternating long note pattern Mulligan uses in measures 55 and 56 becomes the basis of his subsequent backing for Baker.

Finally, the piece draws toward its conclusion with a perfect example of the kind of spontaneous empathy that Mulligan and Baker had. As the trumpet solo ends, Mulligan signals a riff pattern, and immediately he and Baker enter a routine built around this two quarter-note and one half-note phrase, playing the pattern together, but with Mulligan leaving a space of one beat in measures 106 and 107 to create a sense of call-and-response (Example 2.4). It is possible that they had rehearsed this, but

EXAMPLE 2.2 Opening of Mulligan's solo in "Bernie's Tune" (Bernie Miller) (transcription).

given the cue and the way it is picked up, it sounds as if this is just an entirely natural part of the way that the two musicians worked together.

Only a couple of weeks after the quartet's debut session for the newly founded Pacific Jazz label, and before the 78 rpm record's release, the band traveled up to San Francisco. From Monday, September 1, until Saturday, September 6, the group appeared there opposite Dave Brubeck's quartet. The pianist was something of a talent scout for the Bay Area's Fantasy record company, and the gossip among musicians had alerted him to the chemistry between the trumpeter and baritone player who had been appearing at the Haig. Brubeck recalled:

> I was playing at the Black Hawk in San Francisco and Gerry played one night a week at a club in Hollywood, and I liked what I heard about his group. So I said to Gerry why don't you come to where I'm kinda the house band in San Francisco—and then I got him to record

EXAMPLE 2.3 Part of Chet Baker's solo from "Bernie's Tune" (transcription).

> on Fantasy records. My job with that record company was to get good people, and I got Gerry.[25]

The result was a session cut at the club on September 2, which produced some of the quartet's most enduring recordings, namely "Line for Lyons,"

25 Interview with Dave Brubeck, September 2001.

EXAMPLE 2.4 Final part of "Bernie's Tune." Words by Mike Stoller and Jerry Leiber. Music by Bernie Miller. Copyright © 1953, 1954, 1955 Atlantis Music Corp. Copyright renewed. All Rights Reserved. Used by permission. Reprinted by permission of Hal Leonard Europe Ltd. (transcription).

"Carioca," "My Funny Valentine," as well as "Bark for Barksdale," not to mention a second try at "Utter Chaos," which they had attempted at the inaugural Turetsky's house session, but which had now became their sign-off on live events. In most accounts of the quartet, the fact that they then returned to their weekly gigs at the Haig for the rest of September and the first three weeks of October tends to be overlooked. (While back in Los Angeles they made their second Pacific Jazz recording on October 15, at Gold Star Studios, which will be discussed shortly.) However, they had been a great success in San Francisco, so the Black Hawk booked them back as a double headliner for three weeks from October 21 alongside pianist Eddie Heywood's trio. Meanwhile, for the same three weeks, the Haig got its piano out of storage, and Dave Brubeck's quartet became the main act there. This was Brubeck's idea, because during Mulligan's first trip to the Bay Area he had proposed: " 'I'll go down and play where you play in L.A.,' and so we exchanged jobs."[26]

This time around, Chico Hamilton (owing to family and other weeknight gig commitments) did not travel with the group to San Francisco. Instead they were joined by "*Down Beat*'s newest sensation" the drummer Bobby White.[27] To pull in audiences for the three-week season, readers of the local press were told: "A quicky brush-up on your San Francisco where to go includes facts like the 'battle of the bands' at the Black Hawk. Eddie Heywood Trio vies with Gerry Mulligan Quartet with Bobby White on drums."[28] No recordings appear to have survived from the Quartet's work with Bobby White. However, the band was reviewed in *Down Beat*, by the nationally influential journalist Ralph J. Gleason. His article commended their "fantastic, fugue-ish, funky, swinging and contrapuntal sound."[29]

When the Fantasy sides recorded on the group's first visit to the Black Hawk finally appeared, the number that would have the greatest long-term impact was "My Funny Valentine," putting Baker's trumpet in the spotlight and creating a piece that would forever be associated with him throughout the rest of his career. Although he later re-recorded it with his own quartet (and on several other occasions), it is this dark, brooding solo in the Mulligan group that made his reputation with the song, the trumpet's solo line helped immeasurably by the harmonic choices of bassist Carson Smith (who had replaced Whitlock for the trip), as shown in Example 2.5. Smith had some experience as an arranger and he was the one who suggested this piece as the ballad selection for the session.

26 Ibid.

27 Panel advertisement in *Oakland Tribune*, October 23, 1952, p. 80.

28 *Oakland Tribune*, October 25, 1952.

29 Gleason, Ralph J.: "Swingin' the Golden Gate: Mr. Mulligan Has a Real Crazy Gerry-Built Crew," *Down Beat* (October 22, 1952) p. 8. As this was published in Chicago on the day after they opened, Gleason presumably based his review on their September appearance.

EXAMPLE 2.5 "My Funny Valentine" from *Babes in Arms*, words by Lorenz Hart, music by Richard Rodgers. Copyright © 1937 WC Music Corp. and Williamson Music Company (50%) c/o Concord Music Publishing. Copyright renewed. All rights reserved. Used by Permission. Reprinted by permission of Hal Leonard Europe, Ltd. Copyright © 1937 Warner Chappell Music Company Ltd and Williamson Music Company (50%). c/o Warner Chappell Music Ltd, London. Reproduced by permission of Faber Music Ltd. All rights reserved. Opening section, showing the harmonic contrast between Mulligan's and Smith's lines in measures 9–16 (transcription).

Mulligan said of him: "that moving bass line which really makes the arrangement was Carson's idea."[30]

In the opening of the piece, this movement occurs on the second and fourth beats of the initial five measures, whereas the first and third beats of each of these measures remain on a pedal C. But as the example shows, Smith emphasized a simple downward chromatic run, from C to a B natural (emphasizing the major 7th of the C minor chord), then to

30 Jack: *Fifties Jazz Talk*, p. 146.

a B flat, pointing the movement to a simple C 7th chord, and then to an A natural, emphasizing the 6th in a C minor 6th chord, and finally to an A flat, the root note of the chord in the fifth measure. When Mulligan enters on the repeat of the A section, he takes on a similar harmonic movement (though beginning on the first beat of each measure), but now the melody is transposed up a minor third, and the underlying harmonies are altered, because Smith plays an upward-moving sequence of Cm | D dim 7 | E♭ | F | Fm as indicated on the music example, which implies a contrary motion against the harmonies suggested in Mulligan's descending line.

This song had seldom been recorded before, but the clear repeated motif in Richard Rodgers's melody and the stark beauty of the arrangement made it not only accessible to audiences, but also memorable, and there is little doubt that Mulligan's version inspired further recordings by artists as varied as Ella Fitzgerald (1953), Bud Powell (1954), and Miles Davis (on more than one occasion from 1956). Just as "Bernie's Tune" had laid down a paradigm for the band's approach to mid-tempo numbers, the treatment of "My Funny Valentine" would be a similarly important statement of how the group would tackle ballads in the months to come. In his study of the "implied harmony" of the band, Simon Bartlett points out that the harmonic movement in much of the band's repertoire, as in this piece, "was never more than two chords in a bar, and more often than not, one chord in a bar," and that generally, even if the music was not "harmonically familiar material," it offered listeners "time to 'hear' where the progressions were going."[31]

"My Funny Valentine" was the most enduring of the 1952 San Francisco recordings, but the piece with the biggest variation in texture from any of the quartet's other discs of the period was "Carioca." (The name connotes Rio de Janeiro, and the piece prefigures the vogue for the mixture of jazz and Brazilian *bossa nova* that took off later in the decade.) The success of this record is in no small measure due to Chico Hamilton, who created the underlying Latin effects, starting with a roll on the tom-tom with mallets, and then playing on the snare drum with his fingertips rather than sticks or brushes. He said: "That's all it was. I turned the snares off and did the handwork and then picked up the brushes real quick. At that time it was really different. No one had been doing stuff like that.

31 Bartlett, Simon: "An Exploration of the Origin and Expressions of Implied Harmony in the Gerry Mulligan Quartet with Chet Baker (1952–53)" (M.Mus. thesis, Sydney Conservatorium of Music, University of Sydney, 2015) p. 86.

But it gave us a really unique feeling and sound. There was a very good togetherness."[32]

The quartet's togetherness is even more apparent on the opening of Mulligan's medium-paced composition "Line for Lyons," dedicated to Jimmy Lyons, who hosted a late night jazz radio show on KNBC, which, although based in the Bay Area, could be heard along much of the West Coast. Shortly before the Mulligan quartet's first visit to San Francisco, the DJ also hosted a weekly show featuring the Brubeck group, called *Lyons Busy* (for which Brubeck composed a theme tune), and he would later go on in 1958 to found the Monterey Jazz Festival. There was an obvious element of flattery in Mulligan's title, with the quartet and Fantasy surreptitiously pitching for airplay, but the elegant head arrangement (see Example 2.6) shows how the band could stamp its imprimatur on a piece, albeit following the basic template of "Bernie's Tune." Baker sticks to the melody and Mulligan plays a supporting line that sounds composed rather than improvised.

Following the head, just as in "Bernie's Tune," there is a baritone solo, and then Baker solos, accompanied by long notes from Mulligan. The subsequent exchange of phrases between trumpet and baritone is again prompted by a motif from Mulligan, before the band returns to the B section of the head, and takes the piece out on a reprise of the opening. It has a hint of the restraint discernible in some of the Davis Nonet recordings, yet there is, amid the cool relaxation, a sense of pent-up excitement, not least in Baker's solo.

In contrast, "Bark for Barksdale" (also named for a local DJ, the former Oakland basketball star Don Barksdale) is far from "cool." It is an uptempo hard bop number, following the standard pattern of such pieces, with a unison AABA head (dividing into close harmony on the B section) and breakneck choruses from Mulligan and Baker (with subtle saxophone backing) before a lengthy drum solo from Hamilton that is technically exceptional for being played with brushes. His ensemble playing here is also exemplary, with his bass drum (or rather modified tom-tom) accents demonstrating exactly why he had been right to insist on this addition to his reduced kit.

One consequence of the band recording for the established Fantasy label, which had been set up in 1949 by the brothers Max and Sol Weiss, was not only that these discs were well marketed in the United States, but that their international distribution also took off quite quickly. So, for

32 Interview with Chico Hamilton, September 5, 2002.

EXAMPLE 2.6 "Line for Lyons" by Gerry Mulligan. Copyright © 1954 Criterion Music Corp. Copyright renewed. All rights reserved. Used by Permission. Reprinted by permission of Hal Leonard Europe, Ltd. Opening section (transcription).

example, before the end of the year, the American 78 rpm disc of "Line for Lyons" coupled with "Carioca" had been licensed to Vogue in Britain, Swing in France, Karusell in Sweden, and Embassy in Denmark.[33] In the

33 Originally issued on Fantasy 522, then on Karusell K-37, Vogue V-2337, Swing 410, and Embassy 172.

wake of this better-known label's licensing success, Richard Bock's firm was then able to couple "Bernie's Tune" with Chet Baker's composition "Freeway" (cut at the October LA session between the two San Francisco trips) into a single for the British Vogue company, after which the nascent Pacific Jazz business also started to see its product reach an international audience. One longer-term consequence of licensing the quartet's music to the Jazz-Disques company in France, directed by the eminent discographer Charles Delauney (and including both the French Vogue and Swing labels), was that in due course European listeners got the original Mulligan Quartet output from two US companies on a single label, Swing, once the 78s were grouped together for 10-inch LP release. Following the licensing history of the 78s, Volume 1 (M.33.304) was entirely made up of Fantasy sides, but it was soon followed by Volumes 2 and 3 (M.33.305 and M.33.306) containing the Pacific Jazz sessions (Figure 2.1).

The quartet's first two sessions had been, in one respect or another, location recordings, first at Phil Turetsky's house (although the balance he achieved was excellent) and then at the Black Hawk jazz club, which continued to play host to live recordings by bands playing onstage there, until it finally closed its doors in 1963. For the second Pacific Jazz session by the full quartet, Richard Bock booked what was fast establishing itself as Los Angeles's leading independent recording studio, Gold Star, in Hollywood.

Situated at the intersection of Santa Monica Boulevard and Vine Street, it had been founded by acoustic engineer David S. Gold and the recording engineer Stan Ross. Later, working with Phil Spector, their self-designed echo and reverb facilities were a vital ingredient in his "wall of sound" discs, but in 1952, just as Rudy Van Gelder was doing at exactly the same time in New Jersey, Ross was focusing on achieving good fidelity and a "true sound" for his clients in the studio setting. One immediate beneficiary of this was Mulligan, whose baritone has, on these tracks, a depth and clarity seldom achieved in his earlier recordings. Similarly, the brightness in Baker's trumpet tone contrasts favorably to the somewhat low-key timbre of the Black Hawk session. Nowhere is this more evident than on Baker's own piece "Freeway."

This is a startlingly original composition, especially because it does not draw on the same influences as Mulligan's work, which—as demonstrated so far—included the big band tradition, hard bop and the tonal template of his Lawrence, Davis, and Thornhill charts. Even though "Jeru" has measures in different time signatures, and segments of unusual length, it has fewer dramatically effective devices than those present

FIGURE 2.1 Cover of the Mulligan Quartet's first Swing 10-inch LP to contain Pacific Jazz titles.

in the opening section of "Freeway," which has isolated chords played by the entire ensemble in the five-measure introduction, leading to a 2 × 16 measure sequence, in which measures 30–33 (see Example 2.7) have a surprising rhythmic movement into triplet form. Mulligan and Baker's rapport is exceptional, and this is displayed to a greater effect here than on any of the previously discussed examples.

The other significant track recorded at this October Gold Star session was "Walkin' Shoes," part of which had been used in a Kenton chart. It had apparently been written by Mulligan to commemorate his trek across the nation from New York to Los Angeles with Gail Madden. However, by the time of these recordings, the couple had split up. "She

EXAMPLE 2.7 Opening section of "Freeway" by Chet Baker, Copyright © 1954 Atlantis Music Corp. Copyright renewed. All rights reserved. Used by permission. Reprinted by permission of Hal Leonard Europe Ltd. (transcription).

just vanished from the scene, and I never quite understood what went awry," recalled Bob Whitlock.[34]

It seems from piecing together other accounts that, despite Madden's initial success in getting Mulligan straightened out and working, she had

34 Jack: *Fifties Jazz Talk*, p. 157.

EXAMPLE 2.7 Continued

not succeeded in weaning him off heroin for good. After Madden's departure, he took up with one of the waitresses at the Haig, called Jeffie Lee Boyd, and they were soon living together, again having undergone some kind of unofficial "marriage ceremony." Nonetheless, "Walkin' Shoes" stands to immortalize the foot-slogging and hitchhiking that got Mulligan and Madden to California. The piece would be one to which Mulligan returned in the following months in a larger band setting, and it would be a staple of his later quartets.

Although the piece has a simple AABA structure, the melodic line plays with time, notably the eighth-note displacement of the first beat of measure 2 in Example 2.8, which contrasts with the downbeat on the drums; the anticipation of the long-held trumpet F sharp in the sixth measure; and the three groups of eighth notes in measures 7 and 8. The mixture of delay and anticipation is a potent one, and the melody is easily memorable. What is also notable here is that on the first eight measures and the repeat, the trumpet and baritone play a harmonic sequence that is sometimes at odds with the logic of the walking bass line. This is particularly notable in measure 2, where the B flat played by the horns and the A natural in the downward B to A movement of the bass would be expected to sound dissonant, when the major and minor sevenths of the C chord coincide. But Mulligan's strong melodic lines and his skill as writer and arranger overshadow the rules of harmony. This would not work so well outside the context of a "pianoless" group in which the full harmony is implied, rather than explicitly stated. From measure 4, the bass more closely underpins the harmonies of the head, and the chords played by the horns are shown in Example 2.8. It is also notable that these are simplified for the following solos, so that the blowing sequence is:

G	C7	G	Bm7 / E7	Am7	D7	G	Am7 / D7
G	C7	G	Bm7 / E7	Am7	D7	G	G
F♯m7	B7	Em7	Em7	A7	A7	D7	D7
G	C7	G	Bm7 / E7	Am7	D7	G	Am7 / D7

The October Gold Star session gave the fledgling Pacific Jazz label enough material for a 10-inch LP, which was released in the United States before the end of 1952. Adorned by an unusual overhead photograph of the band, taken by Dave Pell from a stepladder looking down on the band from above, at Harte's drum store, and credited to Pell-Thomas,[35] it did much to spread the word about this racially mixed band and its music (Figure 2.2).

Only a few weeks after the band's return to Los Angeles, on January 3, 1953, Fantasy arranged to record the quartet again, so that it could compete in the marketplace by producing an LP of its own. Whereas Pacific Jazz had agreed to pay Mulligan a royalty on sales, Fantasy offered a cash deal with no further payments.[36] This led initially to some reluctance

35 Details from https://jazzresearch.com/the-art-of-william-claxton/ [accessed June 8, 2021].

36 Jack: *Fifties Jazz Talk*, p. 159.

EXAMPLE 2.8 "Walking Shoes" by Gerry Mulligan. Copyright © 1952 Criterion Music Corp. Copyright renewed. All rights reserved. Used by Permission. Reprinted by permission of Hal Leonard Europe, Ltd. Opening section (transcription).

from Mulligan, who felt (despite the earlier San Francisco session) that he owed a moral commitment to Richard Bock for first recording the group and believing in them.

> I got so much pressure from the other guys in the group because they were looking at it in terms of income. Here we were being offered an album, and it's real money, and we're turning it down. I finally

EXAMPLE 2.8 Continued

> knuckled under to their demands. . . . The Fantasy record was on red vinyl, very high-quality stuff. That was the best album we did with the quartet.[37]

This time around, the Fantasy recording was done in Southern California, as by now the quartet was in full-time residence at the Haig, and could not take the time off to return to San Francisco. Carson Smith was now the group's permanent bassist, because Whitlock had been fired by Mulligan after the police spotted a joint being thrown from the window of Baker's car outside the Haig on December 23, 1952. The cops searched the car, in which Baker and Whitlock were enjoying a smoke during the interval, and found more marijuana. As a result, Baker took the rap, and spent Christmas in jail. This event led to what Whitlock described as a "bitter confrontation" with Mulligan, who believed Whitlock was "bad news" for Chet, and promptly sacked him.[38]

37 Josephson: *Jeru's Journey*, p. 31.

38 Jack: *Fifties Jazz Talk*, p. 162.

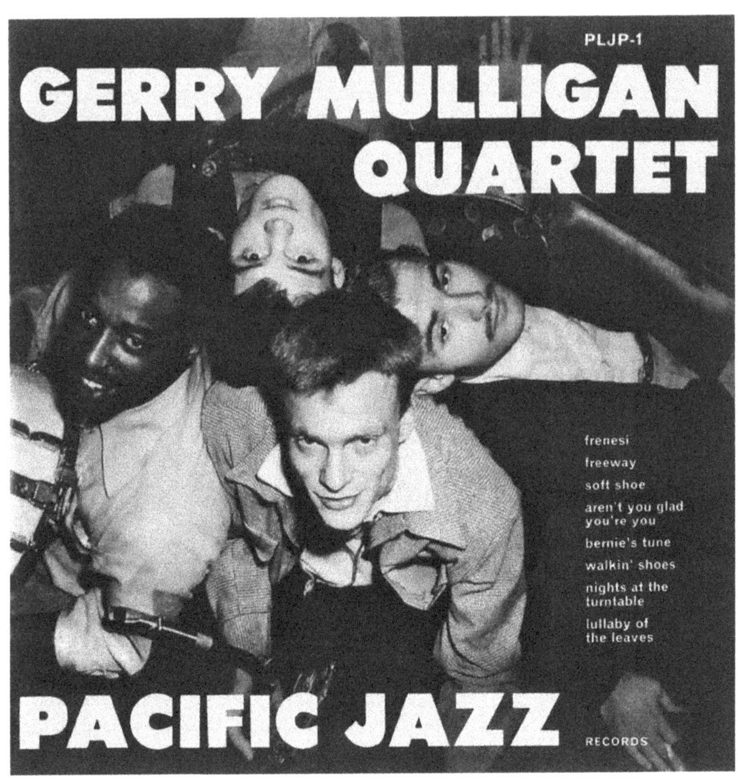

FIGURE 2.2 Cover of the original 1952 Pacific Jazz album, PLJP-1.

Carson Smith had been on tour with Billy May between finishing at the Black Hawk in early November and late December, but he had just returned to Los Angeles when he got the call from Mulligan to rejoin. He stayed throughout the remainder of the quartet's time with Chet Baker. He recalled that he used a hired bass when the quartet recorded, "because mine was literally falling apart."[39]

The studio chosen was one of the longest-established recording facilities in the area, Radio Recorders, at 7000 Santa Monica Boulevard, in West Hollywood. Its engineers were adept at achieving a quick balance for the dozens of radio shows that were relayed from the complex to transmission stations all over the United States, and they did a good job of matching the quality that their more northerly counterparts had

39 Jack: *Fifties Jazz Talk*, p. 159.

achieved at the Black Hawk. However, to avoid any obvious aural dissimilarities, Fantasy issued the four new tracks, "Turnstile," "The Lady Is a Tramp," "Moonlight in Vermont," and "Limelight," on the second side of their 10-inch LP, with the original four tunes on side one. There was also an explanatory note from critic Ralph J. Gleason, pointing out that the Radio Recorders engineers had used "four microphones and an echo chamber to duplicate the acoustical effect of the tunes recorded in San Francisco."[40] Gleason also added his own summary of the group's achievements:

> In these eight renditions there are marvelous moments as the two horns play musical catch with the tune, tossing phases back and forth. There are also delightful examples of parallel thinking on the part of the instrumentalists, whose ideas seem to spring from one central concept, one pattern of thought, and to be spoken in identical accents.[41]

Gleason's writing, particularly as regards his enthusiasm for the band, was important and influential. Before World War II, he had been the founding editor of the periodical *Jazz Information*, and he started as a columnist for *Down Beat* in 1948, also becoming jazz critic for the *San Francisco Chronicle* in 1950. Hence, he was well known among the jazz community from his articles in both a nationally read specialist magazine and a widely distributed newspaper. Yet even though the Mulligan quartet had been enthusiastically received in the Bay Area, and was now consolidating its reputation in Los Angeles, it was not going to get known beyond Southern California just by playing six nights a week at a tiny club that seated so few patrons. Gleason's review of its Black Hawk gigs had indeed been important, but it was the growing press focus on the band's recordings, and particularly its LPs for two different labels, at a time when the 10-inch album was still a relatively new medium, that turned it from a local West Coast phenomenon into a national one during the first months of 1953.

The Pacific Jazz album was favorably reviewed, getting four stars, in the January edition of *Down Beat*, but the writer immediately courted controversy by saying, "we can't hear anything in the music that wouldn't have been even better with a piano." In the next paragraph came an unfortunate mistake, when on the subject of the album's liner notes, the piece

40 Gleason, Ralph J.: *Gerry Mulligan Quartet*, Fantasy LP 3-6 (1953) [liner note].

41 Ibid.

continues: "Gerry Mulligan lays a heavy accent on the lack of a bass with the group."[42] This gave Mulligan the opportunity to reply, and this was printed on February 11, saying: "I'm sure he intended to say 'piano.' . . . On hearing the group, [people] usually remark that they think a piano would 'get in the way' or else they can't imagine a piano with the group at all."[43]

Nothing fuels interest in a record better than such a public disagreement, and both the Pacific Jazz album and, when it appeared in April 1953,[44] the Fantasy LP, were to sell well to jazz lovers, curious to make up their own minds on the back of this lively spat. By the time that Mulligan's riposte to the review was in print, he had, however, been mentioned in a publication that was read by a far wider audience. In early February, *Time* magazine published a feature on the resident band at the Haig under the title "Counterpoint Jazz." Suddenly, the group that was "drawing the biggest crowds in the club's history" was the center of a news story that would define the public perception of Mulligan and the quartet for the decade.

> Mulligan's kind of sound is just about unique in the jazz field: his quartet uses neither piano nor guitar, [it] does its work with trumpet, bass, drums and, of course, Mulligan's hoarse-voiced baritone sax. In comparison with the frantic extremes of bop, his jazz is rich and even orderly, [and] is marked by an almost Bach-like counterpoint. As in Bach, each Mulligan man is busily looking for a pause, a hole in the music, which he can fill with an answering phrase. Sometimes the polyphony is reminiscent of tailgate blues, sometimes it comes tumbling with bell-over-mouthpiece impromptu.[45]

With press attention like this, and (from around the same time) a review in *Metronome*, remarking on the Fantasy 78s that "Gerry's at his best in these sides,"[46] the pianoless quartet became news. And that newsworthiness was

42 "Gerry Mulligan Quartet," *Down Beat*, January 14, 1953, p. 15.

43 "Gerry Mulligan Remarks on Review of His New LP," *Down Beat*, February 11, 1953 [reprinted in Gerry Mulligan and Chet Baker *Complete Pacific Jazz & Capitol Recordings*, Mosaic MD 3-102, liner note].

44 One of the earliest reviews in the syndicated "Tempo" column, *Jefferson City Lincoln Clarion*, April 24, 1953, p. 3, singles out "Carioca" and "Frenesi." "He has kept rather close to the melody but has dressed both these tunes in counterpoint."

45 "Counterpoint Jazz," *Time*, February 2, 1953 [reprinted in Gerry Mulligan and Chet Baker *Complete Pacific Jazz & Capitol Recordings*, Mosaic MD 3-102, liner note].

46 *Metronome* review reprinted on *Gerry Mulligan Quartet*, Fantasy 3-6 (1953) [LP liner note].

somewhat enhanced after Stan Getz sat in with Mulligan and Baker at a jam session at Chet's house. Mulligan recalled: "We worked really well, improvising on ensemble things that were great."[47] Nonetheless it was a surprise when the syndicated "Tempo" newspaper column suddenly reported:

> Stan Getz said in *Down Beat* that he intends to bring back from the West Coast to New York Gerry Mulligan and Chet Baker. Those who have kept up with "Tempo" will remember that Mulligan is the lad who arranges music that does not include a piano. Mulligan concentrates mostly on counter-pointing.[48]

Once again there was a Mulligan response in print very soon afterward: "Gerry Mulligan said in February 24 *Down Beat*, that he did not want anyone coming into his combo with hostile ideas about taking over. He was referring to 'Moon over Vermoth' [*sic*] Stan Getz."[49]

The immediate consequence of this blaze of publicity was that Richard Bock made plans to record the quartet again, starting in January. Early in the month, soon after the Fantasy session, Mulligan, Baker, Smith, and Hamilton were captured in action at the Haig. The resulting sides were "Aren't You Glad You're You," "Get Happy," "Ponciana," and "Godchild." Whereas the 1952 Black Hawk location recording had been done without an audience, this time some of the applause and announcements from a normal night at the Haig were preserved. The fidelity is excellent and this session precedes Rudy Van Gelder's comparable *Night at Birdland with the Art Blakey Quintet* album for Blue Note by over a year, which has been cited as one of the earliest examples of a location recording in a jazz club, which captures the audience noise and general ambience.[50] Unfortunately, Bock's recordings were not issued at the time and they finally appeared some four decades later, well into the CD era. Nonetheless these tracks give us a fine snapshot of the quartet in action at its home base, with three of the original members.

With the exception of Wallington's "Godchild," the other pieces were standards, and by this time the group was playing so much, and so often, that it seldom rehearsed. Carson Smith recalled: "I think in the six

47 Jack: *Fifties Jazz Talk*, p. 147.

48 "Tempo, Stan-Mulligan," *Jefferson City Lincoln Clarion*, February 27, 1953, p. 6.

49 "Tempo," *Jefferson City Lincoln Clarion*, March 13, 1953, p 2.

50 For a full discussion of Van Gelder's innovations see Shipton, Alyn: *A New History of Jazz* (London, Continuum, 2007, 2nd ed.) p. 495.

months I was with him, we might have had about four rehearsals for new material. He often introduced something new by just turning round on the stand and asking me if I knew it."[51]

This occasionally led to difficulties when Smith was not familiar with a tune, but Mulligan told him that as a bassist it was his job to know the standard repertoire, so Smith made it his business to learn as many songs as he could. By this time, although there was sometimes tension between them on stage, Mulligan and Baker (with their respective girlfriends) were sharing a house, and they would apparently sing tunes to one another in the car on the way to the evening's gig, creating the bare bones of a head arrangement.[52] When the horn parts for "Carioca" had been put together the previous year, Mulligan himself recalled that Chet "used to like singing the parts as we drove from his house, and we worked out that arrangement by singing it."[53]

It sounds as if "Aren't You Glad You're You" and "Get Happy" were arrived at by precisely this method. The former opens with a unison theme, which divides into close harmony in the second eight measures, and sees Mulligan play supporting harmonies in the channel. Then we are straight into solos, Mulligan taking a chorus accompanied by just bass and drums, before Baker launches into a bebop-tinged solo, playing runs of eighth and sixteenth notes over a basic harmonic sketch from Mulligan. On the out-chorus there's a role reversal in the "B" section as Mulligan solos over long notes held by Baker. By contrast, after a short trumpet and drum introduction, "Get Happy" is played as a swing number, with the kind of unison head that one might find later that same year in a Buck Clayton Jam Session. The solos are more extended, too, with the players abandoning the constraints of the playing time of a 78 rpm disc to reveal how they tackled these pieces on a normal gig, such as the very one on which Bock's microphones were eavesdropping.

There's an example of Hamilton's command of texture on "Ponciana," recorded almost exactly five years before Ahmad Jamal's celebrated trio version of the song. As on "Carioca," he plays with fingers on the snare drum (with the snare turned off), creating a relaxed Latin feel. On these sides we also catch occasional snatches of Hamilton's singing voice, adding *sotto voce* lines to the harmonies, which he said he often did at the Haig. The most significant of the four tracks cut at the club is

51 Jack: *Fifties Jazz Talk*, p. 167.

52 Gavin: *Deep in a Dream*, p. 57, describes them doing this *en route* to San Francisco.

53 Jack: *Fifties Jazz Talk*, p. 147.

"Godchild," which again shows Mulligan revisiting an earlier piece that he had arranged for Thornhill, and recorded both with Miles Davis and Kai Winding. Here he retains the composer George Wallington's original chord sequence in the solo sections, but the A section of the head is played by baritone and bass for six measures, and then has a two-measure drum break that restores two beats that were not present in the Davis nonet chart. This version, scaled down from the previous forces for which Mulligan had arranged, is well-tailored to the quartet's strengths.

A matter of days after this documentary recording was made at the Haig, Chico Hamilton left the quartet. He had remained on call for Lena Horne all the time he had played with Mulligan, and in the second week of January, she asked him to go back on the road. Furthermore, the Haig could only play union scale, owing to its relatively small size, and Hamilton (who, unlike the others, had a wife and family) could earn substantially more with her. When Hamilton gave his notice, Mulligan—in whom anger often bubbled just under the surface—saw red. "I got really angry," he recalled. "I was so mad, I tossed my horn across the room, stomped out of the place."[54] That temper, maybe fueled by his heroin addiction, but normally kept under wraps, was occasionally directed at the audience in the Haig—something even picked up in the *Time* magazine piece, which noted that Mulligan normally played with his eyes tightly closed, but "opens them only occasionally to glower at customers who are boorish enough to talk against the music."[55]

The new drummer, who, like Carson Smith, would remain with the group until midsummer, was Larry Bunker. A native of the Los Angeles area, he was not only a regular at many jam sessions round the city, but had made a name for himself as a member of Art Pepper's quartet, playing at the Surf Club in Hollywood, and recording for Discovery, for whom Richard Bock had previously worked, in the early months of 1952. There was little or no time for him to rehearse with Mulligan, so he just joined the band and began playing, although he had taken time to familiarize himself with the quartet's records. He recalled:

> It was difficult at first. I was so orientated as to what a rhythm section with a piano should sound like that it took some getting used to, but the transparency became very appealing and I liked it. Gerry, Chet and Carson, who was a good bass player, had some kind of magic

54 Josephson: *Jeru's Journey*, p. 31.

55 "Counterpoint Jazz," *Time*, February 2, 1953.

> chemistry in delineating the harmonic structure with just three voices, so that after a while I didn't miss the piano.[56]

It was a matter of days after Bunker joined the group that Richard Bock brought his microphones back to the Haig, on January 23, 1953, because Lee Konitz, who was in town with Stan Kenton, playing at the Palladium in Los Angeles, came down on one of his off nights to sit in with the quartet. Konitz was not entirely happy with some of his own playing and did not approve of the first piece they recorded, "Too Marvelous for Words," but Mulligan was sufficiently impressed that in the end, complemented by tracks recorded on January 30, and a session at Phil Turetsky's house on February 1, there was enough for an album, Pacific Jazz LP 2, featuring the Mulligan Quintet with Konitz.[57] When I asked Chico Hamilton what he thought about this all-white quintet, which was next to be recorded after the racially mixed group that he had been a part of, he said:

> There was an ethnic thing about it. Even before I left, Lee Konitz used to come down to the Haig and blow. Also Stan [Getz]. But the average white musician from the East Coast—they all played the same way, with the same kinda groove. So it was no problem for them fitting in with the quartet. . . . All the Black musicians played in a different groove . . . like when we worked with Lady Day. That was Wardell Gray, Curtis Counce, Hampton Hawes and myself, can you imagine? That was at one of the clubs in LA called the 331, just around the corner from the Haig.[58]

The opening track, "Too Marvelous for Words" from the first Haig session with Konitz, bears out Hamilton's observation. The band lacks some of the natural groove that Chico had supplied, and which was not only to be heard from the musicians who played at the 331, but in the many African American jazz clubs that still survived in the Central Avenue area of Los Angeles. On this recording, Bunker sticks to simple brushwork, with none of the accents and rhythmic flexibility of his

56 Jack: *Fifties Jazz Talk*, pp. 163–164.

57 These dates are from the discography by Dugelay and Hallqvist, superseding earlier research, which dated these sessions to May. The discography also tallies with billings for Kenton at the Palladium, e.g.: *Long Beach Independent*, January 24, 1953, p. 12.

58 Interview with Chico Hamilton, September 5, 2002.

predecessor's playing. Meanwhile, the altoist produces a *tour-de-force* solo that completely dominates the track, with Mulligan and Baker simply playing supporting harmonies. "Lover Man" is a similar solo vehicle, but "I'll Remember April" begins as a quartet with an ostinato from Mulligan and melodic fragments from Baker, before Konitz again takes center stage with more dazzling inventions. But this time, as the track develops, Baker also solos, with Konitz and Mulligan underpinning his trumpet. The recordings are good enough for a modern listener to get a sense of the intimate setting of the Haig, although musically they are certainly different from the normal work of Mulligan's quartet, especially when Konitz takes off on "All the Things You Are."

The latter two sessions by this impromptu quintet were not recorded at the club (there is some doubt as to the exact location of the January 30 one, though Konitz suggested it was at Joe Mondragon's house), but it is clear that these pieces involved a modicum of rehearsal, and some written charts for the first and last choruses. From the late January date, "Sextet" involves a witty head from Mulligan while his reworking of the standard "Broadway" has the theme of the final measures of the A section repeated as a ghostly echo throughout the bridge. The highlight of the collaboration with Konitz is the final date in February at Phil Turetsky's house, with Joe Mondragon himself, a very experienced session bassist, taking Smith's place. The pieces are tightly organized, each lasting around the 3-minute playing time of a 78, rather than the extended jams from the Haig. Both "I Can't Believe That You're in Love with Me" and George Gershwin's "Lady Be Good" (Example 2.9) have inventive charts framing the solos, and looking back on the three sessions, Konitz asserted, "Gerry was very encouraging and he wrote these very charming arrangements for three horns. . . . I loved the organized pieces very much."[59]

It is not surprising that by the February 1 date with Konitz, not only had the front line jelled into something that sounded more like a regular unit, but that the band was playing proper charts, because as January 1953 progressed, Mulligan was fully back in writing mode. On January 29 and 31, he recorded with his West Coast Tentette, playing eight new arrangements. The *Time* article about the quartet at the Haig, published the same week, noted:

59 Hamilton, Andy: *Lee Konitz—Conversations on the Improviser's Art* (Ann Arbor, University of Michigan Press, 2007) p. 101.

EXAMPLE 2.9 "Lady Be Good" (George and Ira Gershwin). Mulligan's original head arrangement of opening section (transcription).

> After a long evening at the horn, jazzman Mulligan finds he is too keyed up by 2 a.m. to sleep, to he stays up until 6 writing new tunes and arrangements. Next Mulligan objective: an enlarged band. . . . "I've got to keep moving. I've got to grow."[60]

Despite working with the quartet from August 1952, he had kept his arranger's pencil active, as a press report, on New Year's Day 1953, confirmed—noting that "Gerry Mulligan continues to write more music. Lately he has been helping Gene Krupa in recording some new discs."[61] It seems that by the end of January, his desire to "keep moving" was no distant objective, because for the weeks prior to the Tentette sessions, Mulligan had actually been rehearsing this larger band during the daytime, before his nightly gig at the Haig (rather like his informal forays into Central Park in New York leading up to the Prestige recordings). Looking back some years later, he said:

> I started the tentette as a rehearsal band to have something to write for. After a time, Gene Norman, a Los Angeles promoter and disc jockey, came to me and said he'd like to record the band. Since no one else had suggested recording us, I said yes. The irony, as I found out later, was that Gene had no American Federation of Musicians recording license of his own, and planned to offer the date to Capitol, if he could record on their license. Bill Miller of Capitol told me later that he had heard about the band from the musicians and was planning to come to the Haig to discuss recording, when Gene came to him with his proposal. Since Bill felt it would be unethical to pursue the project directly for Capitol we ultimately did the album for Gene.[62]

On the back of this recording, Norman was to found his GNP Crescendo label the following year,[63] the firm's name culled both from a series of concerts he had promoted since the late 1940s under the "Gene Norman Presents" banner, and the Crescendo nightclub in Los Angeles, which he opened in 1954. Norman had already recorded several of his productions

60 "Counterpoint Jazz," *Time*, February 2, 1953.

61 *Kalamazoo College Index*, January 1, 1953.

62 Welding, Pete: *The Complete Pacific Jazz & Capitol Recordings of the Original Gerry Mulligan Quartet and Tentette with Chet Baker*, Mosaic MD 3-102 [liner note].

63 Fox, Margalit: "Gene Norman, Music Producer with an Ear for Jazz, Dies at 93," *New York Times*, November 13, 2015.

over the years, and the label would soon issue judicious selections from these, such as the celebrated Dizzy Gillespie Pasadena concert from 1948, featuring the Cuban percussionist Chano Pozo.[64]

In the interview cited above, Mulligan confirms that the band-within-a-band idea, which he explored in much of his work from Gene Krupa's "Disc Jockey Jump" to the Miles Davis nonet, is the thinking that lay behind several of the compositions and arrangements for this ten-piece group. He makes an explicit connection between using the quartet with Chet Baker as the small group amid a surrounding instrumentation that is similar to the Davis band—save that this time round there are two trumpets, and a second baritone saxophone, allowing Mulligan himself to switch between his own baritone and occasional choruses on piano. Furthermore, for the four tracks recorded on January 29, Chico Hamilton temporarily returned to the fold, before heading East with Lena Horne.

The version of "Walkin' Shoes" from that session exemplifies Mulligan's view that "the ensemble worked perfectly with the quartet concept." Harmonies that are implied by the three tonal voices in the quartet are spelled out in full here, to great effect in the opening head (see Example 2.10) where both the second and final A sections spring to life, and reveal Mulligan to be as adept as ever in corralling larger forces into the service of a simple, memorable melodic chart. The writing behind his baritone solo is particularly effective during the B section, and the third "shout" chorus ushers in a solo for Baker, who floats effortlessly over the larger ensemble. The final measures are introduced by a short solo bass passage from Joe Mondragon, who works extremely well with Hamilton in creating rhythmic support for the eight horns.

From the same session, Mulligan's own composition "Rocker" allows us to make a direct comparison between his earlier arrangement for Davis and this 1953 modification. The Tentette version is more robust than the ethereal-sounding version by the nonet, starting with a bold introductory phrase from Bob Enevoldsen's valve trombone before the head begins. But as ever with Mulligan, the eraser is at work, so the chorus of ensemble melody that follows Konitz's alto solo in the 1950 recording is gone, and the band simply runs through the head (this time with Mulligan's baritone taking the lead on the eighteen-measure B section), followed by trumpet and baritone solos, the latter leading into a reprise of the head that sees the piece out.

64 *Gene Norman Presents Dizzy Gillespie and His Orchestra Featuring Chano Pozo*, GNP Vol. 4; LP 109/110 [10-inch LP, 1955].

EXAMPLE 2.10 "Walking Shoes" by Gerry Mulligan. Copyright © 1952 Criterion Music Corp. Copyright renewed. All rights reserved. Used by Permission. Reprinted by permission of Hal Leonard Europe, Ltd. The Tentette arrangement, opening section (transcription).

EXAMPLE 2.10 Continued

EXAMPLE 2.10 Continued

"Ontet," from January 31, the second session by the ten-piece band, with Larry Bunker in place of Hamilton, picks up on a Mulligan favorite, George Wallington's "Godchild." But this piece is built on the second theme—the shout chorus—of Mulligan's Davis arrangement. This idea had previously been explored by the New York quintet that had been double-headed by Mulligan and Phil Urso, and it had been re-explored in Richard Bock's first experimental trio session at Turetsky's house, with Mulligan on piano, Red Mitchell, bass, and Chico Hamilton drums. Here, with the larger band, Mulligan is again at the piano for the opening measures, and after a lumpy introduction, he continues into the ensemble. Compared to the consistently clean sound of the pianoless tentette on January 29, not least because the instrument seems to need tuning, it would be tactful to say it is an example of "arranger's piano." This woeful heavy-handed level of playing also mars "Flash" from the same session. Although Mulligan only turns to the keyboard for a solo chorus in the standard "Taking a Chance on Love," which is otherwise a fine example of his arranging for medium-sized band, he is no match for some of the fleet-fingered pianists with a lighter touch who would have been available in Los Angeles at the time, such as Hampton Hawes or Jimmy Rowles. The highlight from the second day of tentette recordings is "Simbah," a scintillating uptempo piece (for the pianoless ensemble) that not only coaxes some fine playing from Bunker, but shows exactly how Mulligan could scale up for larger forces the type of number at which the quartet excelled.

As the year went on, Capitol would put some effort into promoting these sides, and with such successful pieces as "Walkin' Shoes," "Rocker," and "Simbah" included, this group was ironically to be more successful in the short term than the quartet. In a national poll for Jazz Record of the Year, the result was a dead heat, announced early in January 1954: "Tying [George] Shearing's group is an all-star tentette. A comparative newcomer to the jazz scene, Gerry Mulligan has assured himself a permanent standing among the few original artists. Besides leading the group, Mulligan composes, arranges, and plays both the baritone sax and piano."[65] But this was almost a year in the future.

Buoyed up by the recording activity with the Tentette and with Konitz, and still pulling in the crowds at the Haig, Mulligan brought the quartet back to Gold Star Studios on February 24, 1953, to record four sides for Pacific Jazz. Issued as 78s, they would also be one of the label's first EPs, EP 4-2. Along with two standards of the kind that Carson Smith recalled being busked into instant arrangements on the bandstand, "Cherry" and "Making Whoopee," there were two originals, Mulligan's "Motel" and Smith's "Carson City Stage." The standards are taken somewhat slowly, but this allows trumpet and baritone to intertwine elements of the melodic lead on both songs, including a neatly harmonized passage on "Making Whoopee" where both horns ease effortlessly into playing together after the main theme statement.

"Carson City Stage" was the only piece Smith wrote for the quartet, and it is yet more evidence of Mulligan's sound editorial judgment. "Gerry didn't like the tune," recalled Smith, "but he loved the introduction, so the intro became the tune, which is all you hear."[66] By contrast, "Motel" has one of Mulligan's most intricate themes, played with their habitual telepathic connection by himself and Baker, and interspersed with pedal notes from Smith. Mulligan's solo is fluent, and Baker tries a high-speed solo that includes a few fluffs, but contrasts with his forceful yet graceful playing elsewhere on the session. Mulligan shares a series of

65 *Salt Lake Utah Daily Chronicle*, January 14, 1954.

66 Jack: *Fifties Jazz Talk*, pp. 163–167.

exchanges with Bunker, and there is a feeling that this track deliberately turns the spotlight on each member of the group in turn.

On March 30, the quartet appeared for Gene Norman at the Pasadena Civic Auditorium, opening for Duke Ellington, and it continued to draw lines of customers at the Haig. But all this was about to change. A police detective, called John Edward O'Grady, was in charge of the narcotics squad with the LAPD, and not least because of the Christmas pot smoking incident, which had put Baker on three months' probation that had just expired, he now had his eye on the Mulligan quartet. He began coming to the Haig, and then, sure that both Mulligan and Baker were using drugs, on April 13, he struck. The press reported the incident as follows:

> Narcotics detectives arrested jazz musicians Gerry Mulligan, 26, and Chesney Baker, 23, and their wives early today, when a raid on the Mulligan apartment allegedly disclosed a supply of heroin and marijuana. Mulligan and Baker, half of a progressive jazz group known as the Gerry Mulligan Quartet[,] were arrested at a nightclub where they appeared. Their wives, Jeffie Mulligan, 21, and Charlene Baker, 22, were arrested at the apartment. Officers said the four had been under surveillance for several days. A search of Mulligan's apartment, detectives said, revealed a gram of heroin, a hypodermic kit, and a can of marijuana. All four denied knowledge of the narcotics or how they got into the apartment.[67]

The heroin was Mulligan's, the marijuana belonged to Baker, and after they were arrested the trumpeter suggested that as, owing to his visible track marks, his housemate was going to own up to the hard drug, maybe he could just admit to the pot as well. In doing so, Mulligan naïvely hoped that he might be sent to get a cure at the drug treatment prison in Lexington, Kentucky. He was not to know if this would happen, as—bailed by Jeffie's mother—the trial was set to take place some weeks hence, so the quartet continued to play at the Haig and to record. Concerned that the band on which his company had been founded was under threat, Bock now convened several sessions on April 27, 29, and 30, and May 20. Gene Norman also took advantage of the quartet's availability, before Mulligan was sentenced, and recorded a set on May 7, albeit in a far more resonant acoustic than any of the band's other discs.

67 "Narcotics Officers Hit Musician's House" (UP), *Yuma Sun*, April 14, 1953.

On these five dates, twenty-eight sides were recorded, including some duplication, notably of pieces intended for both 10-inch and 12-inch 78 release, such as "Swing House," and "I May Be Wrong."

Typically, confronted by the urgent need to record, Mulligan rejigged some of his earlier compositions, and leavened the sessions with standards. Of the former, his pared-down version of "Jeru" confirms his talent for revealing the inner core of a piece, and Baker contributes a solo that owes little to Miles Davis, despite similarities of register and tempo. "Swing House," written by Mulligan and initially scored for both Stan Kenton and Georgie Auld in larger settings, is also brilliantly edited down (particularly in the 10-inch version) to its essence. It makes one of the quartet's most original and effective records. But the swath of standards are, by and large, too formulaic.

The exceptions to the formulae include a version of "I'm Beginning to See the Light," built around a bass riff, but with a staccato statement of the theme so abstract it would be barely recognizable to the average listener. "Tea for Two" has a neatly arranged head, which harks back to Mulligan's January activity in writing charts. "Varsity Drag" from the Gene Norman date is lively and again has a modicum of arrangement, but similar promise from the opening of Miles Davis's "Half Nelson" soon evaporates into something routine. Equally there is a same-ness about the ballad treatments.

Ironically, what would turn out to be the original band's last recording session, which was done at the Haig for Bock on May 20, raises the bar quite substantially. There's a sparkling version of "Five Brothers," a beautifully paced "I Can't Get Started" with some of Baker's most lyrical playing, and a return to "Ide's Side" from the 1951 Prestige sessions (which Mulligan had also re-scored for Shorty Rogers). Less successful is an extended remake of "My Funny Valentine" that lacks the concise discipline of the original recording.

Although record critics in many parts of the country were still discovering the quartet, and reacted favorably as the fruits of these sessions appeared, its original prophet, Ralph J. Gleason became increasingly skeptical. He detected the lack of originality and invention in many of these later sides and wrote:

> Their first discs on Pacific Jazz and Fantasy were a kick when first heard, but . . . the tinsel [has] already considerably dulled. By now, the Mulligan moments are few and far between. . . . I frankly think that the Mulligan Quartet is, with one exception, the most overrated small band in jazz. . . . Mulligan, with or without a piano, and with

> or without his pretentious explanations of what he's doing, is still a child when racked up against men like Duke. Twenty-five years from now, I suggest we will still be playing Duke and Woody and the wonderful Count Basie—yes, and Dizzy Gillespie and Charlie Parker too. Mulligan, I think, will not last as long as Muggsy Spanier.[68]

If the arrest had prompted Bock and Norman into activity, it also made Mulligan think hard about his own life and future direction. He knew things were not going anywhere long-term with Jeffie Lee Boyd, and he reached out to an old flame, whom he had known during the time he had been playing with Kai Winding and Brew Moore, namely Arlyne Brown, the daughter of songwriter Lew Brown, who had been married to the tenor saxophonist Buddy Arnold. She had left Arnold to take up with Brew Moore, but that had fizzled out owing to Moore's addiction to heroin, which was even more severe than Mulligan's. Arlyne Brown recalled:

> I had been thinking a lot about Gerry so I 'phoned him at the Haig and he said, "Will you please get the next plane and come out here and marry me?" . . . I flew out and when I saw him at the airport I knew he was strung out, but the quartet carried on working until the trial took place. Gerry and I got married at the Beverly Hills judge's office on the 8 May 1953 and one of our witnesses was Doe Mitchell, Red's wife. . . . We spent the early part of our marriage driving to gas stations meeting pushers to pick up heroin.[69]

Arlyne was quick to take a more assertive role in Mulligan's life and work than either Gail Madden or Jeffie Lee Boyd had done. Carson Smith observed that within days of her arrival, she had taken over and become Mulligan's *de facto* manager. She would continue in this role well into the mid-1950s.

The trial took place over two months after the initial arrest, and the last week that the quartet is listed as appearing at the Haig is from Monday, June 9.[70] Accounts vary as to the exact date of the trial, but

68 Gleason, Ralph J.: "Ralph Mulls Mulligan: Finds Overrated Child," *Down Beat*, September 23, 1953, p. 8.

69 "Arlyne Brown Mulligan Interview, 2001," kindly supplied by Gordon Jack. Parts of this interview appeared in *Jazz Journal*, June 20, 2019.

70 "More jazz groups working round Los Angeles than anywhere else in the country. . . ." *Jackson Advocate* June 6, 1953, p. 4, lists the area's bands appearing the following week, including

it seems Mulligan was certainly in jail by early September. Far from being sent to Lexington for a Federal sponsored drugs cure, Mulligan was despatched to the Wayside Honor Rancho, a low-security prison at Castiac in California, about forty miles from Los Angeles. Although Arlyne, an indefatigable and well-connected campaigner, worked hard on securing his release, he was not to be a free man again until Christmas Eve, December 24, 1953. While imprisoned, he worked on a road gang, and at one point spent almost a month in a small high-security cell shared with two other inmates, during which time he became seriously depressed.

Yet very positive press coverage of his recordings continued while he was imprisoned. Just before the trial, the original Pacific Jazz LP was described as "hitting on all cylinders,"[71] and midway through his incarceration, Gene Norman released the Tentette sides on Capitol. A review of those tracks is one of the first to use the term "progressive" about Mulligan, rather than "cool" or "West Coast," and is worth citing in full:

> Although he is not new to the music business (he was an arranger for Tommy Tucker, Elliot Lawrence and Stan Kenton Orchestras) Gerry Mulligan is a young and talented new arrival to the often perilous profession of bandleading. His small band, or more technically his large combo, might very easily become one of the leading exponents of the exacting and exciting field of music known as progressive jazz.
>
> Gerry has aptly been described by Gene Norman as "a young composer who somehow combines the restless intensity of a serious and sensitive musician with the levity of a leprechaun." This unusual talent has been displayed to full advantage on his debut as a Capitol recording artist.
>
> "Gerry Mulligan and his Tentette" is the progressive fan's cup of tea. It features highly stylized arrangements of one standard and seven Mulligan originals, in which the ten-piece combo displays itself as a closely knit and technically disciplined organization. Everything about this outfit is unusual in a modern way from the word "go." Its most interesting facets are an intriguing instrumentation and the removal of the piano from the rhythm section. As a result of this, the piano is used only as an occasional solo instrument, with Mulligan

New Orleans musicians George Lewis and Wingy Manone, Howard Rumsey, and the return of Stan Getz to Tiffany's.

71 "Record Review," *Independent Press Telegram*, May 31, 1953.

> doubling on both the piano and the baritone sax. . . . The result is ingenious free expression within the limits of disciplined jazz at its best.[72]

There is little doubt that at the time, the Tentette recordings garnered more press interest in late 1953 than the quartet records. Equally the quintet album with Konitz had appeared and this too got some positive notices.[73] Yet with hindsight, the pianoless quartet was the most remarkable achievement of Mulligan's time in Los Angeles. He also moved from someone who had previously been known principally as an arranger to a recognized virtuoso on his instrument, and was to be voted the principal baritone saxophonist in jazz for forty-two consecutive years starting in 1953.[74]

While Mulligan had been imprisoned, Baker had led his own quartet at the Haig, and had been recorded by Richard Bock. He had tasted the success that goes with being a leader, and was unwilling to surrender that. According to Mulligan, when he ran into Chet, not long after his release, with the expectation that they might re-form the quartet, Baker said, "Gerry I've decided I've got to have $300 a week."[75] This was more than Mulligan himself had earned before his drug bust, and substantially more than the highest-profile sidemen in top bands such as Kenton's were earning. Mulligan simply laughed. He knew that the quartet with Baker was over.

72 Clark, Bob: "New Group May Head Jazz List," *Auburn Plainsman*, October 9, 1953.

73 "Konitz with Mulligan Quartet," *Kalamazoo College Index*, January 1, 1954.

74 https://www.gerrymulligan.com/awards/ [accessed June 9, 2021].

75 Josephson: *Jeru's Journey*, p. 35.

CHAPTER 3

THE SECOND QUARTET

Gerry was a hero as a writer. The scores were very interesting because they were so clear, and so economical.
—BOB BROOKMEYER[1]

IN THE FINAL few days of 1953, Mulligan wasted no time in forming another quartet. To replace Chet Baker, Dave Brubeck suggested a former member of his Octet, the trumpeter Dick Collins, but he was unable to join. Consequently, thinking back to the informal sessions earlier in the year while Stan Getz was at the Tiffany, and remembering an abortive plan from that time to invite Bob Brookmeyer to join the band and make it a quintet, Mulligan called Brookmeyer in New York. He asked him to come West, and to bring a bassist and drummer. As a result, before the end of the year, the trombonist arrived in Los Angeles with drummer Frank Isola and bassist Bill Anthony.[2] This lineup would

1 Interview with Bob Brookmeyer, September 2, 2002.

2 Jack, Gordon: *Fifties Jazz Talk* (Lanham MD, Scarecrow Press, 2004) p. 147.

The Gerry Mulligan 1950s Quartets. Alyn Shipton, Oxford University Press. © Alyn Shipton 2023.
DOI: 10.1093/oso/9780197579756.003.0003

become the Mulligan quartet for the first few months of 1954, although in due course, Anthony was replaced by Red Mitchell. (Red was based in Los Angeles at the time, and, as noted, had rehearsed and recorded with Mulligan at Phil Turetsky's house shortly before Chet Baker joined the first version of the group.)

At the start of January 1954, Mulligan assembled a Tentette again, though without Baker, and presented a "one night only" concert, featuring a set each by this group and his new quartet. It took place at the Embassy Theatre, on S. Western Avenue in downtown Los Angeles, a couple of blocks or so north of Wilshire Boulevard. Arlyne Mulligan recalled: "This was Gerry's first public appearance since his release and he came onstage as the conquering hero—the crowd went wild, you'd have thought he was Elvis Presley. I'd never seen anything like it. They went berserk—just an explosion of love."[3]

After playing close to the very area where he had established his band and his reputation as an instrumentalist, Mulligan now wanted to move the quartet onto the national stage, which meant taking it East. The first press reports of his intention appeared within days of his release from the honor farm (alongside reviews of his pre-incarceration records and his poll successes). A typical piece from the start of January ran: "Lee Konitz and Gerry Mulligan have teamed up on the Pacific Jazz label to record an album, entitled *Konitz with Mulligan Quartet*. . . . Chet Baker and his quartet have invaded the Eastern States and will appear in Detroit on his way to the Coast. . . . Also Gerry Mulligan is playing a similar tour."[4]

The band did not head East with quite the alacrity that this suggests. Instead, there were some weeks of preliminary gigs on the West Coast, before the group headed cross-country. By the end of January, the new quartet was in San Francisco, appearing at the Downbeat, on the junction of Market Street and California Street, close to the waterside Embarcadero district. The local press reported: "Gerry Mulligan does the current jazz beat at the Downbeat."[5] But even at this early stage, there were incipient problems in the band. Bob Brookmeyer remembered:

> We started in January and that was also the start of Gerry's "rich and famous" period. He'd never been rich and famous before, and he

3 "Arlyne Brown Mulligan interview, 2001," kindly supplied by Gordon Jack. Parts of this interview appeared in *Jazz Journal*, June 20, 2019.

4 *Kalamazoo College Index*, January 1, 1954.

5 *Oakland Tribune*, January 30, 1954, p. 6. The band was still advertised there in the same paper, February 10, 1954, p. 30.

was married to a lady who was from a rich and famous family. We did OK rehearsing in California, because in LA we played a couple of concerts. And then we went to San Francisco for two weeks, and Gerry began to announce at length between tunes what we were going to play next, interspersed by jokes, which were not funny. Frank Isola the drummer and I complained. "Let's knock off this stuff, it's really embarrassing." He said, "I'm doing this stuff because the quartet is not ready." We said, "We're not ready for this!"[6]

Tensions in the band also ran high because, firstly, Mulligan was often angry with himself as he worked to recapture the easy instrumental fluency he had before his incarceration, and secondly, the group's management had changed. In 1952, there had been no manager, simply informal growth into the potential that had been observed by Dick Bock when the quartet arrived at the Haig as a unit. During 1953, Gene Norman, who was starting to extend his interests beyond concert presentation and recordings, had taken a hand in promoting the band. But now things were different. Having gotten involved in looking after the group's business before Mulligan's imprisonment, as Carson Smith observed, Arlyne Mulligan now made matters more formal (Figure 3.1). She said, quite categorically: "He was getting offers like crazy but he said he wouldn't take the quartet on the road unless I managed it, so I took over as Gerry's manager and being Lew Brown's daughter I helped negotiate better fees for the group."[7]

After staying in the Bay Area well into February, including a return to the Black Hawk, the band moved East via a flurry of one-nighters and short-term gigs. Arlyne Mulligan remembered everyone "living out of suitcases . . . and the only time we were not working was when we were travelling to the next job."[8] After crisscrossing the nation, they spent some time in Philadelphia, following which an informal recording exists of the quartet at the Storyville in Boston at the start of April.[9] From there they moved to a longer residency in New York, at the Basin Street club, on 51st Street at Broadway. Here they might well have been perceived as "rich and famous," because they followed Louis Armstrong and the All Stars at the venue, and were billed opposite Gerry's former boss, Gene

6 Interview with Bob Brookmeyer, September 2, 2002.

7 "Arlyne Brown Mulligan Interview," as above.

8 Ibid.

9 Online Mulligan discography by Gérard Dugelay and Kenneth Hallqvist [pdalbury.files.wordpress.com/2012/09/gm-discography-2011.pdf; accessed May 16, 2021].

FIGURE 3.1 Gerry and Arlyne Mulligan. Photo courtesy Gordon Jack.

Krupa, and his trio.[10] The club occupied part of the Roseland Theater building, and was managed by Ralph Watkins, who had also been involved in running the Royal Roost and Bop City. In the same way as he had with those clubs, he attracted big names to play at the venue, and coming in to New York opposite Krupa, Mulligan had very certainly "arrived," at a very different level from his ignominious departure from the city just over two years before, with Gail Madden.

Just as the first quartet's rise to fame in early 1953 had been helped by positive press and a dash of controversy, the very day the band opened at Basin Street, the *Baltimore Afro-American* ran a story that was to fuel public curiosity once more. It has already been mentioned that some Jazz

10 *Daily Princetonian,* April 1, 1954, p. 5. Panel ad for Basin St, 51st and Broadway, New York, "Appearing nightly Louis 'Satchmo' Armstrong and His All Stars. Opening April 6th: Gene Krupa Trio / Gerry Mulligan."

at the Philharmonic Concerts involved the piano dropping out from the rhythm section while certain soloists played, but now a musician, who would some years later be a prominent member of the Mulligan quartet himself, cast doubt on the originality of Mulligan's "pianoless" concept.

> "The idea of leaving the piano out of ensemble playing by small combos did not originate with Gerry Mulligan like most people think." So says trumpeter Art Farmer. . . . "Why man, that cat just picked up on something that Thelonious Monk himself started in New York a few years ago. Thelonious would just 'stroll,'" he went on. "He would 'cool' on the piano and leave the other guys to blow by themselves. In fact," continued Farmer, "the 'Monk' would even leave the bandstand. Then the bass would come up real loud while the other instruments would go down soft. After a while the horns would swell back up loud, and the bass softened down and it would sound like a whole lot of instruments playing."[11]

While such controversy about the band's pianoless style was again being stirred up, Mulligan's earlier reputation as an arranger was being boosted by another former employer, when Claude Thornhill released a couple of 10-inch LPs on the Trend label. Reviews of the second of these described "his band playing a flock of arrangements by the ace Gerry Mulligan."[12]

For quite different reasons from the new group's time in San Francisco, Brookmeyer found the Basin Street residency tough. This was largely because, compared to playing in a city where the group already had a reputation and could explore some new material, the band reverted to playing much of the repertoire recorded by the original quartet. It was the music from those LPs that East Coast audiences expected to hear. He recalled:

> There was no replacing Chet, and I was very aware of that. I would quit every night and after a few drinks say, "What this band needs is a trumpet player! I quit!" It got to the point where we were in New York . . . and Gerry called me at 6 a.m. He said, "Are you okay?" I growled, "What's wrong?" He said, "Well you didn't quit tonight, so I was worried!"[13]

11 Jackson, Reid E: "Art Farmer Discusses the History of Jazz Combos," *Baltimore Afro-American*, April 6, 1954, p. 7.

12 *Cedar Rapids Gazette*, January 31, 1954, p. 81.

13 Interview with Bob Brookmeyer, September 2, 2002.

Gradually, the musical side of the band settled down. In May, the quartet headlined in a concert at the Philadelphia Academy of Music, as part of a package show alongside its Basin Street counterpart, Gene Krupa's Trio, plus Sarah Vaughan and the George Shearing Quintet.[14] It also garnered speculation that it might be about to move to a major label, when reports appeared saying: "Columbia Records, who recently signed pianist Dave Brubeck's quartet, is now making generous overtures to Gerry Mulligan."

This followed discussions that Arlyne had with her family contacts at the company, including the legendary producer George Avakian, although in this case Mulligan himself decided to stick with Pacific Jazz, because Richard Bock had been such a support in getting the band started.[15]

During the quartet's appearance in Philadelphia in March, at the Blue Note on 15th Street, they were heard by the French pianist and record producer Henri Renaud, who, on his return to France, was quick to mention to his colleagues that he thought the band was exceptional.[16] This, plus the success of the first quartet's records in Europe, enthusiastic reviews in the Francophone press from the critics André Hodeir and Charles Delauney, and subsequent news of the warm reception in New York for the new version of the band, led to its being invited to appear for several nights in the third edition of the Paris Salon du Jazz, at the beginning of June 1954.[17]

These events had begun in 1949, and the second festival in 1952 had drawn over 50,000 visitors to the Salle Pleyel concert hall, and to its associated trade fair, which had stalls for instrument makers, record companies, and music publishers. In 1954, the concerts were underwritten by the French Ministry for Commerce and Industry, and the minister himself was to open the festivities. There had been complaints from certain factions in the Parisian artistic community that this subsidy was focused on "commercial" art, rather than something more aesthetic, so to counter this, there was also a special exhibition which ran in parallel with the concerts and trade fair, showing paintings, drawings, prints, and sculpture by (among others) Chagall, Braque, Matisse, and the family of the co-organizer Charles Delauney (whose parents were

14 *Philadelphia Jewish Exponent*, April 30, 1954, p. 31.

15 *Jefferson City Lincoln Clarion*, May 21, 1954.

16 Carrière, Claude: *Gerry Mulligan Quartet, Pleyel Concert Vol. 1*, BMG France 74321429232 (1993) [liner note].

17 Perchard, Tom: *After Django, Making Jazz in Postwar France* (Ann Arbor, University of Michigan Press, 2013) p. 55.

recognized artists in the post-Impressionist tradition). The 1954 Salon du Jazz ran for a week from June 1, attracted 90,000 attendees, and was—on the surface—a resounding success. It later emerged that there were serious underlying financial irregularities, which caused a long-lasting schism between Delauney and his fellow promoter Jacques Souplet, who between them took several years to pay off the festival's sizable debts.[18]

Although the event's own problems remained under the surface while the concerts were running, the difficulties within the Mulligan band reappeared at the very moment its members arrived in France. Bob Brookmeyer said:

> There was an anger that Gerry had all his life which he needed to express. He liked to have scenes. I did not understand anger then. That came for me much later. Then I had no train stops between "love" and "kill." So these big episodes of anger used to really upset me. And finally after six months, when we were landing in Paris, there was a big scene on the tarmac, between Mulligan and the promoters. And I said, "That does it. I quit." So his wife was very upset and so was he. "How can you quit the first night, when Gerry's not feeling well?" But I said, "No, I quit." So we played the festival, you could say, under slightly strained circumstances.[19]

Once on stage, despite this, the band behaved professionally, and if its recordings are anything to go by, for much of the time it seems to have enjoyed itself almost as much as the ecstatic audiences. Indeed, an eyewitness, in the form of Charles Delauney, wrote: "Contrary to so many modern musicians, whose attitude seems to be one of utter boredom, the members of the Mulligan Quartet showed their evident pleasure in what they were playing."[20] The group's concerts, on June 1, 3, 5, and 7, were all recorded by the French Vogue label, which Delauney still supervised. The band briefly left France on June 2, making a lightning trip to Basel in Switzerland, where it played a concert at the Mustermesse (the home of the city's sizable trade fairs), which was also recorded, and broadcast by the Swiss Francophone station Radio Lausanne, in its series *Jazz Partout 1954*. In both locations, as it had been at the Basin Street club in

18 Tournès, Ludovic: *New Orleans sur Seine, Histoire du Jazz en France* (Paris, Fayard, 1999) p. 131.

19 Interview with Bob Brookmeyer, September 2, 2002.

20 Carrière: *Gerry Mulligan Quartet.*

New York, the repertoire was mainly based on that of the original group with Chet Baker. So, spread across all five of the recorded concerts we find four versions of "Makin' Whoopee," three each of "Love Me or Leave Me," "Motel," and "The Nearness of You," and a couple of runs through "Bark for Barksdale" and "Five Brothers."

The opening number from the quartet's first concert, "Bernie's Tune," has plenty in common with the original, not least Isola's drumming, which catches something of both Hamilton's lightness with the brushes and his effective punctuations. Brookmeyer's second chorus is very much his own, whereas his first has Baker's specter hanging over it. Mulligan, by contrast, is far more extrovert than he was on the earlier recording, and Red Mitchell's nuanced playing is much less workaday than Whitlock's. "Walkin' Shoes" is also a clear attempt to capture the essence of the 1952 recording, but of the pieces that look backward, the least successful is "My Funny Valentine," where Brookmeyer fails to create such a vividly personal interpretation as Baker's original version. There is not a wrong note to be heard, and he plays quite beautifully, but he lacks the combination of fragility and passion that Baker brought to the piece. In this regard, Mulligan's biographer Jerome Klinkowitz talks of Brookmeyer's "timidity."[21]

Yet this is to miss the aforementioned trap into which many a band trying to sell records is lured, by needing to play recognizable versions of the recorded repertoire, so that the public buys plenty of LPs. Owing to the press buildup prior to the festival from Hodeir and Delauney, Mulligan felt it incumbent on him to play familiar music that chimed with the positive reviews of the records released in France on the Rhythm label, not least because he was now the only member of the original band present. Moreover, he had a point to prove, particularly to Delauney, not so much as co-organizer of the Salon du Jazz, but because he had written in *Jazz-Hot*: "Gerry Mulligan, like all talented composers, has something to say. His music is driven by simplicity: it is clear, logical and tasteful. The future will show whether his first records are an experience with no future, or alternatively the point of departure for a new style, capable of renewing jazz music."[22]

One piece that the quartet recorded a couple of times in Paris, but which, by being newly added to the repertoire, did not hark back to

21 Klinkowitz, Jerome: *Listen: Gerry Mulligan—An Aural Narrative in Jazz* (New York, Schirmer, 1991) p. 85.

22 Delauney, Charles: quoted in liner note for *The Gerry Mulligan Quartet*, Swing M 33.304 (1953) (translated by the author).

the Chet Baker era was David Raksin and Johnny Mercer's "Laura." This points forward to the sound of Mulligan and Brookmeyer's subsequent collaboration later in the decade, and the June 7 version in particular shows how they could create something original and fresh. Mulligan's opening theme statement is backed by a countermelody from Brookmeyer that is far more harmonically adept than Baker's supporting lines on the earlier records. Equally, the trombone solo breaks free from the shackles of the trumpeter's recordings (see Examples 3.1 and 3.2). The other piece from that final Salle Pleyel concert that shows a departure from the earlier group is "Come Out, Come Out, Wherever You Are," and this too has a head that shows a different kind of empathy between Brookmeyer and Mulligan from the music of the previous two years with Baker.

The atmosphere on stage may have been relatively relaxed, but off stage it was claustrophobic, contributing to Brookmeyer's decision to leave, and this mostly had to do with Arlyne Mulligan's style of management. The British critic Alun Morgan was in attendance, not least because the Musicians' Union made it virtually impossible for American jazz musicians to play in the United Kingdom at that time, and he was keen to report on this novel pianoless quartet for his English readers. He recalled:

> We failed almost completely to converse with the star of the show Gerry Mulligan, and it was here that we realised that the Gerry Mulligan Quartet is in effect a Quintet. The fifth member, Gerry's wife and personal manager Arlyne, threw an almost impenetrable screen around Mulligan. She cut short his conversations with journalists and French musicians and spent most of her husband's on-stage appearances in directing photographers and leading the audience applause from a visible position in the wings of the stage.[23]

When the band returned to the United States, although Mitchell and Isola had threatened to resign at the same time as Brookmeyer, they stayed. Not long after their return, Mulligan was being widely billed to appear at the first ever edition of what was to become one of the world's great jazz festivals. Along with a photograph of him and his baritone, captioned to suggest the grandstands might need reinforcement to accommodate

23 Letter from Morgan quoted by Gordon Jack in an email to the author, July 16, 2020.

EXAMPLE 3.1 "Laura." Lyrics by Johnny Mercer. Music by David Raksin. © 1945 (Renewed) Twentieth Century Music Corporation. All rights controlled and Administered by EMI Robbins Catalog Inc. (Publishing) and Alfred Music (Print). All Rights Reserved. Used by Permission. Reprinted by permission of Hal Leonard Europe Ltd. Opening section (transcription).

his fans, the syndicated column by the nationally respected critic Irving Kolodin reported:

> Not too many years ago when "ball" at Newport R. I. was mentioned, it cost upwards of six figures and caused a considerable stir in the

EXAMPLE 3.2 Brookmeyer's solo from "Laura" (transcription).

society pages. In work now are plans for a different kind of "ball" in which such leading figures in the jazz world as Ellington, Condon, Tatum, Gerry Mulligan, and Benny Goodman will take part on a July weekend.[24]

24 Kolodin, Irving: "Fashionable Newport R.I. Plans New Kind of 'Ball,'" *Tucson Daily Citizen*, June 26, 1954.

EXAMPLE 3.3 Fruscella's solo on "Bernie's Tune" showing use of a repeated motif.

This was to be the inaugural Newport Jazz Festival, and Mulligan's quartet duly played on the outdoor stage in the Casino Gardens there on July 17, with trumpeter Tony Fruscella replacing Brookmeyer. Fruscella was perhaps a somewhat unusual choice. The British author Dave Gelly wrote that, after a troubled childhood in an orphanage, he was "virtually a vagrant. He rarely had a fixed address and almost never a telephone number. He carried his trumpet around in a brown paper bag."[25] Yet what we hear in the little recorded evidence there is of his playing suggests a sensitive, responsive, and somewhat romantic-sounding musician.

The quartet's program again delved back into the catalog of Baker recordings, including "Bernie's Tune," "The Lady Is a Tramp," and a truncated "Lullaby of the Leaves." These survive as part of a broadcast that went out later the same night as the concert, in the weekly *Strictly from Dixie* show on the national ABC network.[26] Although Mulligan had a slight problem with one of the stage microphones, his band sounds rehearsed and confident. In particular, Mulligan himself produces a storming solo on "The Lady Is a Tramp" and as he gets into his stride, Mitchell and Isola raise their game to give him splendid hard-swinging support. Fruscella seems slightly inhibited among the other members of this regular working unit, but he adopts two mannerisms that distinguish his solos from Baker's. On both the first two pieces he improvises by building on a series of short motifs, or at times just figures built of repeated notes (see Examples 3.3 and 3.4), and he also tends to draw out his long notes, slightly altering both pitch and volume, which is not an unattractive effect. This is particularly apparent on the closing reprise of the head in "Bernie's Tune."

The most interesting recording is the surviving fragment of "Lullaby of the Leaves," cut off as the program reaches its allotted time slot, where

25 Gelly, Dave: *Stan Getz, Nobody Else but Me* (San Francisco, Backbeat Books, 2002) p. 68.
26 Issued on *Newport Jazz Festival No. 1* (Sounds of Yesteryear, 2237).

EXAMPLE 3.4 Fruscella's solo on "Bernie's Tune" showing use of repeated notes.

Fruscella hints at a somber, introverted ballad style, that works well both in his brief solo statements and in a chorus where his lines interweave with Mulligan's. It would have been interesting to see how the band might have developed such ideas further with Fruscella, but Mulligan found him difficult to work with, so the association ended there and then. Mulligan recalled:

> Tony had that fuzzy introverted tone that Chet had, although Chet's was more outgoing, while Tony's was introverted. It sounded nice but one concert at the Newport Jazz Festival was enough for me to realize that having Tony travelling with me and being onstage together night after night would have driven me crazy.[27]

Away from his own quartet that weekend, Mulligan was a guest with several of the other musicians appearing on the festival, including Billie Holiday and Buck Clayton, Ruby Braff and Teddy Wilson, and tenorist Warne Marsh.

Back in New York, Mulligan needed to recruit a new trumpeter, because there were engagements in the diary. The quartet was scheduled to open on August 17 for a residency at the Club Tijuana, known as "Baltimore's house of modern jazz," on the city's Pennsylvania Avenue, following on from the Billy Taylor trio.[28] Not for the last time in this period of his life, Mulligan left his decision about whom to hire until very late, and only a few days before its debut in Baltimore, the quartet was still only a trio. According to the author Gordon Jack, it was almost by chance that Gerry and Arlyne found their eventual fourth member: "Jon Eardley was appearing at the Open Door in Greenwich Village when the Mulligans were in the audience. Arlyne apparently asked the trumpeter

27 Jack: *Fifties Jazz Talk*, p. 149.

28 Panel advertisement, *Baltimore Afro American*, July 31, 1954.

how many white shirts he had. On being told he had three or four, she took him over to Gerry who asked him if he would like to join the quartet. They opened three days later in Baltimore."[29]

Within a couple of days of the group's debut at the Club Tijuana, a press story did the rounds of the regional papers, attempting to categorize the band's music, but harking back to the Fantasy LP release from the Chet Baker era. Interestingly again, the word "cool" still does not appear.

> "New jazz" is the latest addition to the wide world of music. Gerry Mulligan and Chet Baker have released one on the Fantasy label. When it first came out, the astonished explorers of music called the new jazz "bop." Now it is termed intense. Who termed it? Why Gerry Mulligan himself. Gerry, a saxophonist, and Chet, a trumpet player, are striving for complete musical individuality. So they say![30]

Fortunately, during the band's residency in Baltimore, although Jon Eardley was already in the grip of heroin addiction (which Mulligan himself had finally quit a short while after his time on the honor farm), he proved himself to be a good, competent replacement for Baker and Brookmeyer. His frontline partnership with Mulligan breathed some new life into the familiar Fantasy and Pacific Jazz numbers. There were some new additions to the repertoire, but the main element of Eardley's arrival was to reinvigorate the band after the falling out with Brookmeyer. This was important, because that fall the Quartet was to be part of a package tour organized by Norman Granz, who, using his Jazz at the Philharmonic organization to book major concert halls, had put together a series of evenings featuring the Duke Ellington Orchestra, supported by three small groups. The press release—now deliberately emphasizing the word "cool"—ran as follows:

> [The] Modern Jazz Concert combines hot and cool music in one busload. Duke Ellington and His Merry Men provide the hot stuff, and the cool music comes from three quartets led by Stan Getz, Dave Brubeck, and Gerry Mulligan. The tour will hit 16 cities from Boston

29 Email to the author, July 16, 2020.

30 *Kenosha Evening News*, August 20, 1954.

to Los Angeles in late October and early November. Dig that crazy itinerary.[31]

If not crazy, it was certainly hectic. And the interpersonal relationships between the Getz and Mulligan bands were slightly complex, as both Brookmeyer and Bill Anthony were now in the Getz lineup (a quintet rather than "quartet" as in the press release), and their sets tended to overrun somewhat, provoking Mulligan's ire. The average duration of a complete concert was, notwithstanding overruns, supposed to be close to three hours, and on Saturday, October 16, the day after the tour opened in Philadelphia, the troupe undertook two shows—a 2:30 matinee at the Mosque Theatre in Newark, New Jersey, and a midnight event at Carnegie Hall in Manhattan. The package then visited Baltimore, Columbus, Cleveland, Chicago, Madison, and Indianapolis, before coming back to Carnegie Hall on October 30, "returning, according to Granz, because so many were unable to be accommodated last time the show appeared here."[32] The package then traveled west via Macon, Missouri, to play at the San Francisco Municipal Auditorium, and at the Berkeley Community Theatre, before winding up at the Shrine Auditorium in Los Angeles on November 8. Stan Getz's set from the Shrine was recorded by Granz for his Norgran label, and this was supplemented by two studio tracks cut the following day, for which Getz "borrowed" Frank Isola from Mulligan's quartet. *Stan Getz at the Shrine* went on to be one of his most successful albums.[33]

Meanwhile, Fantasy Records put some of their advertising muscle behind the tour itself, promoting the two bands they had previously recorded by placing panel ads in the music press, These offered 10 percent off Brubeck and Mulligan albums during the month of October.[34] Quite clearly, from the high attendances it achieved across the United States, this was a successful package, many concerts being completely sold out.[35]

31 *Cedar Rapids Gazette*, October 12, 1954.

32 "Jazz at the Phil to Come Back to Carnegie," *Indianapolis Recorder*, October 23, 1954.

33 Dates culled from: *Chicago Austin News*, October 13, 1954; *Wilmington News Journal*, October 14, 1954; *Madison Wisconsin State Journal*, October 21, 1954; *Indianapolis Recorder*, October 23, 1954; *Macon Chronicle Herald*, October 28, 1954; *Oakland Tribune*, November 5, 1954; *Indianapolis Recorder*, November 6, 1954.

34 "Special Announcement," *Billboard*, October 2, 1954, p. 39.

35 "Norman Granz's Carnegie Hall concert two Saturdays ago was the third successive sell-out in two days: Friday in Philadelphia, and on Saturday both at the Mosque Theatre . . . and Carnegie Hall," *Phoenix Arizona Sun*, November 5, 1954, p. 3.

But Granz himself was not happy, later saying: "I could never put on a cerebral concert. I'd rather go the emotional route. The biggest flop I've ever had was the tour I put on with some of the cerebral musicians like Brubeck and Gerry Mulligan."[36] While going out of his way not to criticize Getz, with whom he had a recording contract, he made clear that he preferred the adrenaline rush of the jam sessions and jousts in JATP concerts, and he also felt that Mulligan's and Brubeck's sets strayed too far from the blues.

Yet, although reviewers of the concert tended to heap most praise on Ellington, one typical report saying, "Duke and crew need no 'package,' "[37] it was generally the Mulligan quartet that received the most enthusiastic notices among the supporting bands. Typically, under the title "The Duke Still Wears the Crown," Leo Lesser Jr., the African American jazz critic for the *Indianapolis Recorder*, wrote:

> Mentions must be made of the aggregations appearing with Ellington on the bill. Stan "The Man" Goetz [*sic*] opened the concert and got things off to a flying start. Outstanding sax solo work by Goetz put concert-goers in a mood for the introduction of the Dave Brubeck combo. Brubeck has been touring colleges and enjoys quite a following among the younger set. Brubeck's piano solos were a bit monotonous in spots but the alto sax solos of Paul Desmond overruled any of Mr. Brubeck's shortcomings. Gerry Mulligan's instrumental quartet was the best-received "jazz" group that performed during the night. The Mulligan group does not use a piano on several selections. The results achieved by Gerry in omitting the piano are astounding.[38]

After the tour finished, both the Mulligan quartet and Bob Brookmeyer (who elected at that point to leave Stan Getz) remained in California. And it seems from one press report that, for a short time at least, Mulligan returned to the Haig, where for some weeks in late 1954 another very distinguished musician had been playing, rather as Mulligan used to do, on Monday nights. Aline Mosby of Universal Press, finding yet more adjectives to describe the contemporary jazz of the time, wrote:

36 Hershorn, Tad: *Norman Granz: The Man Who Used Jazz for Justice* (Berkeley, University of California Press, 2011) p. 210.

37 Butler, Henry: "Duke and Crew Need No 'Package,'" *Indianapolis Recorder*, November 6, 1954.

38 Lesser Jr., Leo: "The Duke Still Wears the Crown," *Indianapolis Recorder*, November 6, 1954.

> The new "progressive" jazz that has made Southern California its headquarters now has lured a classical music director from MGM into the act. By day, pianist Andre Previn draws down a four-figure paycheck at MGM as the town's youngest stu [*sic*] music director, conducting and composing film scores. By night, not known to his movie bosses, their 25-year old boy genius often can be found bending over a hot piano at a little Wilshire Blvd. bistro to beat out the new jazz, "just for fun."
>
> "I sit in now and then when the regular entertainers take a night off," said Previn. "I get $12 I think. In this kind of club I can play anything I want until two in the morning. I get my fun out of it. I sit at MGM so much with a pencil in my hand, I don't get to play. I couldn't play modern jazz at places like Ciro's or Mocambo. And this place couldn't afford to pay me my regular fee. So I just come in at the union scale. Nobody's going to tell me what to play."
>
> "Progressive" or "modern" jazz, for those un-cool readers, has been collecting devoted addicts since World War II. Trumpeter Shorty Rogers and drummer Shelly Manne play on Hollywood Blvd. The regular act at Previn's place is the Gerry Mulligan Quartet, another top progressive group.[39]

Being back in Los Angeles, and playing at least part of the time at his former base, Mulligan set about both recording his current quartet for Richard Bock at Pacific Jazz, and also writing and rehearsing charts for a new idea, a sextet that would bring Zoot Sims and Bob Brookmeyer into the lineup alongside himself, Eardley, Mitchell, and either Chico Hamilton or Larry Bunker (Frank Isola having returned East). The resulting sessions took place at high school concerts approximately a month apart, on November 12, at Stockton, California (with just the quartet), and at Hoover High School, San Diego (with both bands), on December 14.

Although the second session has slightly better fidelity and is more fulfilling musically, owing to the contrast between the two lineups, there is nonetheless plenty to enthuse about in the November quartet recording. Not least, particularly compared to the slightly nervous feel of the July Newport Festival set, it has a sense of relaxed spontaneity

39 Mosby, Aline: "Previn Leaves Classical for Jazz and Pay Check," *Brownsville Herald*, December 15, 1954.

EXAMPLE 3.5 "Blues Going Up" (traditional 12-measure blues). The Mulligan / Mitchell / Eardley exchanges (transcription).

from the outset, as Mulligan tells the audience as he comes on stage that "maybe I'll play some blues while you get seated," before asking Mitchell and Hamilton to "play some Count Basie." The resulting opening chorus of the impromptu "Blues Going Up" immediately catches the feel of a laid-back Basie band introduction, not least because of the flowing lines from the double bass, on which Mitchell improves even further in the second chorus, as baritone and trumpet join in, while Hamilton provides some Jo Jones–style hi-hat. Eardley's solo is pleasantly behind the beat, leading to a fine exchange between Mitchell and Mulligan, with Eardley then joining as well; (see Example 3.5).

This is some of the most accomplished bass playing to be heard in any of the Mulligan quartet recordings so far, with Mitchell contributing as a soloist on an equal level to the horns. On the following "Little Girl Blue" there's a theme statement from Eardley that clearly shows he owes nothing to Baker and is confident of his own place in the ensemble. As reissue producer Michael Cuscuna put it, "Jon Eardley is a wonderful surprise for those not familiar with him. . . . A well-rounded and distinctive player, he has a great sense of swing and is a thoughtful, fresh improviser."[40] A rather lumbering "Piano Blues" aside, which features Mulligan's not very eloquent pianism, the band is on fine form, and pieces from its earlier repertoire like "Soft Shoe" and a high-speed "Bark for Barksdale" take on a new life. The highlight of the concert is a splendid rendition of Charlie Parker's "Yardbird Suite." Taken at a medium fast tempo, the band keeps the sense of relaxation with which it opened the concert, and Mulligan's first baritone solo is some of his most free-blowing uninhibited playing—giving us just a flavor of what Leo Lesser Jr. heard in the Norman Granz concert package. Equally, Eardley takes a well-constructed solo with some fine underpinning from the baritone (Example 3.6). Here again, Mitchell is featured in exchanges, this time with both saxophone and trumpet. Throughout, Hamilton's playing is exemplary, underlining what an asset he was to the original quartet as well as to this later edition.

The most consistent recordings by this late 1954 version of the quartet come from the second college concert in San Diego. Four of the five pieces revisit the repertoire of the first group with Chet Baker: "Makin' Whoopee," "Nights at the Turntable," "Frenesi," and "Limelite," though each seems to take on a fresh personality with this lineup. But then, building on his exchanges with the horns from the previous month's concert, Red Mitchell is featured on his own composition "Blues for Tiny." The head is simple, suggesting the almost impromptu stringing together of a phrase that players might hum to one another behind a horn solo to create a backing riff. This works brilliantly in the first two choruses for solo bass (see Example 3.7), where Spartan riffs are sporadically interjected between Mitchell's busy phrasing. This is quite unlike anything by the earlier quartets.

The principal revelation in this second high-school concert is not the quartet with Eardley, but the Mulligan Sextet. The highlight, "Western Reunion," has a simple riff head on a thirty-two-measure AABA chord sequence (Example 3.8). The middle eight is collective improvisation around Eardley's lead, harking back to the earliest days of ensemble jazz. The band's power and enthusiasm still leap out of the speakers almost seven decades after it was recorded. Each solo shows strength and energy, beginning with

40 Cuscuna, Michael: *California Concerts Vol. 1*, Pacific Jazz, CDP 7 46860-2 [liner note to 1998 reissue].

EXAMPLE 3.6 "Yardbird Suite" (Charlie Parker). Part of Eardley's solo (transcription).

Zoot Sims, and then moving toward a show-stopping couple of choruses from Brookmeyer that draw spontaneous applause from the crowd. Behind Mulligan's equally high-voltage solo, Brookmeyer shows his talent for creating spur-of-the-moment riff backings. Eardley takes a fluent boppish trumpet solo (revisiting in passing some of the ideas from Brookmeyer's choruses) before the spotlight falls on Mitchell. The first bass chorus has a slightly chaotic backing riff, but the second reveals a fluent solo with minimal drum support from Bunker, who then goes to trade fours with the horns (Example 3.9). This extrovert, hard-blowing, mainstream, yet bop-influenced band is the antithesis of the more introverted quartet recordings with Baker. There's no requirement for Bunker to stick to brushes, and he comes into his own as a forceful, hard-swinging drummer, both backing the ensembles and as a soloist. Brookmeyer recalled:

> When we started the sextet with Mulligan . . . the ghost of Chet sort of vanished. . . . And Red Mitchell played like Charlie Parker on bass.

EXAMPLE 3.7 "Blues for Tiny" (Red Mitchell). Mitchell's bass solo (transcription).

> I'd never heard anybody do that. Oscar Pettiford and I were friends, and Oscar was probably one of the best bass soloists I ever heard. But [in comparison] Red Mitchell made a new world, he did things that were not possible.[41]

41 Interview with Bob Brookmeyer, September 2, 2002.

EXAMPLE 3.8 "Western Reunion" by Gerry Mulligan. Copyright © 1955 Criterion Music Corp. Copyright renewed. All Rights Reserved. Used by Permission. Reprinted by permission of Hal Leonard Europe Ltd. Opening section for sextet (transcription).

Of the other sextet pieces recorded at San Diego, Mulligan's "I Know, Don't Know How" extends the palette of the group with a piece that makes the implied harmonies of the quartet explicit, and indeed extends them (Example 3.10). Mulligan takes the lead on the head and Eardley and Sims answer in harmony around him, with Brookmeyer taking a third layer of response. In the opening head, the rhythm section reverts to the approach of the quartet, playing four even beats to the measure, and with Bunker on brushes. For the closing head, the bass reverts to a 2/4 feel, but Bunker again uses brushes.

This piece and "The Red Door" (co-written by Mulligan and Sims) would become staples of the sextet repertoire, reappearing in the following year's US concerts and on a subsequent European tour. For the latter piece, Brookmeyer shifts to piano, proving himself a far more adept

EXAMPLE 3.9 "Western Reunion," Red Mitchell's second bass chorus (transcription).

keyboard player than Mulligan, and changing the sound of the group from its "pianoless" origins toward a more conventional jazz sextet. The drums and piano also provide a firm platform for another outstanding solo from Mitchell. "Polka Dots and Moonbeams" (a piece Mulligan had first recorded as a member of Claude Thornhill's band) is just a quartet for baritone saxophone, piano, bass, and drums.

The concert also included an Ellington medley ("In a Sentimental Mood/Flamingo/Moon Mist"), which showed the sextet's range of timbre in tackling ballads, and a sprightly version of "It Don't Mean a Thing (If It Ain't Got That Swing," which is every bit as forceful as "Western Reunion."

When the recordings came out on Pacific Jazz in the spring of 1955, they were universally welcomed. The familiar sound of the Mulligan quartet offered a jumping-off point for reviewers to lead in to discussing the larger ensemble. One typical review read:

> Concert jazz is on the uptake nowadays. . . . Gerry Mulligan isn't one to be left out. His latest is from two high school concerts for Pacific Jazz. Mulligan with his baritone and piano is joined by such standouts as Zoot Sims, tenor, Bob Brookmeyer, trombone, plus his regular trio. Casualness of this session makes it go. Best numbers are

EXAMPLE 3.10 "I Know, Don't Know How" by Gerry Mulligan. Copyright © 1955 Criterion Music Corp. Copyright renewed. All Rights Reserved. Used by Permission. Reprinted by permission of Hal Leonard Europe Ltd. Closing head (transcription).

EXAMPLE 3.10 Continued

> "Yardbird Suite," "I Know, Don't Know How" and "Western Reunion." Brookmeyer and Zoot cop the honors.[42]

And another contemporaneous piece singled out two other members of the lineup:

> The young sax virtuoso stands sponsor for the new talents of trumpeter Jon Beardley [*sic*] and bassist Red Mitchell. They are well worth knowing especially as heard in the late Charlie Parker's "Yardbird Suite." Zoot Sims and Bob Brookmeyer also sit in.[43]

However, by the time the records and these reviews appeared, Mulligan had taken the decision to curtail the activities of both ensembles. In early January, after his return to New York, the press reported: "Gerry Mulligan is disbanding his famous pianoless jazz group and plans to spend the next six months searching for a new sound."[44]

This did not go well. Almost immediately Mulligan hit an unexpected problem—writer's block. For someone who had almost always been able to produce arrangements and compositions in almost every circumstance since his teens, apart from that brief period at the very height of his heroin addiction before Gail Madden took him in hand, this came as an unexpected blow. He took an unusual route to deal with the problem, by deciding to appear as a guest with the small group led by none other than Chet Baker. "It was sick, very sick," he recalled. "I didn't know what else to do with myself. To go back and play with Chet Baker's group was just frustration."[45] He could, of course, have simply reconvened his own quartet with Jon Eardley and managed to make more than a good living, but the decision not to do so was at least in part because he and Arlyne believed that, as he tried to get back to serious writing, he could earn substantially more as a solo star, appearing as a guest on concerts and broadcasts. An early example was a solo appearance with the TV studio orchestra on the *Steve Allen Show*.[46] Following this, he rather laconically

42 *Los Angeles Southern Californian Daily Trojan*, March 25, 1955, p. 2.

43 "Record Round Up: Gerry Mulligan and Quartet," *Tucson Daily Citizen*, April 9, 1955.

44 *Dover Daily Reporter*, January 13, 1955.

45 Gavin, James: *Deep in a Dream: The Long Night of Chet Baker* (London, Chatto and Windus, 2002) p. 109.

46 Online Mulligan discography by Gérard Dugelay and Kenneth Hallqvist [pdalbury.files.wordpress.com/2012/09/gm-discography-2011.pdf; accessed May 16, 2021].

recalled that "In 1955, I sometimes appeared as a guest in Chet Baker's group."[47]

It was a little more than "sometimes," in that there was a sporadic national tour lasting overall from March to May 1955. As with the previous year's Norman Granz show, Carnegie Hall was an early stop on the itinerary for the new package, this time with Carmen McRae on the bill as well. One press report said:

> Dave Brubeck, Gerry Mulligan and Chet Baker will walk out with more than just bags of money after their Carnegie Hall jazz concert Saturday March 12. They'll be presented with gold plaques by *Downbeat* for winning the 1955 popularity poll for best combo, baritone saxist and trumpeter, respectively.[48]

There were two houses and Mulligan did extremely well financially from jointly headlining this single event, guesting on just a few numbers with Baker and his quintet with Russ Freeman, piano; Jack Lowler, bass; and Peter Littman, drums. According to one report: "The lure and influence of modern jazz was demonstrated at Carnegie Hall in New York City when the Dave Brubeck Quartet, Gerry Mulligan and the Chat Barker [*sic*] combo grossed $18,000 in a two-performance one-night appearance."[49] Ironically Chet's regular frontline partner up to and including the first part of these concerts was none other than Phil Urso, Mulligan's former colleague from the Elliot Lawrence days. But the Carnegie Hall event was Urso's last appearance with Baker for some time, as Mulligan effectively took his place. The British *Jazz Journal* critic Douglas Hague was impressed by the ballad playing of Baker's band on this concert and commented, "The audience was the most quiet and intense that I have ever witnessed at Carnegie Hall."[50]

There were more shows to follow with this package, as well as a one-off late April gig for the Mulligan-with-Baker quintet at Princeton, on a bill with Erroll Garner and Lionel Hampton. The tour with Brubeck then continued, taking in the Music Hall in Cincinnati on May 6,[51] and further appearances in Pittsburgh and Houston.[52]

47 Jack: *Fifties Jazz Talk*, p. 150.

48 *Towanda Daily Review*, March 14, 1955.

49 "Carnegie Jumps," *Indianapolis Recorder*, August 20, 1955.

50 *Jazz Journal* review, quoted in Gavin: *Deep in a Dream*, p. 109.

51 *Middletown Journal*, May 3, 1955.

52 *San Antonio Light*, June 3, 1955.

By mid-May, Mulligan was in residence with an ad hoc group of his own at the Basin Street club in New York. This quintet was unusual in that he shared frontline duties with tenor saxophonist Al Cohn, and he had coaxed Gil Evans into playing piano. Bassist George Duvivier and drummer Herb Wasserman completed the lineup. Yet this time around, it wasn't the music that drew press attention, but Mulligan's star status. Gossip columnist Dorothy Kilgallen wrote:

> Gerry Mulligan is getting unprecedented red carpet treatment from the management at Basin Street. Most jazz cellars don't worry much about "little touches" in their backstage area—even a big star of the music world is lucky to get an ill-lit, peeling, cubby hole to change his shirt in after a long set. But Gerry's dressing room behind the bandstand is outfitted with a cushioned basket bed for his French poodle and a frilly, feminine little armchair for Mrs. Mulligan. Because he never goes anywhere—even to work—without his dog and his wife.[53]

The reason, it seems, that Arlyne had installed her armchair and home comforts at the club was that she was pregnant, but sadly at the end of June she suffered the first of a series of miscarriages.[54] Aside from the gossip, there is one report that mentions the extremely high quality of Mulligan's band. The other band on the bill at Basin Street was the West Coast traditional septet led by Bob Scobey, featuring banjoist Clancy Hayes. In a profile of Scobey published the following year, an anonymous Californian columnist described the challenge of making an impact in New York opposite Mulligan's very accomplished and much more modern quintet, calling it the traditionalists' "stiffest test." However, apparently: "Scobey's trumpet and the singing of his vocalist Clancy Hayes falls winningly on the ears of two-beat and cool partisans alike."[55]

Within a few days after the personal tragedy of losing a baby, Mulligan's professional life had to continue, and he was reunited one more time with Chet Baker's quartet, during a series of guest appearances at the Newport Jazz Festival. With no current band of his own, it was announced that "Gerry Mulligan, king of the baritone saxophone, will sit in with various groups. He was one of the hits of 1954 here."[56] During the July weekend,

53 "Dorothy Kilgallen," *Sarasota News*, May 13, 1955.

54 "Songwriter Lew Brown's Daughter, Mrs. Gerry Mulligan, Mending," *Uniontown Morning Herald*, July 8, 1955.

55 *Oakland Tribune*, July 1, 1956.

56 "Armstrong to Brubeck—They'll All Be at Festival," *Newport Daily News*, June 10, 1955.

he played informally with several ensembles apart from Baker's, including those of Wild Bill Davison, Kai Winding, and Dave Brubeck. But perhaps the star turn was a sextet that also included Miles Davis, Zoot Sims, Thelonious Monk, Percy Heath, and Connie Kay. Columbia producer George Avakian was in the audience, and said: "The second piece they played was 'Round Midnight.' It was a spellbinding performance. My brother was listening with me, and he said, 'Why don't you go ahead and sign Miles, because somebody else will after tonight!' "[57]

That is exactly what Avakian did, starting a thirty-two-year relationship between the trumpeter and the Columbia label. However, despite his earlier discussions with Arlyne, Avakian did not rush to sign Mulligan. But another of the baritonist's guest appearances at Newport led to his being signed by a different producer. The previous year Bob Shad had been given the job of founding EmArcy, the jazz subsidiary of Mercury Records. His artists included the Clifford Brown–Max Roach Quintet, and shortly after midnight on the night of July 16, Mulligan, Brown, and Roach wandered on to the stage where Brubeck's quartet was playing, and joined in. "The Brubeck group took the invasion with good grace," reported the local paper. "A jam on 'Tea for Two' went on for about 15 minutes until producer Wein signaled a frantic halt."[58] In fact a bootleg recording of the piece suggests it only lasted around ten minutes,[59] but it's clear that following this, Shad took an interest in Mulligan, and by September had signed him to his label, which had far greater reach than Pacific Jazz or Fantasy.

Still suffering to some degree from writer's block, Mulligan's logical conclusion, with a new contract on the horizon, was that he should reform the sextet. In its West Coast incarnation, it had predominantly been a jamming band, and used fairly simple head arrangements. Brookmeyer and Sims agreed to rejoin, and initially Mulligan invited trumpeter Idrees Sulieman to make up the front line. Rehearsals were set to take place in mid-August at Nola Studios, and there would be some out-of-town warm-up gigs toward the end of the month at the Loop Lounge in Cleveland, and at George Wein's Storyville Club in Boston. Neither Red Mitchell nor Larry Bunker was available, and—in much the same way that Eardley had come into the quartet the previous year—the new members of the rhythm section were almost accidental last-minute

57 Interview with George Avakian, February 24, 1999.

58 *Newport Daily News*, July 18, 1955.

59 It is timed at 9:44 on Retro R2CD 40-86.

replacements. Mulligan was trying out various musicians at the studio rehearsals, sometimes reading through sextet charts, and on one occasion, playing through some of the tentette arrangements. Drummer Dave Bailey, who had gone along that day to listen with his friend, the bassist Peck Morrison, said:

> The drummer and the bass player didn't show up. The drummer was Osie Johnson and the bass player was Oscar Pettiford. But he had two novices, me and Peck, sitting there. And Idrees Sulieman, who was playing trumpet in the tentette, told Gerry that Peck Morrison was a bass player, because he knew Peck. So Peck rented a bass in Nola's, which you could do at that time, and started rehearsing with the group. And Gerry said, "Gee, I'm stuck, because I need a drummer." And Peck Morrison looked over at me, and said, "There's a drummer." So Gerry asked me would I play, and I said yes. I was nervous as all hell, but I sat down and played with the group and it sounded pretty good.
>
> So at the end of the rehearsal, I'm ready to go home, and Gerry asked Peck if he wanted to join his group. This was to be in Cleveland, Ohio. The rehearsal was on a Thursday and they were to open in Cleveland on the Monday. And so Peck Morrison said, "Yeah! I'll go, but of course I've gotta talk to my wife." And then Gerry said, "What about your buddy?" Peck says, "You mean Dave? Oh yeah, he'll go!" Without even asking me! So as I was leaving, Gerry said, "I'll see you in Cleveland." And to make a long story short, we opened the next week in Cleveland with the Sextet.[60]

The brief Cleveland and Boston residencies both featured Idrees Sulieman on trumpet, but by the time the band returned to New York in mid-September 1955, Jon Eardley had been asked to rejoin. Mulligan later reflected that Sulieman was an interesting choice, and might have taken the music in a very different direction, but "we had a hard time getting together on a style for the ensemble."[61] The sextet opened at Basin Street in New York on Tuesday, September 20, and in the weeks that followed it played opposite the Clifford Brown–Max Roach Quintet and Gene Krupa's small group.[62]

60 Interview with Dave Bailey, September 5, 2002.

61 Jack: *Fifties Jazz Talk*, p. 150.

62 Kilgallen, Dorothy: "Broadway Scene," *Sarasota News*, September 20, 1955; and Online Mulligan Discography by Gérard Dugelay and Kenneth Hallqvist.

On the two days after their first evening at Basin Street, the Sextet was in the studio for EmArcy, making the first of the eight tracks that would comprise their debut for the label. The resulting album, a 12-inch LP titled *Presenting the Gerry Mulligan Sextet*, appeared before the end of the year. (It also included some pieces from a further session in late October.) The opening "Mud Bug" has a comparable impact to that of "Western Reunion" from the previous year, except that the rhythmic drive of Morrison and Bailey is even greater than that of Mitchell and Isola, both in the ensemble sections and behind solos. Morrison was not the adept or inventive bassist that Mitchell was, and his own solo choruses in the sextet tend to consist of walking bass lines. But his playing experience, not least through having worked briefly in the Duke Ellington Orchestra in late 1954,[63] meant that what he lacked as a soloist he more than made up for in drive. He locked on to Bailey's drums with an energy that reflected their joint apprenticeship among New York's community of African American jazz musicians, Bailey having previously worked with Lou Donaldson, Charles Mingus, and Johnny Hodges, among others, and Morrison with Lucky Thompson, J. J. Johnson, and Kai Winding.

The rest of the sextet repertoire from this first EmArcy LP revisits a number of pieces from the first quartet with Chet Baker. So we find "Nights at the Turntable," "Broadway" (which had been one of the tracks made with Lee Konitz), "The Lady Is a Tramp," and "Bernie's Tune." Three of these same pieces then turn up in the surviving airshots from the Sextet's residency at Basin Street, recorded in October and December 1955, so they were clearly part of the group's core live repertoire, along with "The Red Door" from the earlier California concert. The focus of this book is mainly on the quartet recordings, but it is instructive to hear how some of the harmonies that are implied on the earlier records are opened up and played in fuller form by the larger group. Also, "Nights at the Turntable" becomes more of a jamming vehicle, largely losing the tag at the end of each chorus between solos once the head has been played, so that these extra measures only appear sporadically in the sextet version.

The head of "Bernie's Tune" (retitled "Bernie's Theme" on the sextet album) is a clear example of implied harmony made explicit, by comparing the two versions, as in Examples 3.11 and 3.12. What

63 Nielsen, Ole J.: *Jazz Records 1942–80, Volume 6: Duke Ellington* (Copenhagen, Jazz Media, 1991) p. 147.

EXAMPLE 3.11 "Bernie's Tune" by Bernie Miller. Head from original Mulligan Quartet recording, August 16, 1952 (transcription).

is obvious is that this was a tight-knit ensemble, which had the improvisational capability and collective understanding to work with the minimum of formal arrangements. Brookmeyer and the group's subsequent bassist Bill Crow both attested that the heads involved passages that had to be learned, such as the harmonies behind Mulligan's lead on "Sweet and Lovely," or the somewhat circular backing phrase in "The Lady Is a Tramp." But for the most part we hear six musicians of high caliber jamming together on repertoire that lends itself to impromptu riff-making and—in several instances—polyphonic collective improvisation. Mulligan's biographer Jerome Klinkowitz describes this as Mulligan's "happiest group by far," and goes on to state perceptively that "in the sextet's hands, numbers that once seemed pro-forma exercises in musicianship and composition theory now come across with the feel of good time blowing."[64]

64 Klinkowitz, Jerome: *Listen: Gerry Mulligan* (New York, Schirmer, 1991) p. 98.

EXAMPLE 3.12 Sextet voicings of head for "Bernie's Tune" showing the spread of harmonies between the horns in measures 1–2 and 5–6, despite a reduced role for the bass (transcription).

The sextet played at Basin Street through to the end of October, save for a week at the Patio Lounge in Washington, DC, early in the month. Its broadcasts from the New York club include a beautifully written version of "Moonlight in Vermont" that harks back to some of Mulligan's earlier big band writing, though again the elaborate voicings evaporate after a couple of choruses, once the solos start. As the piece progresses, Brookmeyer's backings for Sims show his talent for creating sympathetic riffs, which would resurface the next decade in Mulligan's Concert

Jazz Band. It is worth noting that Morrison's uncomplicated bass lines, staying close to root notes and fifths, give Mulligan perfect support for his half-chorus solo.

Club work was one thing. Playing huge concert halls was another, and in November the sextet set off on that fall's package tour, dubbed "Modern Jazz of '55" and booked by Louis Armstrong's manager Joe Glaser, in partnership with prominent local promoters. The press notice stated:

> In the all-star line-up will be Dave Brubeck and his quartet featuring Paul Desmond, the Gerry Mulligan Sextet with Zoot Sims and Bob Brookmeyer, singer Carmen McRae and the Australian Jazz Quartet.[65]

During the month of November, the package not only played what might almost be seen by this time as a routine visit to Carnegie Hall, but also appeared at the Philadelphia Academy of Music; Symphony Hall, Boston; the Erlanger Theater, Buffalo; Toledo Arena; Orchestra Hall, Chicago; and the National Guard Armory in Washington, DC. (For this final date the Sauter-Finegan Orchestra was added to the program.)[66]

The sextet mainly lived on the road during this period, but in a brief moment in New York between the Philadelphia and Boston concerts, there was more distress in the Mulligan household. On November 9, the gossip columns announced: "Jazz star Gerry Mulligan and his Arlene [*sic*] are knitting tiny garments for a June '56 arrival."[67] But the following day there was an update: "Sad news for the Gerry Mulligans. The talented jazz musician and his wife lost their expected baby."[68] Their relationship was not helped by Mulligan having to leave almost immediately for the tour.

Nonetheless the tour pulled the band together in the way that only playing for concert audiences every night can, and on its next broadcast from Basin Street, after returning to the club in early December, it has a swagger and confidence that was only just beginning to emerge before it set out. There is a hard-swinging medium-tempo version of "Soft Shoe" as well as a brisk run through "The Red Door," not to mention a

65 "Modern Jazz show of '55," *Chicago Austin News*, November 9, 1955.

66 *Chester Times*, October 18, 1955; *Buffalo Spectrum*, October 21, 1955; *Chicago Garfieldian*, November 9, 1955; *Boston Heights*, November 10, 1955, *Norwalk Reflector Herald*, November 11, 1955; *Baltimore Afro American*, November 27, 1955.

67 *Sarasota News*, November 9, 1955.

68 *Middletown Journal*, November 10, 1955.

relaxed "Making Whoopee" that starts out in the same way as the original quartet version, until all the sextet voices pile in behind Mulligan's lead. His own solo is minimal, understated, and he resists the temptation to play too many notes. Their Basin Street set on December 3 rounds off with what must be one of the fastest versions of "Bernie's Tune" that Mulligan ever recorded, but with the band clearly enjoying the adrenaline rush.[69]

Regardless of the obvious synergy between the band members, and despite—on that very same version of "Bernie's Tune"—an exhilarating walking-bass chorus on which the frontline players take it in turns to jam a few bars each with Peck Morrison, the bassist had nonetheless already decided to leave the sextet by this point. This was because there was a lengthy European tour on the horizon, slated to run from February to April 1956, and Morrison simply did not want to be away from home for that long. So at the end of 1955, Mulligan called the bass player who was currently working at the Hickory House in Marian McPartland's trio alongside drummer Joe Morello. This was Bill Crow, who had previously worked with Brookmeyer in Stan Getz's quintet. He had spent part of 1953 in Claude Thornhill's Orchestra, and had also briefly known Mulligan in his pre-West Coast days, at the time of the Central Park rehearsals and his relationship with Gail Madden. Crow recalled:

> Peck Morrison didn't want to go on the road with them, so he resigned and Gerry was looking for a bass player. I don't know whether Bob recommended me, or whether he knew of my work from having stopped by the Hickory House, but anyway I got a call from Gerry to come join the sextet. I couldn't turn that down. I had a good steady job in town with Marian, but the chance to play with all those guys was just too attractive. So I resigned from the Hickory House and joined the sextet. They had been recording an album for Mercury and Peck had done the first part of it, and we did a little more of it, and a couple of jobs around town, and then came the European tour.[70]

The two tracks recorded for EmArcy on January 25, 1956, that were first released reveal that Bill Crow had the ideal balance between the burnished tone, variety of phrasing and virtuosity of Red Mitchell and

69 *Gerry Mulligan Sextet/Quartet Rare and Unissued 1955–56 Broadcasts*, Rare Live Recordings 88660 [released 2010].

70 Interview with Bill Crow, September 4, 2002.

the drive of Peck Morrison. In particular the fine recording of the Count Basie/Buster Harding piece "Ain't It the Truth" recalls Mulligan's instruction to Mitchell to "Play some Basie," back in California. The Mulligan arrangement of this number (a piece originally recorded by the full Basie band in 1942) pares the original chart down to the essentials, and the rhythm team of Crow and Bailey sound closer to Basie's contemporaneous "New Testament" rhythm team of Eddie Jones and Sonny Payne, than the original pairing of Walter Page and Jo Jones who played on the Count's recording. This is straight-ahead mainstream jazz (to use the critic Stanley Dance's term), and the album itself was to be titled *Mainstream of Jazz*.

This name derived from Mulligan's new composition, called simply "Mainstream," which was a medium-tempo swing number, though the recording has a rather jumbled opening chorus shared between Sims and Mulligan, rescued when Sims plays some almost exaggerated swing licks to pull the baritone into line. What these two tracks also show is that—even in a limited way—Mulligan was writing again, and his new charts have a directness and swing that had little to do with notions of "West Coast cool." An interesting parallel is the 1954 album *Shorty Rogers Courts the Count*, which (with a lineup also including Zoot Sims) explores Basie material, and where Rogers uses baritone saxophonist Bob Gordon to add depth to a track such as "Jump for Me" in a very similar way to Mulligan's scoring of his own part on "Ain't It the Truth."

Just a matter of days after the EmArcy recording, the sextet was in Europe, and its tour began in Italy, with a concert on February 22 in Rome. It then set off on an itinerary that took it from Italy to France, and then to Switzerland, Belgium, Germany, and Holland, returning to L'Olympia in Paris on April 11.[71] (See Figure 3.2). We have a snapshot of one of the earlier concerts in the tour, from the Teatro della Fiera in Milan, from which part of the soundtrack to a television recording survives. There's a slightly less frenetic "Bernie's Tune" than the previous year's broadcast from Basin Street, on which Bill Crow acquits himself well on the bass chorus toward the end, which Morrison had used as his opportunity to joust with the front line. There's also a version of "Ontet"

71 The tour dates are: February 22, Rome; 24, Genoa; 25, Milan; 26, Turin; 27, Bologna; 29, Versailles, France; March 1–3, Paris; 5, Lyons; 6, Lille; 7, Rouen [then no details available for two weeks]; 21, Geneva, Switzerland; 22, Lugano; 23, Basel; 24, Zurich; 25, Brussels, Belgium; 30, Ramstein, Germany; 31, West Berlin; April 7 (matinee), The Hague, Netherlands; 7 (evening), Amsterdam; 11, Paris, France, L'Olympia.

FIGURE 3.2 The sextet rehearsing at the Deutschlandhalle on March 31, 1956, prior to a triple bill with the groups of Chet Baker and Stan Getz. Baker is sitting in here with the sextet. Left to right: Mulligan, Crow, Bailey, Baker, Eardley, Brookmeyer, Sims. Picture © Bill Crow.

with Mulligan at the piano, proving once again that he was not in the same league as a pianist as Brookmeyer. But the highlight is "Walkin' Shoes," neatly expanding the old quartet version into a compelling vehicle for the larger group, but with plenty of space for extended solos. Brookmeyer again shows his prowess as a riff-maker, backing Mulligan with a phrase that is momentarily mimicked and then harmonized by the baritone, before Mulligan presses on with his solo. Sims's playing is relaxed and the rhythm section has the same unforced swing that it had achieved in the studio on "Ain't It the Truth."

The Amsterdam concert on the evening of April 7 was recorded from the stage at the Concertgebouw in a small studio set up for the purpose by the Philips record company.[72] Almost the entire concert survives, opening with a storming version of "Mud Bug." There's an equally impressive live rendition of "Ain't It the Truth," Mulligan's opening baritone solo flowing with none of the hesitancy of his piano work on "Ontet." Again, this is hard-swinging mainstream jazz, albeit with nods to the bebop vocabulary in some of the solos, and after just over six weeks on the road, the band sounds completely relaxed and at ease with the material, and even some slightly scrambled ensemble work on the outchoruses of "Ain't It the Truth" is quickly overcome as the band reverts to the head. There's also a consistent sense of good humor and fun among the participants.

"Line for Lyons" is a quartet feature for Mulligan and Brookmeyer, and their improvisational interplay (see Example 3.13) points to the way that they would continue to develop in the four-piece band in the months that followed.

The highlights of the full sextet's work at the Amsterdam evening are Eardley's contrafact of "Sweet Georgia Brown" named "Demanton" (with Crow and Bailey goading the soloists into better and better playing), "Broadway" (with a fine solo from Sims, and Eardley creating sufficient space to solo more economically than he sometimes did), and the closing piece, "Western Reunion." The press reviews were uniformly favorable, talking of "intensively concentrated improvisations on a high artistic level."[73] Now it seemed, with the EmArcy label backing him and a band that was very different from the quartet with Baker, that Mulligan's future looked promising.

By early May the sextet was back in residence at Basin Street in New York, and the press was advertising its forthcoming appearance at that summer's Newport Jazz Festival in July. "Jazz Festival Tickets are now on sale," ran the release, ". . . those scheduled will include Duke Ellington's Orchestra, the Gerry Mulligan Sextet, the Chico Hamilton Quintet, vocalists Jimmy Rushing and Anita O'Day, and the George Shearing Quintet."[74] Prior to this, at the end of May, the sextet set off to Chicago for a two-week engagement at the Modern Jazz Room, but the after-effects of the European touring, followed by the effort of plunging straight back into club dates, were taking their toll on Mulligan. Three days after the sextet's return from Chicago, columnist Dorothy Kilgallen reported: "Gerry Mulligan's doctors have told him to go easy on the

72 *Gerry Mulligan Western Reunion* (Dutch Jazz Archive Series) MCN 0801.

73 Ibid., quoted in liner note by Lex Lemman.

74 *Newport Daily News*, May 11, 1956.

EXAMPLE 3.13 “Line for Lyons” from the April 7, 1956, Amsterdam concert, showing ensemble interplay between Mulligan, Brookmeyer, and Crow in the jamming section after the solos (transcription).

playing. The jazz star will devote more time to composing—like a good boy.”[75] The band’s appearance was pulled from the Newport program,

75 Kilgallen, Dorothy: “Voice of Broadway,” *Anderson Herald Bulletin*, June 15, 1956.

and this was followed by the syndicated reporter Dick Sinnot not only speculating that this might be the last ever Newport Jazz Festival, owing to difficulties between the organizers (George Wein and the Lorillard family) and the townsfolk of Newport, but stating: "The sizzling saxophone of Gerry Mulligan won't be heard. Mulligan recently was advised by physicians to 'take a rest.'"[76]

This hiatus almost led to the dissolution of the sextet. Immediate bookings were canceled, but there was a tour looming in the late fall with some prestigious dates. Mulligan would manage to re-form the band then, but it was at this point in the summer of 1956 that Eardley left for good. As Bill Crow recalled:

> Zoot was a little impatient with having to memorize all those little parts that Gerry had written, and he didn't get much solo space. Jon Eardley was the one that complained the most, even when Gerry explained to him: "It's a sextet, and it's my band, so I'm going to get the most solos. Zoot's my featured player, so he's gonna get the next most, and Brookmeyer is a wonderful player, so he's gonna get the next most! You're just going to have to be satisfied with what's left."[77]

Despite having to cancel appearing at Newport and the sextet's upcoming club dates, Mulligan was back leading a quartet of himself, Brookmeyer, Crow, and Bailey by the end of July, when the band appeared on the CBS *Camera 3* television show. This has survived as an audio recording, and the fragment of "Line for Lyons" that exists shows Brookmeyer and Mulligan indulging in what Mulligan calls (in his announcement) "contrapuntal interplay" as they move toward the closing head. This is the great strength of what would subsequently emerge as the mature Mulligan/Brookmeyer quartet, with these two instinctive arrangers playing off each other, embellishing both melody and harmony, and sounding as spontaneous in their collective improvisation as a traditional New Orleans band. The version of "My Funny Valentine" that follows uses the bass line from the original recording, but with Mulligan taking the lead, and Brookmeyer harmonizing behind him. The "ghost

76 Sinnot, Dick: "American Jazz Festival May Start Swan Song July 5th," *North Adams Transcript*, July 2, 1956.

77 Interview with Bill Crow, September 4, 2002.

of Chet" has indeed vanished and this version is a quantum leap forward from the Salle Pleyel quartet record from 1954.

The best of these July 29 television pieces is a sprightly version of "Five Brothers" that has the easy forward momentum of the sextet's best work, with Crow and Bailey settling into the same driving swing as on the larger band's "Ain't It the Truth." Apparently the rest of this edition of *Camera 3* involved a classical string quartet in a deliberate contrast to the Mulligan group's collective four-part improvising, and explains Mulligan's reference to counterpoint in his announcement.[78] Back in the television studios the following month for another broadcast, the Mulligan quartet eases through yet another relaxed version of "Line for Lyons," suggesting that far from the leader "devoting more time to composing," as Dorothy Kilgallen had speculated, he was reverting to playing material that involved little or no arrangement and allowed the band to busk through his "greatest hits." Mulligan also made some media appearances as a guest speaker during August 1956, for example joining Dave Brubeck and George Shearing in an edition of the *Mitch Miller Show* on CBS radio, to discuss the state of jazz and "the past and future of their art."[79]

Later in the month, the quartet with Brookmeyer, Crow, and Bailey made a high-profile appearance in New York. The Associated Press wire announced:

> The first Annual New York Jazz Festival will be held here at Randall's Island Stadium on August 24 and 25. The most glittering array of jazz talent ever assembled for one function already includes Count Basie and His Orchestra, Dave Brubeck, Erroll Garner, Gerry Mulligan, Lester Young, Billie Holiday, The Modern Jazz Quartet, Gene Krupa, the Don Elliott Quartet and Anita O'Day.[80]

On the day of its concert, the quartet was joined—for a couple of numbers—by Lee Konitz, thereby harking back to the 1953 Haig club collaborations. The following weekend, Mulligan was to make the trek to the Lenox Music Barn in Massachusetts, for the season closer at that Berkshire venue. This time he did not take his own group, but appeared

78 "An experiment in treatment of a musical theme featuring Gerry Mulligan and a jazz quartet in contrast with a traditional string quartet will be illustrated in *Camera 3* WIN-T 15," "TV Guide—10.30am," *Defiance Crescent News*, July 28, 1956.

79 *Lubbock Avalanche Journal*, August 19, 1956.

80 *Indianapolis Recorder*, August 18, 1956.

as a guest with the Modern Jazz Quartet. It would have been interesting to hear him with this ensemble that had also experimented with contrapuntal ideas, through the writing of John Lewis and his interplay with Milt Jackson's vibraphone. Clearly in this company, Mulligan adopted the persona of the free-blowing improviser of the sextet and his recent quartet, judging by the local paper's review:

> The final part of the program found Gerry Mulligan adding his big sound to the MJQ in three numbers, which showed the versatility and top technique of the West Coast Flash. Mr. Mulligan gave bassist Percy Heath and drummer Connie Kay a chance to move out a bit, and they seemed to enjoy the novel experience. Jimmy Giuffre joined the group for two exciting numbers in which he and Mulligan exchanged some fancy counterpoint. This was the high point of the evening.[81]

In late September, the Mulligan sextet returned to the studios for EmArcy to complete work on two albums that would also draw on the unreleased material recorded in late 1955 and January 1956. For this session and the subsequent fall live dates, Mulligan recruited trumpeter Don Ferrara to replace Eardley, who by this time had gone to Florida to try to quit his drug addiction.[82] Ferrara had big band experience with Georgie Auld and Woody Herman, he had played in a service band with Red Mitchell, and as well as working quite frequently with Lee Konitz, in 1956 he was studying with Lennie Tristano. Yet he was also something of a Roy Eldridge disciple and he brought to the sextet just the right mixture of improvisational daring and intellectual appreciation of the group's aims.

However, before Ferrara joined, Mulligan was back in the newspapers for another reason. As Dorothy Kilgallen reported: "The Gerry Mulligans are (1) expecting a tiny tootler. And (2) searching madly for a nice big soundproof apartment where Gerry and his pals can jam and no neighbors will complain if the baby joins in on vocals."[83] They might not have found exactly the apartment described here, but by the time their son Reed Brown Mulligan was born on February 10, 1957, Gerry and Arlyne Mulligan had moved to a home on 58th Street in Manhattan, just a block below Central Park and close to Columbus Circle. In the months

81 Bass, Milton E.: "Music Barn Ends Season," *Berkshire Eagle*, September 4, 1956, p. 8.

82 According to Bill Crow, September 4, 2002.

83 *Middletown Journal* (OH), September 1, 1956.

following Ms. Kilgallen's announcement, before Reed's arrival, the sextet made its final recordings and briefly went out on the road.

From the September 26 EmArcy sextet session, a couple of tracks stand out. Notably, "Igloo" is another example of a lightly arranged number that lends itself to relaxed jamming. Brookmeyer turns in a highly fluent solo, which prefigures his sound in the quartet in the months to come. Ferrara also reveals himself as a strong soloist, well suited to this type of mainstream ensemble. The dramatic high-speed dash of "Lollypop" (composed by the band's former drummer Chico Hamilton and West Coast pianist Gerry Wiggins) hardly sounds like a studio recording, it is so vibrant, and it gives a sense of why this band was appreciated so much for its live concerts. The sessions with Ferrara also included a return to one of Mulligan's earliest compositions—a new version of "Elevation" from the Elliot Lawrence days, although at times this sounds over-arranged compared to the lightness of touch in "Igloo" and "Lollypop."

In the weeks after that recording, the sextet fulfilled its contractual obligations, but in between these, Mulligan was already beginning to focus on the quartet with himself, Brookmeyer, Crow, and Bailey. This smaller group would soon become his main working ensemble until August 1957. It broadcast as one of a number of live relays on *Bandstand USA*, a syndicated radio program, on Saturday, October 13 (along with groups led by Art Tatum, Max Roach, Chris Connor, and Phineas Newborn Jr.).[84]

November saw the full sextet return to one of the large package shows that had characterized the closing months of the last two years, its Chicago appearance (spread over two nights on November 21 and 22) being billed as "The Big Jazz for Moderns Show":

> The all star line-up will be Count Basie and his Orchestra with Joe Williams, Erroll Garner with his concert trio, Gerry Mulligan and his Sextet featuring Bob Brookmeyer, the Australian Jazz Quintet, Chico Hamilton and His Quintet and the Kai Winding Septet with Carl Fontana.[85]

This Chicago event seems to have been the sextet's last ever appearance, because four days later the Mulligan quartet was headlining at Massey Hall in Toronto. "We ended up working with the quartet that was left,"

84 *Robesonian* (Lumberton, NC), October 12, 1956.

85 *Chicago Austin News*, November 14, 1956; and *Chicago Austin News*, November 22, 1956.

recalled Bill Crow, "which was a very good quartet: Dave Bailey, Bob Brookmeyer and myself, with Gerry."

Reflecting on the demise of the larger group, Brookmeyer had a characteristically individual view of the transition back to a four-piece band. He said:

> I never liked the sextet. It was okay, and it was nice to play together. I didn't like Jon Eardley, and never did. I loved Zoot of course, and then we had Don Ferrara later on. He was a great trumpet player. The results were interesting sometimes, but it was not something that I really enjoyed. When it broke up, I was not at all sad, and when we started the quartet, I said, "Thank God!" The thing we'd needed in the sextet was a more creative rhythm section, and to get rid of Jon Eardley! If Zoot had really wanted to participate [it would have been different]. . . . We needed to find someone who was willing to give themselves to the ensemble, and then Gerry and I and other people could write, so we could really have things happen with six people. You didn't have to have six people playing all the time. One piece could be a solo. And next you could really go "orchestral" with all six, but we never really thought about that. When we were in Europe on the road for those two and a half months in early 1956, the problem was keeping people sober enough to play the concert! So there were opportunities missed there. Also, I wasn't a great pianist, and Gerry was a lousy piano player, so that wasn't an immediate help either. If I'd known then what I know now, we could have really expanded the scope of the sextet, and done much more with it. Some of the improvising was pretty good. This was ensemble playing by Gerry for one, who can play with other people. Me for another, I can play with people. He proved it in many combinations, and I proved it with Stan Getz, and later with Clark Terry. Playing *with* someone is a talent. You learn and you build from that. The good things that happened in the sextet were done by people who were used to "giving to get," whereas the various bebop bands of the time, Blakey and so on, were about the individual soloist. Mostly those bands were not about playing together. Ornette was about playing together, but John Coltrane wasn't. A bit later, when he and Elvin got going, you might as well have left McCoy and Jimmy Garrison at home because you couldn't hear them. That was playing together with two people, but not playing together with four people, like Gerry's band. His group was about the art of listening and giving of yourself for a greater good. You take the little ego part of yourself that says, "look at me!" and you submerge that into a

mush with three other people, or in the case of the sextet—five others. The sextet had a good start but, as I said, we didn't know quite what to do with it. I don't think Gerry had a lot of help from me, or Zoot and Eardley. So Gerry was at the rudder of a wandering vessel, and we didn't have the foresight to see its full potential.[86]

Despite Brookmeyer's criticism of the rhythm section, it seems that once Bailey and Crow became part of a four-piece lineup, after the comparative freedom of the sextet, it compelled them to think harder about what they were doing. This had begun in the summer of 1956, following Mulligan's return to playing after he had been ordered to rest. Looking back at that period, Bill Crow said:

> Early in the life of the quartet, when we were just bare bones, Gerry said something about, "You're playing my notes!" And I said, "What makes them your notes?" And then he explained that he expected me to hang around the roots and thirds and fifths of the chord, so that he could play patterns that were based on higher partials of the chord. And also the "rich" notes, the major seventh, the minor seventh and ninth. He liked to make lines with those. And I realized when he played a third and I played a root, because he was an octave above me, that made a tenth, which if you play it on the piano shows that it implies the fifth and maybe the seventh, even though nobody's playing them, because the notes just resonate that way. So with that in mind, I put a little more thought into what I was choosing as a bass line, and I was able to follow the direction of his harmony. Sometimes we would end up staying a tenth away from each other, and it would really sound rich, and I'd think "Oh! We'll keep that!" He never really said any more to me about that, and he kept hiring me, so I assumed I was doing the right thing![87]

Dave Bailey, after his initial months in the sextet alongside Peck Morrison, and then the continuation of the group with Bill Crow, felt that soon after they adopted the quartet format, he and the bassist understood their roles very well:

86 Interview with Bob Brookmeyer, September 2, 2002.

87 Interview with Bill Crow, September 4, 2002.

> Bill Crow and I, we were like a hand in a glove. We felt rhythm the same way, and had a ball. Gerry was very demanding on bass players, and I can understand in retrospect why he was, because of the lack of piano. The bass player needed to play notes that gave a sense of where the melody and the chords were going. I learned that, so my ear now is very attuned to bass players and chords, and the extension of chords. In the few rehearsals that we had, Gerry explained why he wanted *this* note, and that kind of thing, and it gave us—me particularly—an insight into tonics and fifths and so on. Gerry didn't want to play the notes the bass player was playing. That was the whole thing. So he'd say, "Take a turnaround here," and so forth. And Bill Crow understood that.[88]

It did not take long before the quartet produced what was to be its definitive set of recordings. Five days after the Massey Hall appearance, the band began a week's residency at George Wein's Storyville Club in Boston, and the best of its performances there were collected for a Pacific Jazz LP.[89]

As ever, Mulligan raided his own back catalogue for material on these sessions, and in this case "Bweebida Bobbida" made a worthy candidate, the quartet version being beautifully pared down from the earlier big band and tentette scores (see Chapter 1, Example 1.5), and now using the bass as an essential ensemble voice (Example 3.14). Brookmeyer's backing to Mulligan's solo and the baritone behind his energetic trombone choruses demonstrate exactly Bob's point about the soloists playing *for* one another (Example 3.15).

Otherwise the repertoire is largely material that Mulligan's various bands had not recorded before. The standards include "Birth of the Blues," "Baubles, Bangles and Beads," and "That Old Feeling." Of these, the last-named is the standout performance, Mulligan's melodic lead being sensitively backed by Brookmeyer, who then takes an inventive solo that moves far from the melody but gives Mulligan the opportunity to hint at the tune in his accompanying figures. The other two standards recorded at Storyville would appear regularly on the group's later concerts including a disc recorded in Europe in early 1957.

Original pieces by the band members were equally important in this quartet's work. Mulligan's "Storyville Story" is just a twelve-measure blues

88 Interview with Dave Bailey, September 5, 2002.

89 *Gerry Mulligan Quartet: Recorded at Boston in Storyville*, Pacific Jazz 1228.

EXAMPLE 3.14 "Bweebida Bobbida" by Gerry Mulligan. Copyright © 1951 Mulligan Publishing Co. Inc. Copyright renewed. All rights administered by Universal Music Corp. All rights reserved. Used by permission. Reprinted by permission of Hal Leonard Europe Ltd. Head of the 1956 quartet version (transcription).

EXAMPLE 3.15 Mulligan's interplay with Brookmeyer's solo on the 1956 recording of "Bweebida Bobbida" (transcription).

with some rather lumpy piano playing from the composer, but it also became a regular part of the repertoire. By contrast his Spooneristically titled "Bike Up the Strand," a contrafact of Gershwin's "Strike Up the Band," is pianoless and buoyant. Most significantly, Brookmeyer's beautifully written (and played) "Open Country" would become a regular item in this quartet's repertoire, even after it re-formed in the 1960s. The "shout" chorus that starts at 4:42 into the track (see Example 3.16) is a fine example of Brookmeyer's riff-making (very similar to the two-horn lines he would later produce for the quintet with Clark Terry), and the two horns and bass state the harmonies so clearly that it is obvious that Brookmeyer completely understood how to produce effective material for the "pianoless" quartet.

Brookmeyer's composing and arranging would come further to the fore in the Concert Jazz Band from 1960 onward, but in 1956 this aspect

EXAMPLE 3.16 "Open Country" shout chorus (transcription).

of his talent clearly marked him out as a very different musical partner for Mulligan from Baker. Brookmeyer's "Rustic Hop" from Storyville, with echoes of the rural dances that showed up in the works of Aaron Copland and Virgil Thomson, did not feature very often in future concerts, but it was ideal material for the quartet, with a tightly written head, yet a loose enough feeling to hint at some of the spontaneity of the sextet at its best.

Although the Storyville recordings were to become something of a template for this edition of the quartet, its first personnel change took place just a few weeks later, at the start of 1957. After a year of traveling and playing with Mulligan, Bill Crow decided to leave the band, to spend more time in New York. He joined Don Elliott's group at Cy Coleman's club close to Central Park. Apart from a brief spell in Detroit with Lou Stein, he then stayed on in Manhattan for much of 1957, once again playing in Marian McPartland's trio, at a club called the Composer (which was situated on West 58th Street, immediately opposite Gerry and Arlyne Mulligan's apartment).[90] His place in the quartet was taken by Joe Benjamin, who was best known at the time for having worked regularly during the preceding couple of years with Sarah Vaughan.

In January 1957, aside from club work, the quartet played for refugees from the Hungarian uprising, which had occurred during October and November the previous year. Those who had fled to the United States were quartered at Camp Kilmer, an army base in New Jersey. The press reported:

> Several weeks before in their war-torn homeland, some of them had listened to the Voice of America and heard one of the greatest in jazz, Gerry Mulligan. Now they were to see him in person.[91]

The following month, the quartet travelled to State College, Pennsylvania, for a major jazz event, described as follows:

> The largest assemblage of jazz musicians yet brought to university music fans, featuring such names as Chris Connor, and the Gerry Mulligan Quartet will arrive on campus February 24. The Jazz Revue, sponsored by the Penn State Jazz Club, will draw prominent modern jazz groups from the East Coast area. The Kai Winding Septet, Chris Connor, the Les Jazz Modes and the Gerry Mulligan Quartet will perform for the revue. . . . Mulligan's band is the first piano-less group since Dixieland was at its peak during the 1920s. The present quartette features Bob Brookmeyer on valve trombone, bass, drum [*sic*] and baritone saxophone.[92]

90 Crow, Bill: *From Birdland to Broadway* (New York, Oxford, 1992) pp. 151–152.

91 *Star News*, February 15, 1957.

92 "Largest Jazz Review Scheduled for Feb. 24," *State College Daily Collegian*, February 14, 1957.

All this was preparation for a European tour that was to run from late April to the end of May, starting at the Royal Festival Hall in London.[93] In the early months of the year, members of the quartet had joined Mulligan in recordings with Billy Taylor and Manny Albam. Shortly before the band left for Europe, not only did it broadcast from the Red Hill Inn, Pennsauken, New Jersey, on the syndicated *Bandstand USA* show, but on April 19 it was subsumed into a Columbia record date for which Mulligan fronted a big band. This was to be part of an eventual LP called *Gerry Mulligan the Arranger*,[94] which also featured tracks by Elliot Lawrence and Gene Krupa. The tracks included—as was often the case—reworkings of earlier compositions, in this case "Mullennium" and "Motel."

From concert programs that have survived from the European tour, it seems that the quartet played a mixture of the early 1950s repertoire, such as "Walking' Shoes," "My Funny Valentine," and "Bernie's Tune," alongside the more recent tracks from the soon-to-be-released Storyville sessions, such as "Open Country" and "Birth of the Blues." Fortunately the majority of the Stockholm concert from the tour was recorded, so we have the opportunity to hear how the band had matured since December the previous year.[95] "Open Country" has a new introduction, and is played with a swaggering confidence and familiarity by both horns, backed judiciously by Benjamin and Bailey. Meanwhile "Birth of the Blues" is taken at a slightly faster tempo than at Storyville, which works much better, and again the band sounds utterly confident and secure in the material. On that piece Brookmeyer's solo, which opens with a figure that corkscrews upward from the head, is both highly melodic and inventive. Mulligan then takes up the challenge, playing with time, but also showing his melodic talents. Benjamin solos, with a powerful lower register sound, but employing none of the inventiveness and facility of Mitchell or the ability across the range of the instrument displayed by Crow. Nonetheless, overall we get the sense of a band, just like the sextet, that had honed its sound on the road, and had a clear group identity. The

93 The tour dates were: April 27, Royal Festival Hall, London; 28, Dudley; 29, St. Andrew's Hall, Glasgow; 30, Usher Hall, Edinburgh; May 1, City Hall, Hull; 3, Philharmonic Hall, Liverpool; 4, Rialto Theatre, York; 5, Davis Theatre, Croydon; 6, Guildhall, Southampton; 7, De Montfort Hall, Leicester; 8, The Dome, Brighton; 9, City Hall, Newcastle-upon-Tyne; 10, City Hall, Sheffield; 11, Free Trade Hall, Manchester (2 houses); 12, Stoll Theatre, London; 16, Gothenburg, Sweden; 17, Stockholm; 18, Gothenburg; 20, L'Olympia, Paris.

94 Columbia PC 34803.

95 *Gerry Mulligan*, Editions Atlas/Charly WIS CD 633 (reissued 1995).

opening of "Baubles, Bangles and Beads," for example, is almost abstract, but gives way to a spellbinding solo from Mulligan.

Its greatest achievement is that when Mulligan and Brookmeyer returned to the Baker era repertoire, the ghost of Chet was entirely absent. "Lullaby of the Leaves" is a good example, and now sounds completely consistent with what Mulligan refers to in his announcements as "our newer arrangements." Even the ones from what he calls "the middle" period, such as "Yardbird Suite," are subsumed by this band's collective personality. So it was the more tragic that after its return from Europe, this group would only last for another two and a half months.

During that time it appeared at the Newport Jazz Festival,[96] gaining some extremely positive reviews. According to critic Ted Hunter, Mulligan's "baritone sax wandered at will among the chord patterns, smooth and complex. If applause meters are any indication of success, the quartet's third number 'My Funny Valentine' would walk off with tonight's popularity poll."[97] Soon after its Rhode Island success, the band traveled to Stratford, Ontario, for a broadcast with Lee Konitz, and then played regularly in New York in a series of summer concerts at the Wollman Memorial Theatre in Central Park, before heading to the West Coast for a JATP concert at the Hollywood Bowl.

It seems to have been during July, while the band was playing for several successive nights in Manhattan, that matters came to a head. Brookmeyer described it to the author as a "personal matter" between him and Mulligan. In fact it was more a personal matter between him and Arlyne, as during that month in New York, he started an affair with her. She recalled:

> Gerry was already cheating on me when Bob and I started our romance. "You're having an affair with him?" He finally noticed! What did he think we were doing?
>
> Gerry insisted I invite Bob round for dinner, which is when he said, "How could you have an affair with my wife?"
>
> Bob replied, "To have a wife you have to be a husband. I've been on the road with you and you're no husband." Gerry was pretty shocked of course.

96 "Utter Chaos" and "My Funny Valentine" from this concert were issued on *The Teddy Wilson Trio and the Gerry Mulligan Quartet with Bob Brookmeyer at Newport*, Verve MGV 8235.

97 Hunter, Ted: "Attendance Records Broken at Newport Jazz Festival," *Lowell Sun*, July 7, 1957, p. 1.

> Unfortunately Bob had a drinking problem, which didn't affect his playing, but it did affect the rest of his life, which is why we [eventually] broke up.[98]

When Arlyne and Mulligan separated, Dave Bailey took over her role as the band's manager. She stayed in New York, bringing up Reed, whom Mulligan visited from time to time, when he was not on the road.

The last concerts by the 1957 edition of the Mulligan quartet, with Brookmeyer, Benjamin, and Bailey, took place on August 2 and 3 in California. The first of these, at the Hollywood Bowl, on August 2 involved a set lasting just under half an hour. It included the "new" versions of "Baubles, Bangles and Beads" and "Bweebida Bobbida," as well as a nod backward to the Salle Pleyel concerts of 1954 with "Come Out, Come Out Wherever You Are" and "Laura." Only the Mulligan theme tune, "Utter Chaos," reminded local listeners of the band's beginnings, in the lineup with Chet Baker, a few miles away at the Haig. Just over three years on from its first recording of "Laura," it is the best representation of how far this quartet had developed. There is an easy confidence about it, and however difficult the interpersonal relationship had become between Brookmeyer and Mulligan (an echo of how things had been in Paris) there is no hint of it in their playing. Brookmeyer's solo shows plenty of the variety in his playing from his dramatic pick-up from Mulligan, to repeated higher register phrases, and rapidly executed runs, all of which are backed by Mulligan.

The next night, the band was at the Berkeley Community Theatre, opposite the groups of Stan Getz and Shelly Manne, but Mulligan was already experimenting with various frontline partners to take Brookmeyer's place, and at a session in the small hours of the morning before the Hollywood Bowl concert, he, Benjamin, and Bailey recorded a few tracks with Paul Desmond, whom Mulligan knew well from all the tours alongside Dave Brubeck. These are discussed in the next chapter, alongside their East Coast studio reunion later in the month.

98 "Arlyne Brown Mulligan interview," as above.

CHAPTER 4

THE QUARTET WITH ART FARMER

MULLIGAN WAS BACK in New York two days after the Berkeley event, and billed to appear in another of the Wollman Memorial Theatre concerts in Central Park on August 5, but it is not clear with whom he was playing, in a program that also featured the Hi-Los, Chris Connor, Buddy Rich, and Maynard Ferguson. What is clear is that exactly one week later he was in the studio with a very different quartet from his own, making the album *Mulligan Meets Monk*, with Thelonious Monk's regular trio—its other members being bassist Wilbur Ware and drummer Shadow Wilson. The producer of the session for Riverside Records, Orrin Keepnews, recalled:

> The pairing of Monk and Mulligan came about because one day Monk dropped in at our office. He happened to mention "Gerry dropped me off at the corner." So I discovered there was a considerable personal

The Gerry Mulligan 1950s Quartets. Alyn Shipton, Oxford University Press. © Alyn Shipton 2023.
DOI: 10.1093/oso/9780197579756.003.0004

friendship between Mulligan and Monk. They hung out together a lot, they talked about music with each other, and Monk was not the kind of man who would say, "Guess what?"—he was just giving a factual report. So I was able to say to him, "How about you recording with Mulligan?"[1]

Only a few weeks before, Monk had made the famous studio recording of "Trinkle Tinkle" with John Coltrane, again backed by Ware and Wilson, and this was the period when he and Trane worked together quite frequently at the Five Spot, culminating in their Carnegie Hall concert in November 1957. But whereas Monk's partnership with Coltrane had evolved through live performances and several studio dates, he and Mulligan had barely played together before, apart from a brief jam in Paris in 1954 and the informal concert with Miles Davis at Newport in 1955.

Mulligan—always the perfectionist—regretted that they had not had more opportunities to work alongside one another before they ended up in the studio. He said:

> Unfortunately I never had that much chance to play with Monk. At that particular period we were neighbors. We only lived about a block apart on the West Side of New York, and we became great pals, and spent a lot of time together. In fact we were together just about every day. We spent a lot of time talking and working on music and writing things, and didn't play at all. He was supposed to do a record date, and Monk said he wanted me to make the record with him. And so I did, and I was delighted to do it. But it was also the learning process being recorded, at a point when I would very much liked to have had more time playing and adapting myself to the way Monk thought. He had a very unusual approach to chord progressions and clusters. One of the things he talked about was the use of the keyboard and different tensions on different notes, changing the rhythmic stress and the impact of the attack. That was Monk's thing—the attack. Hitting one note harder than another note so that they would ring together. He was absolutely in love with orchestrated textures on the keyboard, and we never had a chance to explore any of that. I was struggling to hear his chord progressions, which were very angular, and different to

1 Interview with Orrin Keepnews, February 1999.

what I was used to. If I'd played enough with Monk, I'd have learned a lot more of what to leave out, to make it into a unity.[2]

When the *Mulligan Meets Monk* album came out, only a few weeks after it was recorded, Keepnews hailed it in his liner notes as "one of those once in a lifetime meetings of giants."[3] He also put into print a sentence that has become part of jazz folklore: "Bop begins with Monk and cool jazz begins with Mulligan." We have seen how relatively slowly the "cool" label was applied to Mulligan, but by 1957 (the year the Davis nonet sides were first reissued under the title *The Birth of the Cool*) this simple comparison resonated with the jazz public and journalists alike, although one of the first reviews somewhat mixed up the ideas:

> Thelonious Monk, one of the leading exponents of the "cool school" of modern jazz, is back on the musical track with a new LP album for Riverside entitled *Gerry Mulligan and Thelonious Monk*, in which the goateed virtuoso teams with the famed baritone saxist for a session of fine improvisation.[4]

In his interview with the author, Keepnews averred that they worked particularly well together owing to the fact that, although they were both modernists, each was also equally deeply rooted in the jazz tradition. And while this is true, the highlight of the session, "I Mean You," is a fully integrated quartet performance of a 1948 Monk original that plays to their respective strengths.[5] On the fourth take, which was the one originally issued on LP, Mulligan deftly negotiates the theme in unison with the piano in the opening A section of the head, during which Wilson's punctuations underline the slightly off-balance melody line. In the B section, Mulligan's flared long notes give Monk an opportunity to play answering phrases and he does so with aplomb, from a widely spaced set of single notes to one of his typical downward cascades. From there, right through to the closing repeat of the head, and benefiting from the "learning process" of the previous takes, the performance sounds like a well-rehearsed group, and there is no sense that this is a one-off studio meeting.

2 Gerry Mulligan interviewed by Charles Fox, Glasgow Jazz Festival, July 1988.

3 Keepnews, Orrin: notes to *Mulligan Meets Monk*, RLP 12-247 (1957).

4 *Baltimore Afro-American*, August 31, 1957.

5 After a gap of some years, Monk had returned to this piece just a few weeks earlier for his May 14 Atlantic session with Art Blakey.

This is not quite the case when, instead of his own music, we hear Monk tackling a standard, "Sweet and Lovely," to which his introduction is anything but. However, his playing on Mulligan's comparatively mainstream composition "Decidedly" (based on Charlie Shavers's "Undecided") includes some almost conventional swing comping, while Mulligan's powerful solo impels the performance forward, including a couple of sections where the baritone duets with Wilson, and also a chorus or so of "strolling," when Monk drops out to leave only bass and drums providing the backing (exactly as had been described by Art Farmer in the article cited in the previous chapter).

The saxophone lays down a harmonic carpet under the first part of the piano solo, after which Monk's playing becomes increasingly abstract, before Ware walks his way through a chorus with hi-hat accompaniment. What this track and "I Mean You" show is that each of the principals could come a fair distance to meet and collaborate with the other, without sacrificing their respective original contributions to jazz. The remaining tracks are Monk compositions, all regularly recorded by him in various combinations, and certainly successful enough to justify Keepnews's decision to abort a projected larger band session scheduled for the following day, in order to use the studio time to complete the quartet album.[6] The majority of critics seem to have agreed with Keepnews's assessment that this was a productive and interesting summit meeting, only Whitney Balliett demurring, and proposing that the two men's rhythmic approaches were too "hopelessly different" for the album to succeed.[7]

The 27th of the same month saw Mulligan and his regular colleagues, Joe Benjamin and Dave Bailey, making their second recording session with alto saxophonist Paul Desmond (who was still a member of the Brubeck quartet at the time) to complete the album that they had begun in Hollywood for Verve. The idea had been mooted some time earlier, indeed, according to Nat Hentoff, as early as the fall of 1954 when Mulligan sat in on "Tea for Two" with Brubeck at Carnegie Hall during the "Modern Jazz Concert" tour with the Ellington band.[8] The two saxophonists discussed the idea again at Newport in early July 1957, at

6 "Rhythm-a-ning" from this session unusually has a sixteen-measure channel, as opposed to Monk's original version of the piece, which is a contrafact of "Christopher Columbus."

7 Balliett, Whitney: "Monk," in *Collected Works: A Journal of Jazz 1954–2000* (London, Granta, 2000) p. 49.

8 Hentoff, Nat: *The Gerry Mulligan–Paul Desmond Quartet*, Verve MGV 8246 (1957) [liner note].

which point Norman Granz offered to sort out any contractual difficulties with their respective labels and produce the LP himself. They then had to wait until both players were in the same place at the same time, which happened at the very start of August.

Across the two sessions, each principal contributed three compositions (including Desmond's original "Battle Hymn of the Republican") and they also included one standard, "Body and Soul." The engineers did not manage quite such a close acoustic match between locations as the Fantasy team had achieved in the early days of Mulligan's first quartet. The Hollywood sides, such as Desmond's "Blues in Time," were made with quite a resonant acoustic, and in this reflective studio atmosphere the alto, in particular, sings out, almost like a trumpet. The New York sides are closer-miked and have a more intimate feel. Nonetheless, throughout the album, here are two musicians who know each other's playing well, and their chemistry is apparent. Sadly, Desmond's commitments to Brubeck prevented him and Mulligan from working live as a quartet, but they were to convene again in the studio during 1962 (with a number of different bassists and drummers, plus a guest appearance from guitarist Jim Hall) to make the *Two of a Mind* album for RCA Victor. They also went on to appear informally at various festivals where both Mulligan and Brubeck were on the bill.

According to Desmond, there was little or no preparation for the 1957 dates. "About all we came in with," he reported, "was a list of typewritten tunes. There were some obvious unison things written, one-chorus lines on two short tunes Gerry wrote, but everything else, including the counterpoint, was off the cuff."[9] Mulligan's own observation on the sessions was that Desmond "always wanted to do the pianoless quartet thing, with the alto playing lead instead of trumpet."[10] This is exactly what Desmond achieves on the opening chorus of "Line for Lyons," although he offers no countermelody on the following solo from Mulligan, as Baker or Eardley might have done. His own solo, however, has some subtle underpinning from Mulligan, who clearly thrives on Desmond's lyrical inventiveness, and when the two horns combine for some collective interplay in the chorus before the final head we hear them sparking ideas off one another (Example 4.1). By contrast, Desmond's composition, the ballad "Wintersong" is—to a large extent—an alto saxophone feature. Mulligan makes a relatively brief appearance, almost four minutes

9 Ibid.

10 Jack, Gordon: *Fifties Jazz Talk* (Lanham MD, Scarecrow Press, 2004) p. 151.

EXAMPLE 4.1 The penultimate chorus of "Line for Lyons," from the *Gerry Mulligan–Paul Desmond Quartet* (transcription).

in to the seven-minute track, but for the most part it is a long lyrical Desmond solo, although at one point, somewhat abandoning the lyricism, he builds almost half a chorus out of short motifs that are then repeated, transposed, and repeated again.

The track that points most to what this quartet might have achieved had it been a regular working band is Mulligan's "Stand Still," a contrafact of Richard Rodgers's "My Heart Stood Still." There's a strong unison head, with one of Mulligan's characteristic catchy themes, before the baritone ushers in an alto solo, adds harmonies in the channel, and then builds a solo out of Desmond's final phrase. The rhythm section drops its volume back so far on the ensemble chorus after the solos that there is a momentary illusion of the horns playing unaccompanied (something this group was ideally capable of doing, and no doubt would have done, had it been together more) and after Bailey's subtle punctuations as the head returns, there's a witty false ending.

The experience of working with Desmond, backed by Benjamin and Bailey, led to a solution for Mulligan's late autumn tour, which had been booked by Norman Granz. Billed as "Jazz for Moderns," it was planned to start in mid-November in Chicago, and then wend its way to San Francisco, where a slightly different combination of musicians would appear as part of the "Jazz à la carte" concert series. Promoters had already been promised the Mulligan Quartet, so having split with Brookmeyer, Mulligan co-opted Lee Konitz to take on a very similar role to that which Desmond had proved would work well. The publicity for the tour was helped by the fact that it coincided with the release on Pacific Jazz of the first 12-inch LP of the 1953 recordings of Konitz with the original Mulligan Quartet including Chet Baker.

It seems that the quartet was in abeyance from the end of August 1957 until those November tour dates, but in the interim Mulligan, who now seemed to have found favor with Norman Granz (despite the producer's negative comments about the 1954 tour that involved the Ellington band), was asked to fly out to California to record for Verve with Stan Getz. The two saxophonists had recorded together in early August (the day before the Desmond quartet session) with the *Jazz Giants of 1958*,[11] namely the Oscar Peterson trio, trumpeter Harry Sweets Edison, and drummer Louie Bellson. But now this was to be their own session, which Granz initially titled *Gerry Mulligan Meets Stan Getz*.

According to his biographer, Dave Gelly, Getz made more recordings in October 1957 than in any other month of his life.[12] Yet despite that conveyor belt of sessions, this one does have some fine moments, although three tracks that involved Mulligan and Getz swapping horns are the least successful of the eight numbers they recorded. Nothing had been

11 Verve MGV 8248.

12 Gelly, Dave: *Stan Getz, Nobody Else but Me* (San Francisco, Backbeat Books, 2002) p. 79.

prepared ahead of time and in contrast to the session with Desmond, Mulligan was unhappy about this lack of planning, saying:

> The jam session idea is alright, but it has never been my bag, and it wasn't my idea to switch horns on some numbers. Stan or Norman suggested it. I liked Zoot's and Brew Moore's mouthpieces, but I never liked Stan's and I didn't like the sound I got on it.[13]

Of the tracks on which they played their own instruments, there's a breakneck version of "This Can't Be Love," with a coruscating solo from Getz after he has asserted his personality on the head, but Mulligan rises to the challenge with an equally fluent improvisation, at the same time asking some more subtle harmonic questions. The rhythm section is expertly propelled by bassist Ray Brown and drummer Stan Levey, but Lou Levy's piano playing is very understated, and while being very neat and orderly, he fails entirely to catch the energy of the saxophonists. The best moment here is a chase chorus for the two reed players after Levy's insipid piano solo.

An unnaturally fast version of "That Old Feeling" has some similarly aggressive soloing from the front line, but the highlight of the original six-track album is Mulligan's composition "A Ballad," ravishingly introduced by Getz, who is joined after a half chorus by Mulligan's subtle accompanying harmonies. A little later, Mulligan's solo almost goes into double time, neatly mirrored by Brown and Levey, but settles into an equally beautiful exploration of the piece. Both players see the number out with some collective interplay, before Getz restates the theme at the end, sensitively underpinned by Mulligan's deft harmonic backing. If ever there were a lesson that "less is more," this is it.

Only forty-eight hours after this session in Los Angeles, Mulligan was back in the studio in New York, to record trumpeter Phil Sunkel's *Jazz Concerto Grosso*,[14] for which the concertino parts were played by Sunkel, Mulligan, and Bob Brookmeyer. This might have been awkward on the personal front, but the vision for the piece was consistent with Mulligan's own "band-within-a band" concept that dated back to "Disc Jockey Jump." Sunkel said: "My idea of a jazz band is something between a small combo and a big band, incorporating the good features of both. Here we have the flexibility of a small group which allows the soloist a

13 Jack: *Fifties Jazz Talk*, p. 150.

14 ABC-Paramount LP, ABC-225.

maximum of freedom, plus the color and drama produced by the different ensemble sounds."[15]

Following that recording date, which also involved some septet sides, Mulligan returned to writing, prior to the November tour. This began in Chicago on November 12, but on that initial concert several members of the troupe were unexpectedly laid low by the national epidemic of Asian flu. Reviewer Ken Broun reported:

> The flu bug took its toll of performers at Thursday's *Jazz For Moderns*, but some fine bits of solid jazz entertainment managed to peek through. George Shearing could not make the performance because of our Asiatic friend and Chico Hamilton had to leave the stage in the middle of his set for the same reason. Gerry Mulligan's drummer played for the Hamilton Quintet, the Miles Davis group and his own quartet. Davis and his swinging trumpet showed up halfway through his group's set.
>
> Confused? So were most of the large audience that expected to listen to an evening of organized jazz. But the crowd managed to bear through the situation. Perhaps the most interesting event of the evening was Mulligan playing piano for the Shearing sextet [*sic*]. Mulligan, an accomplished pianist along with his incomparable sax styling, did a commendable job, considering that he has a very different idea from Shearing about how jazz should sound.
>
> Mulligan's own group was by far the most outstanding of the evening. Comparatively unhampered by injuries to the first team, the quartet blended in some very swinging counterpoint. Cannonball Adderley, a fine alto sax man, led the Davis group until the boss arrived. The quintet had its moments but lacked its noted drive due to the situation.[16]

Fortunately, when the players reconvened in Cleveland four days later, everyone had recovered enough to play, and the Mulligan Quartet with Lee Konitz held its own alongside some other formidable talents.[17] One reviewer (previewing a later date on the tour) summed up the band thus:

> The bass is the main thread around which the two saxophones, Mulligan on baritone and Lee Konitz on alto, weave their counterpoint

15 Sunkel, Phil: *Jazz Concerto Grosso* [liner note to the 2006 reissue: Fresh Sound 2223].

16 Broun, Ken: "Asian Flu Hits Jazz Leaders," *Chicago Daily Illini*, November 15, 1957.

17 Tour dates: November 12, Chicago; 16, Cleveland; 17, Detroit; 19, Rochester, NY; 21, Syracuse; 22, Carnegie Hall, New York; and Mulligan's group then joined "Jazz à la Carte" in San Francisco on November 30.

> type of jazz. The other two members of the quartet are Joe Benjamin, bass and Bill [*sic*] Bailey, drums. Mulligan himself does most of the arranging for the group, having been considered one of the top arrangers in jazz today.[18]

It does not appear that any of the concerts with this group with Konitz were recorded, but we do get a chance to hear his playing of the time in Mulligan's next recording project after the band returned to New York. However, despite being the "main thread" of this quartet, within days of that return, Joe Benjamin left the lineup. So to replace him, Mulligan recruited Henry Grimes, a virtually unknown bassist from Philadelphia. He had heard Grimes working with Anita O'Day at the Red Hill Inn in Pennsauken, New Jersey, and Dave Bailey suggested that they should try out the twenty-two-year-old youngster. In one of his characteristic figures of speech, Grimes recalled for the author the way he was invited to join the group, by playing informally with Mulligan and Bailey, and thereby realizing that he had to supply all the underlying harmonies.

> That was a very valuable exercise. I was sort of auditioned by Gerry. His way of auditioning was like you are laying on a rug that was made by the man before you. But when the new man who is you comes up to that rug, then you all come into something a bit different.[19]

Grimes was to settle in to the group in due course, but for his first recordings in New York, on December 4 and 5, as a member of Mulligan's octet, expanded from the quartet to explore a set of the baritonist's compositions, Gerry took the precaution of adding guitarist Freddie Green to the rhythm section. He said that Green "seemed to center the tonality. It made a range for the bass to play in so that the intonation was much more clear-cut. Intonation seems to be a problem for the bass sometimes, playing without a piano."[20] This is a rather courteous and graceful way of saying that when he first joined the band, Grimes was not always dependable in terms of his tuning. Dave Bailey, however, suggested that Green's presence on this record was also due to the fact that "saxes are noted for making the tempos drag a little, and he wanted a really solid sound."[21]

18 *Oakland Tribune*, November 22, 1957.

19 Interview with Henry Grimes, May 2009.

20 Hentoff, Nat: *The Gerry Mulligan Songbook*, World Pacific 1237 (1958) [liner note].

21 Jack: *Fifties Jazz Talk*, p. 18.

The Gerry Mulligan Songbook adds another three saxophonists to the quartet front line of Mulligan and Konitz. Allen Eager and Zoot Sims double on alto and tenor, while Al Cohn doubles on tenor and baritone. The repertoire is—as the title suggests—all written by Mulligan, going back as far as the Krupa days with "Disc Jockey Jump," to the Davis nonet with "Venus De Milo," and to the 1949 New York Prestige sides with "Four and One Moore." All but one of the pieces were arranged for this session by Mulligan's onetime Stan Kenton colleague, Bill Holman, but Mulligan did flex his own writing and arranging muscles with a new piece called "Crazy Day."

In one of his best charts, Holman takes "Turnstile" (also known as "Gold Rush") from the quartet repertoire and neatly expands it for the larger lineup. Here his ensemble writing is denser than Mulligan's tended to be, and the more intriguing for that, but it is the soloing, and the exchanges of eight- and four-measure turns between the members of the "sax section" as the band was billed on the record sleeve, that capture the attention most. The rhythm team with Green, Grimes, and Bailey has all the urgency and swing of a Basie small group, and once again places Mulligan's larger band work in the "mainstream of jazz."

Mulligan was to be reunited with Freddie Green just three days after the octet session, when he sat in with a version of the Basie orchestra itself on the *Sound of Jazz* CBS telecast. This program had been planned by the writers Nat Hentoff and Whitney Balliett as a jazz spectacular in the *Seven Lively Arts* series, sponsored by Timex. The one-hour show was to bring together musicians from all eras of jazz, from New Orleans trumpeter Henry "Red" Allen to Thelonious Monk, and the Basie assemblage included four members of his current band, Joe Newman, Joe Wilder, Freddie Green, and bassist Eddie Jones, along with past alumni such as Vic Dickenson, Earl Warren, Lester Young, and Jo Jones. Basie's three numbers, however, were eclipsed by a mainstream band led by pianist Mal Waldron, and specially assembled to back Billie Holiday on her blues "Fine and Mellow." In a saxophone section that included Coleman Hawkins, Lester Young, and Ben Webster, and despite the emotional charge of Holiday's on-screen reunion with Young, Mulligan holds his own, charting a clever course between the sparse swing tropes of the first half of his solo chorus and the more rapidly moving figures nodding toward bebop with which he leads back into Holiday's vocal.

It was not with Holiday, but another singer, that Mulligan's quartet recorded that same month, namely Annie Ross. And recruited for these December dates, a mixture of vocal and instrumental sessions for World Pacific (as Dick Bock's label was now called), was a surprising choice of trumpeter—Chet Baker. Dave Bailey speculated that (urged on by Bock) Mulligan agreed to do these recordings with Chet because following Brookmeyer's departure and the stop-gap measure of hiring Lee Konitz, he "wanted the two of them to get back together."[22] Pacific had released some very successful recordings with Baker after the original pianoless quartet split in 1953, and the brief period in which Mulligan had toured as a guest soloist with Baker's group made him consider that this might be the right moment for them to pair up again. However, once they got into the studio, from Mulligan's perspective of the reformed addict, plus his greater experience as a bandleader, and long months of working alongside Brookmeyer (who shared an arranger's attitude to the quartet), he swiftly realized it was not to be. "Music requires discipline, and he once had it," Mulligan told Baker's biographer James Gavin. "He was serious about it and he worked hard. And heroin is the opposite of that."[23]

In the event, the sessions with Annie Ross have endured better than the quartet's purely instrumental ones, partly because by late 1957 she was at the top of her game, working regularly at Julius Monk's Upstairs at the Downstairs nightclub on West 56th Street in Manhattan, and partly because Mulligan completed the album the following year with his "new" quartet with trumpeter Art Farmer. We shall return to this music shortly, but first it is worth a brief exploration of the instrumental *Reunion with Chet Baker.*

The adjective that springs to mind, and which would not apply to any of Mulligan's own recordings since the foundation of the original quartet, is "insipid." With the exception of the title track "Reunion," a new composition by Mulligan, where both horns recapture something of their original vigor, it is clear that the trumpeter is just a passenger, being carried by the other members of the band. Mulligan mostly introduces each melody—possibly to remind Baker of what they are supposed to be playing—and whereas he supplies harmony behind Baker's solos, the favor is barely ever returned. Grimes has a tendency to over-compensate, and it is not surprising that the original liner note describes him as "more percussive and a little less sustaining than is usual."[24] Yet this comes in useful when he rescues "When Your Lover Has Gone," during what sounds as if it is going to be a final chorus, led by the trumpet. Around

22 Jack: *Fifties Jazz Talk*, p. 18.

23 Gavin, James: *Deep in a Dream—The Long Night of Chet Baker* (London, Chatto and Windus, 2002) p. 143.

24 Colket 3rd, Tristram C.: *Reunion with Chet Baker*, Pacific Jazz 1241 [liner note].

halfway into the sequence, Baker fires off a couple of rapid runs, and seems to get lost. One can visualize Mulligan frantically nodding in the direction of the bassist, who responds quickly and begins a solo to carry them through without sacrificing the entire take.

Aside from "Reunion," there's one more hint of what the band might have achieved if Baker had been on better form, which is the final chorus of "Stardust." It would seem that this is the only time Baker ever recorded the standard, which is beautifully introduced by Mulligan, stating the melody with a minimum of ornamentation, underpinned by a straightforward bass line from Grimes. Baker then solos simply and slowly—despite a few minor fluffs—paraphrasing the melody, before Mulligan plays a similarly melodic half chorus. Baker takes the final half, accompanied by the baritone, and deftly edits the melodic line, before a neat ending with the two horns playing the coda together (see Example 4.2). This is a rare glimpse of their former magic.

Maybe realizing that he had a less-than-perfect session by two of the biggest names on his label, Richard Bock commissioned an otiose liner note, which glossed over any of the album's shortcomings with a torrent of verbiage. After citing Kierkegaard and Kafka, it focused on the "mind of Mulligan":

> Within its terse crucible so very much is happening. The provocative tensions that inter-weavingly and multi-thematically present both themselves and their infinitely possible resolutions, so tangibly sift through its textured dimensionality that it is difficult to believe that the vertical moment will be invariably reconciled to the horizontal reality.[25]

The writer goes on to assert that Mulligan is not "mainstream," and to discuss the "mathematical purity" of the Baker/Mulligan partnership.

This same partnership is the weakest element of the album *Annie Ross Sings a Song with Mulligan.*[26] James Gavin reports that during the first session, according to Ross, Chet "went to the loo and never came back."[27] Indeed, he is not present on the best track originally issued from those New York recordings, "It Don't Mean a Thing, If It Ain't Got That Swing," which is accompanied by the remaining trio of Mulligan, Grimes, and

25 Ibid.

26 World Pacific 1253.

27 Gavin: *Deep in a Dream*, p. 143.

EXAMPLE 4.2 The final sixteen measures of "Stardust" (by Hoagy Carmichael and Mitchell Parish) from *Reunion with Chet Baker* (World Pacific T-90061) (transcription).

Bailey. On that piece, despite an over-resonant acoustic, Ross matches the instrumentalists well, and demonstrates that she clearly understands the meaning of the lyric. She told the author: "When I was younger I didn't really know what jazz was. I knew what I was doing was jazz-related, but it wasn't until I went to Paris in 1947 and started singing with Coleman Hawkins, Kenny Clarke, James Moody, and Dizzy and Bird, people like them, that I really found out what 'swing' was. It's one thing to be a singer, it's another to be a swinging singer. The first time that feeling comes to you it's indescribable."[28]

British-born and American-raised, Ross returned to the United States from that stint in Paris in 1952, after which she recorded her famous version of "Twisted." She went back to Europe in 1955 with Lionel Hampton, and the following year appeared in London and on Broadway in the revue *Cranks*. Along with a growing international reputation, her jazz credentials were excellent, and the word was already out when she first came into the studio with Mulligan that she had been hard at work during the last three months of 1957 on overdubbing vocal parts for a new album to be called *Sing a Song of Basie*, with fellow singers Dave Lambert and Jon Hendricks. Between them they sang the lines of all the brass and reeds, not to mention vocalese versions of the original solos, on a series of Basie's best-known numbers.

That album had yet to appear when the first Mulligan sessions took place, but it had just been issued when Mulligan, Baker, Grimes, and Bailey were reunited with Ross in Los Angeles on February 11, 1958, with the intention of completing their record. In the event, the *Annie Ross Sings a Song with Mulligan* album was still unfinished by the end of that day, although they did manage to record "This Time the Dream's on Me," "Between the Devil and the Deep Blue Sea," "How about You," and "Let There Be Love."

On the last-named, Ross's vocal is exceptional, playing with the time, lingering on syllables to accentuate the meaning, and yet never losing her jazz sensibility as she teases out the vocal line. Mulligan plays an assertive solo, backed by some of the cleanest, hardest-swinging walking bass that Grimes recorded during his time with the group. However, on "How about You," Ross's vocal dexterity is inhibited by a funereal accompanying figure scored for trumpet and baritone. Baker contributes a solo that has a modicum of pace, after which Mulligan's energetic playing suggests that they can really develop the piece, but then it returns to the leaden head arrangement. "This Time the Dream's on Me" is perfunctory and "Between the Devil and the Deep Blue Sea" is plodding. It would be hard to disagree with this perceptive review from syndicated jazz critic Bob Snead:

> Annie Ross is one of the most gifted and perhaps one of the most truly jazz vocalists. Gerry is certainly one of the outstanding baritone

28 Interview with Annie Ross, April 1999.

voices of his day. However, there are some things that just don't mix. One of them being the voice of Annie Ross, backed by the baritone sounds of Mulligan. It seems to us that someone at WP got carried away with two names without thought about the sounds that they would produce. We found it hard to listen to Annie render what was without doubt a very good solo because we just couldn't help but feel that Gerry was going to move in and take over before her solo was completed. Then at other times we found Mulligan, although the accompanying voice, way out in front of Annie. Perhaps we can put it another way. We like Annie Ross and when she sings we like to listen to her without distraction—this we could not do listening to Mulligan + Baker combo in the background. Reading this far, you are no doubt wondering why we have given this session a rating of good. Well, good isn't the word for the improvement on side 2. There are five excellent tracks here. The only explanation we can offer is that side 1 must have been recorded on a separate date, or the producer, recognizing the above faults, corrected them on side 2. Mulligan not only subdues his sound, but gives out with a remarkable solo on "This is Always," with Annie really putting herself into this ballad. She also creates a swinging mood on "Give Me The Simple Life."[29]

The perception and the supposition here are both accurate. The five tracks cut in Los Angeles on September 25, 1958, are not only a return to Mulligan's usual high standards, but the quartet now has Bill Crow back on bass, and Art Farmer on trumpet. Crow's bass lines are both inventive and functional, providing the harmonic framework the band needs, and locking on to Bailey's drumming in a way that Grimes never quite managed, so as to inject effortless swing into every track. And unlike Baker, Farmer is both fully present in the lightly arranged heads, and spurs the others on with his solo vignettes. "All of You" benefits from some particularly fine playing from Farmer and an arranged out-chorus that differs from the opening head, working up toward one of Ross's spectacular high-note finishes. The overall highlight is the track picked out by another of the contemporary critics, Fred Sherman, who accurately realizes that in this setting Ross has a musical voice as potent as the other four members of the band:

29 Snead, Bob: "Jazz Corner," *Cleveland Call and Post*, March 21, 1959, p 24.

> A voice like a jazz instrument turns the Gerry Mulligan quartet into a quintet. . . . You won't hear better jazz than is played here. About the singer, you must make the decision yourself. The test is easy, for it is offered forthright in "I Feel Pretty," a deliriously happy tune by Leonard Bernstein.[30]

Not only is this song a fine match between vocalist and instrumentalists in terms of the arrangement, but it has some deft touches such as a unison phrase (drawn from the head) for baritone and voice that punctuates Mulligan's solo. It also maintains a sprightly tempo that the Baker reunions failed to achieve. For Ross, working on such a neatly worked-out arrangement had an additional challenge. She said:

> We would run down the chords, and I had a very good ear. I was very lucky to have that, because I don't read music, so it helped me enormously! There are a lot of people who read those dots on the page beautifully, without any kind of problem, but they don't swing. Technically they're wonderful but they don't have that necessary ingredient.[31]

Playing by ear in the context of the Mulligan quartet went back to its very origins and the head arrangements that the two principals learned by singing to one another in Chet Baker's car on the way to the Haig. Bill Crow observed that "Annie always had wonderful ears," and that he particularly enjoyed working with her on the Mulligan album because, first, he had long admired her vocal prowess, and secondly, she had known him for a long time. When she initially began singing with Dave Lambert, he and Dave had been sharing a basement apartment (if that's not too grand a word for it) on 10th Street in New York City. Crow recalled:

> It was just a big basement that used to be a coal cellar, and when the building went on to natural gas, it left all this empty space that the guy was able to rent out cheap, and we had turned it into quite nice living accommodation, just one big room with a kitchenette and a bathroom. We'd found a poker table that we'd mounted on some boxes, and an old curved seat, an upholstered bench that had been thrown

30 Sherman, Fred: "Voice Like Jazz Instrument," *Miami Herald*, March 22, 1959, p. 188.

31 Interview with Annie Ross, April 1999.

> out by the bar across the street, and this was the perfect place for vocal groups to sit and sing. Dave had a lot of stuff that he had written and when Annie came to town, she just gravitated down there because there was a lot of singing going on. So we got to be very good friends.[32]

Bill Crow also suggested that the genesis of Lambert, Hendricks, and Ross dated to that period when he was sharing with Dave, and indeed, as mentioned, that trio's Basie album was in preparation just as Annie Ross made her initial sessions with Mulligan. Bill marveled that she was able to negotiate the vocal group's tricky arrangements and all the overdubbing on *Sing a Song of Basie*, without being able to read music.

Art Farmer's first public appearance with the quartet seems to have been on the CBS Timex "All Star Jazz Festival" broadcast from New York on April 30, 1958. This was a very high profile event, widely covered in the press, and also featured Louis Armstrong, Lionel Hampton and His Orchestra, the George Shearing Quintet, Jack Teagarden's Band with Cozy Cole and Henry "Red" Allen, Gene Krupa, and the Dukes of Dixieland.[33] Still with Grimes and Bailey in the lineup, the part of the band's performance that was broadcast included "Bernie's Tune" and "Utter Chaos." The arrival of Farmer galvanized the quartet to a level comparable to, if not even better than, its final days with Brookmeyer the previous year. Dave Bailey was unequivocal:

> When Art came in it changed a lot of the flavor of the Gerry Mulligan Quartet. Instead of being cool, we became hot! Very hot. I think it was the best quartet—in my humble opinion—that Gerry Mulligan ever had. We used to blow 'em away. Wherever we played concerts, people used to go out feeling a lot better than when they came in.[34]

Farmer had mainly worked on the West Coast from 1945, before joining Lionel Hampton in 1952, and then relocating to New York the following year. Mulligan would have known his subsequent work with Teddy Charles and then with Horace Silver, but there was a much closer connection, in that soon after Farmer's move East, he began recording

32 Interview with Bill Crow, September 4, 2002.

33 "All Star Jazz Show," *Dubuque Telegraph Herald*, April 27, 1958; further listing from *Oakland Tribune*, April 30, 1958.

34 Interview with Dave Bailey, September 5, 2002.

for Prestige, still run by Mulligan's friend Bob Weinstock, and by this time also involving critic and producer Ira Gitler, who recalled:

> When he was with the Lionel Hampton Band in 1953, he came to New York, and that's when we did a session with him. At the time I was producing, Bob had backed off from producing for a while, and so we did a thing called *Work of Art*, which included members of the Hampton band. Quincy Jones was playing trumpet in the section and that was Art's first actual 10-inch LP as a leader. And of course in those days they always made 78s out of the LPs, because they were still a viable entity. So I think he was pretty well-known by the time he went with Gerry, later in the 50s.[35]

In the wake of the Timex festival, Farmer's first formal recorded work with Mulligan turned out not to be with the regular quartet. Dave Bailey was still working as Mulligan's manager, but he remembered that at this point "Gerry tended to work sporadically," taking long periods off.[36] So, in what was expected to be down time, Bailey accepted as many gigs as he could around New York, with the likes of Ben Webster, Coleman Hawkins, and Chris Connor. The quartet was next to convene for Newport in early July, and Mulligan had already called Bill Crow to ask him to rejoin, as Henry Grimes had been booked to play the festival with Sonny Rollins's trio (with whom he later went to Europe the following year) and he was also to do a set with Thelonious Monk.

Then prior to Newport, and somewhat unexpectedly, Mulligan was invited to make his way to Hollywood to appear in and play on the soundtrack for a movie called *I Want to Live!* This was a fictionalization of the true-life story of Barbara Graham, who was convicted in 1955 for the murder of another woman, but who maintained her innocence right up to the moment she was sent to the gas chamber. It offered actress Susan Hayward the opportunity for a *tour-de-force* performance as Graham, which she delivered brilliantly, winning an Oscar in the process. The relatively short notice for the shoot was because pre-production had taken some time, with Don Mankiewicz's original screenplay (based on the investigative journalism of Ed Montgomery) being partially re-written

35 Interview with Ira Gitler, March 25, 2002. *Work of Art* was originally released in 1956 as *The Art Farmer Septet* (Prestige 7031) with Gitler's session from 1953 and a follow-up date produced by Weinstock in 1954.

36 Jack: *Fifties Jazz Talk*, p. 18.

by Nelson Gidding. But in April 1958, with a final script acceptable to the production team, the principal photography began, and Mulligan and Farmer made their way to Los Angeles during May. (Although the movie was set in San Francisco, it was filmed in and around Hollywood.) Owing to his New York commitments, Bailey could not make the trip, and Crow had not yet rejoined the quartet, so Mulligan and Farmer found themselves in somewhat different musical company.

It transpired that in real life Barbara Graham had been a jazz fan, and her particular love was the music of Gerry Mulligan, so the producer and director not only wanted Mulligan in the movie, but they invited Johnny Mandel (whom Mulligan had known since his Gene Krupa days) to write an all-jazz score to feature him. There had been several films up to this point where at least part of the score featured jazz, or was jazz-related, but very few had abandoned the traditional studio orchestra to create a consistent jazz soundtrack throughout the entire movie. Mandel, who had previously worked not only as a big band player and arranger, but also as the musical director on several radio and TV programs, including comedian Sid Caesar's *Show of Shows*, recalled:

> The first movie I ever did was *I Want To Live*. I had a music editor that showed me the ropes, right away, and I said, "My God! Where have I been all my life?" It combined what I'd learned working for the radio, working to the clock, and working to sight cues in vaudeville, which is really what the *Show of Shows*, or Broadway shows are. It was like I'd been doing it all the time, and I'd learned the technique. . . . *I Want To Live!* was really the first all jazz score. I used no traditional underscoring at all. It came about through a fortunate combination of circumstances, Walter Wanger, who was the producer, and Bobby Wise, who was the director, just made it all work. They decided they wanted to document the life of Barbara Graham, the first lady ever to go to the gas chamber. And at that time that was a big deal, as far as selling a movie, because it had never happened before. She was a big Gerry Mulligan fan, and that's another thing, she loved jazz, so we had Mulligan in the movie, not acting, just playing with a group. So I wrote a whole album's worth for the Mulligan Septet, because I wanted four horns. Bud Shank, and Gerry, Frank Rosolino, trombone, and Art Farmer on trumpet. Not too shabby! It was an all-jazz score, and when she was executed and when she was arrested—those dramatic scenes—I did them all with jazz. It was a real education for me, because usually they'd go to traditional stuff for that. It got a tremendous amount of acclaim, but it was not even eligible for an

> Academy Award for the music, because the old-timers didn't like this sort of thing. It was a marvelous experience, but for a while I didn't work except for occasional jazz things. Until people started using jazz scores all the time, because the producers quickly caught on that you could do it—make a whole lot of music with a small group.[37]

In fact, the small group plays only six soundtrack cues, and, as Mandel said, another sixteen, which covered most of the main dramatic moments, such as "Gas Chamber Unveiling" and "Preparations for Execution," were recorded by a twenty-six-piece jazz big band. But the septet (which included Mulligan's former bass colleague Red Mitchell, alongside drummer Shelly Manne and pianist Pete Jolly) has some fine moments, including an on-screen club appearance where the shirt-sleeved Mulligan is deliberately visually distinguished from the formal jackets of Farmer, Rosolino, and Shank (see Figure 4.1). Farmer's on-screen presence would not only coincide with the planned future tours of the "New" Gerry Mulligan Quartet when the film was released, but made certain that, in keeping with most of Mulligan's 1950s bands, this one was racially integrated.

Mandel's skill admirably lived up to what the author of the notes to the soundtrack LP, William Johns, described as the "provocative challenge . . . to write in terms of the picture, and at the same time in a manner that would be firmly in the Mulligan mode."[38] His most successful achievement is to use a seven-piece band that includes a piano, yet leaving sufficient space in most of the numbers for the audience to hear—from time to time—something resembling the familiar sound of a Mulligan quartet (even if there's a degree of trombone and trumpet unison and either unison or very close harmony with the reeds, plus some very discreet piano). A good example is the first 2:20 of "Night Watch," which has a head that could easily have been drawn from the quartet repertoire, followed by fine solos from Mulligan and Farmer, before the piano takes over. The linear theme at the very start of "Black Nightgown" has similar quartet echoes, notably (following a bass and drums intro) in the opening A section with the trombone in unison with the baritone.

Following the filming, Mulligan and Farmer returned to New York, and by the time of the Newport Jazz Festival in July, Bill Crow had

37 Johnny Mandel interviewed by Guy Barker, July 2004.

38 Johns, William: *The Jazz Combo from "I Want to Live!"* (United Artists UAL 4006) 1958.

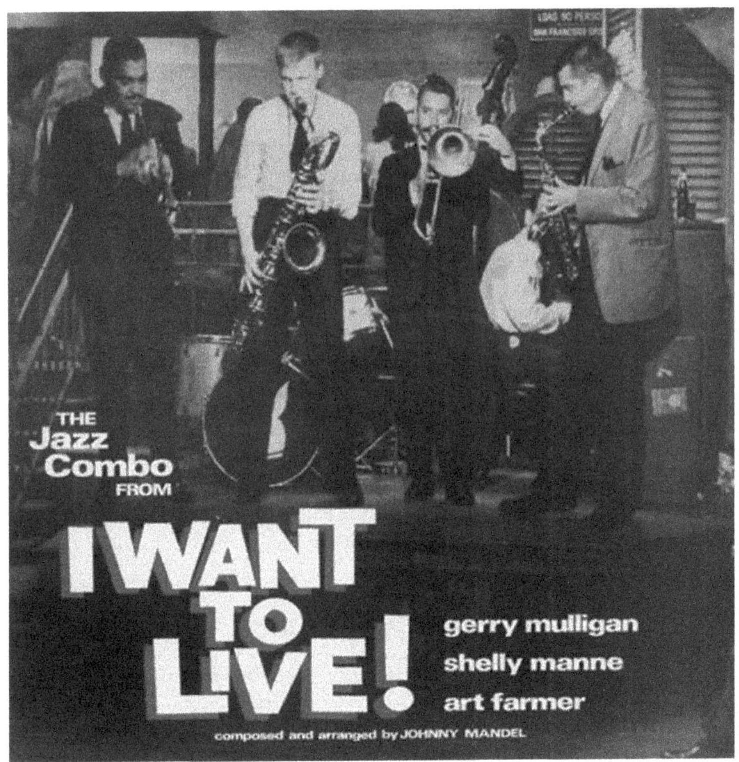

FIGURE 4.1 The cover of the soundtrack album for *I Want to Live!* with a still shot from the club sequence in the movie showing (left to right) Art Farmer, Gerry Mulligan, Frank Rosolino, and Bud Shank.

rejoined the quartet. There the band not only played a high octane set for the festivalgoers, but from it, their performance of Mulligan's "Catch as Catch Can" was featured in the film *Jazz on a Summer's Day*, as well as on the soundtrack album. Mulligan and Farmer negotiate the tricky head, both play invigorating solos, and the spotlight also falls on Crow and Bailey for brief solo outings, during what was the closing number of their concert. What is immediately obvious in Farmer's playing is that he employs far more bebop phrasing than either Baker or Eardley had done, but yet the overall impression is still that of a hard-swinging mainstream band (see Example 4.3).

This track and other material that survives from that Newport appearance attest to the accuracy of Dave Bailey's assessment that far from

EXAMPLE 4.3 The final sixteen measures of Farmer's Newport solo on "Catch as Catch Can" (transcription).

being cool the band was "hot," although the opening "Festive Minor" (a recent Mulligan piece first recorded at the Chet Baker reunion sessions the previous December) starts rather coolly, if not uncertainly, before the quartet hits its stride with "Bernie's Tune."[39] In the rehearsals before the festival, Mulligan made clear that he wanted this "new" quartet to play some more fresh material, but there was a problem, as Bill Crow recalled:

> He said: "Gee, I just can't seem to get down to writing new stuff. Why don't you guys bring in something?" So Art brought a tune called "Blueport" and I brought a tune "News From Blueport"—those were both Gerry's titles.[40]

So—as the puns on the festival's name suggest—Newport saw the first public airings of these pieces, both of which would be featured in virtually every one of the quartet's subsequent festival and concert appearances that year, before eventually being recorded in December on an album for Columbia.

Both are twelve-measure blues (alluded to in their titles), and they mark a change in the band's approach. Previously, a blues was an infrequent ingredient in any set by the quartet. For example, in all the 1954 Paris concerts by the original edition of the Brookmeyer quartet, there was not a single blues. And when Norman Granz complained that on the 1954 tour with Ellington, Getz, and Brubeck, Mulligan had been "too cerebral," he had specifically mentioned that his music went "too far from

39 The full set is on *Gerry Mulligan / Art Farmer Quartet Complete at Newport 1958*, RLR 88639.

40 Interview with Bill Crow, September 4, 2002.

EXAMPLE 4.4 As played at Newport, the head of "Blueport" by Art Farmer. Copyright © 1959 Criterion Music Corp. Copyright renewed. All Rights Reserved. Used by Permission. Reprinted by permission of Hal Leonard Europe Ltd. (transcription).

the blues." As mentioned in Chapter 3, there had been some forays in this direction when Red Mitchell was the group's bassist, but Farmer's arrival injected a natural blues feeling into the heart of the band, whether in a catchy theme such as his own "Blueport" (which owes more than a little allegiance to Jimmie Blanton and Duke Ellington's "Mr. J. B. Blues"; see Example 4.4) or playing over Mulligan's backing on the slower-paced "News from Blueport" (see Example 4.5).

Following its appearance before the estimated 60,000 fans at Newport that summer[41] the Mulligan Quartet also reached a wider public in ways

41 Audience estimate from Stratemann, Klaus: *Ellington Day by Day and Film by Film* (Copenhagen, JazzMedia, 1992) p. 390. (Mulligan sat in with the Ellington band for one number on their set at Newport.)

EXAMPLE 4.5 "News from Blueport" by Bill Crow. Copyright © 1958 Othello Music. Copyright renewed. Used by permission. Head from 1:49 into the Newport recording, but showing the "three over four" ideas inherent in the piece, which subsequently mutated into being played in 3/4 time.

that earlier editions did not. For example, later in July, after Newport, it played four short sets every day for a week to entertain visitors at the Boston International Car Show. Then it appeared before 10,000 people in an outdoor concert at the Lewisohn Stadium in New York on July 24, in a double bill with the Ellington band. Three days later the quartet headlined at the second annual Great South Bay Jazz Festival at the Timber Grove Club in East Islip on Long Island. The press notice advertised that there would be:

> A twilight concert . . . on Sunday featuring jazz singer Chris Connor and her quartet, Gerry Mulligan and his Quartet with Art Farmer, and the Willie The Lion Smith Septet with Maxine Sullivan handling the vocals.[42]

In fact, Mulligan topped the bill that Sunday evening, and Maxine Sullivan was coaxed back to the stage to sing "Mack the Knife" and "Ace in the Hole" with the quartet, in a set that otherwise spanned the band's history from "Bernie's Tune" via "Catch as Catch Can" to "Blueport." A couple of weekends later, the group was to take part in a new festival venture promoted by George Wein. One preview ran:

> You people who want something right next to Newport can find it pretty close to home next month at French Lick, Ind. The old spa is inaugurating a series of music festivals in August with the jazz show due 15, 16 and 17. George Wein who has been permanent music director of the Newport Jazz Festival since its inception five years ago is producing the show at the French Lick Sheraton Hotel amphitheater. The site is a natural grove on the grounds of the 1,700 acre spa, and 5,000 seats are available. Wein teaches the history of jazz at Boston University and operates the Storyville, one of the country's finest jazz clubs. Opening night will feature Duke Ellington's band and the Erroll Garner Trio. Saturday night brings Krupa's Quartet, some fine blowing from Gerry Mulligan, the Eddie Condon All Stars and Chris Connor.[43]

Playing outdoor gigs, and performing for audiences that were often substantially bigger than in previous years, Mulligan had decided to smarten the band up. In the Brookmeyer days they had generally worn matching sports coats (from the Andover store in Boston), but prior to Newport he had taken the band to Breidbart's on 6th Avenue in New York, and bought smart gray suits for the other three musicians, while kitting himself out in similar pants, and a red coat. It is clear from

42 "Jazz Festival Sat. at Timber Grove," *East Hampton Star*, July 24, 1958.

43 *Lima News*, July 19, 1958.

the *Jazz on a Summer's Day* footage that—even at night—the band got exceedingly hot in these garments under the stage lights. So before the Great South Bay Festival, in an effort to keep the musicians cooler, Mulligan took them back to Breidbart's to buy matching dark blue linen pants, and short-sleeved cotton shirts with inch-wide red and white stripes, plus shoestring neckties. Thus attired, the band turned up to do their set. According to Bill Crow, the pants fit the somewhat ample figures of Bailey and Farmer rather too snugly, and they weren't best pleased meeting Dizzy Gillespie just before going on stage to hear him shout: "You cats got some *buns* back there!"[44] The striped shirts and dark pants were retired gracefully after the French Lick event, and the quartet went back to its gray suits.

Shortly before that August festival, Art Farmer and Mulligan had appeared in Art Kane's famous "Great Day in Harlem" photograph, taken at 17 East 126th Street on August 12 to bring together fifty-seven musicians from the current New York jazz scene. Then, following their concert at French Lick on 16th, the band headed West to California, where after recording the balance of the tracks for the album with Annie Ross in Los Angeles, they traveled to Monterey for the very first edition of the jazz festival there. This was produced by Jimmy Lyons, the former San Francisco DJ commemorated in "Line for Lyons."

The new quartet went down extremely well, with critics and audience alike, although their concert was almost identical in repertoire terms to the one they had played at Newport. A ten-minute version of "Blueport" survives on a multi-CD release commemorating forty years of the festival.[45] But Mulligan's own appearance there drew acclaim for another set altogether, the late night jam session on which he was one of the guests who sat in with Dizzy Gillespie's quintet. Writer Michele Ellis remarked: "This swingin' affair owed most of its success, besides the rhythm section, to Gerry Mulligan and Sonny Rollins, who 'blew' once in a million performances."[46]

Back in the East, the quartet performed several gigs in late October and early November, including playing for students at Columbia University in New York and MIT in Cambridge. The highest-profile concert was at New York Town Hall on November 28, opposite Miles Davis's quintet, Thelonious Monk's quartet, and the Jimmy Giuffre Trio (with

44 Crow, Bill: *From Birdland to Broadway* (New York, Oxford University Press, 1992) p. 166.

45 *Monterey Jazz Festival: Forty Legendary Years*, Malpaso 9 467032.

46 Ellis, Michele: "The Monterey Jazz Festival Hits High and Low Notes," *San Rafael Daily Independent*, October 18, 1958.

Bob Brookmeyer and Jim Hall). The Mulligan quartet also played on the WNTA television show *Art Ford's Jazz Party* that same month, but all this was preparation for an imminent return to the recording studios, and the move to a different label—Columbia.

Compared to the rate at which the earlier quartets with Baker and Brookmeyer had added to their repertoire, it is noticeable that this edition seldom changed its setlists, but relied on increasingly inventive solos to hold its audience's interest. It seems that (as he had been prior to Newport) Mulligan was still suffering from writer's block, this time brought on by his increasing fame, and by gossip column interest in his burgeoning affair with the actress Judy Holliday. She had been starring on Broadway in the Comden and Green show (shortly to become a movie in which she also starred) *Bells Are Ringing*, and by late 1958, already involved with Mulligan, she had just gone through a somewhat public divorce from her husband David Oppenheim. Bill Crow recalled:

> We had a Columbia album coming up and Gerry only contributed the arrangement for "What Is There to Say?" and he only did that because I gave him the keys to my apartment and told him there was nobody there, nobody'd know where he was. There was a piano there. I would go to stay with my girlfriend, and he could write us some stuff. He came out with this one beautiful chart, on "What Is There to Say?" but that was as much as he was really able to do. He had become popular with some of the theater world, and if he stayed home, he didn't really have any "alone time." And especially now he wasn't hungry. He used to always write when he was hungry, when he was poor, and I think it had changed a little bit![47]

The album takes its title from, and opens with, Mulligan's new chart, as mentioned by Bill Crow,[48] but once recording had gotten under way—as a nod in the direction of Judy Holliday—he did manage a skeletal arrangement of a song from *Bells Are Ringing*, namely, "Just in Time," composed by Jule Styne to Comden and Green's lyrics, but which, after Mulligan ushers in a faster tempo following a short, measured introduction, becomes a straight-ahead blowing vehicle. The rest of the album, which also revisits the earlier quartet's "My Funny Valentine," draws

47 Interview with Bill Crow, September 4, 2002.

48 *What Is There To Say?*, Columbia CL 1307.

FIGURE 4.2 Recording for Columbia: Farmer, Mulligan, Bailey, Crow. Photo by Don Hunstein © Sony Music Entertainment. Used by permission.

on the setlist the band had been playing for the last six months (see Figure 4.2).

Both "Blueport" and "News from Blueport" have developed over six months in terms of the band's confidence and swagger. The former is a far more powerful performance than the Newport one, whereas "News from Blueport" is still a twelve-measure blues, but it now has a different time signature from its earlier incarnation, settling easily into 3/4 meter after the head, giving it a very different feel from the group's more standard 4/4 repertoire. "Festive Minor" which suffered from being the set opener at Newport, where it is obvious that the band had been adjusting to the open air stage and to the acoustic, is excellently played here, and bears scant relation to the earliest version of the piece recorded a year before during the reunion with Chet Baker (but unissued at the time). Whereas Baker appeared to be a nervous passenger, entering late with his hesitant phrasing and occasionally insecure pitch, not helped by Grimes's woeful intonation, the new version, cut in January 1959 is a masterly four-way conversation between the group members. Farmer's muted trumpet sets a somber atmosphere for the piece, and Crow's mixture of repetitive patterns and walking fits excellently with Bailey's restrained brushwork. But the highlight of *What Is There to Say?* is "As

EXAMPLE 4.6 "As Catch Can" by Gerry Mulligan. Copyright © 1959 Criterion Music Corp. Copyright renewed. International Copyright secured. All Rights Reserved. Reprinted by permission of Hal Leonard Europe Ltd. Showing the head at 0:07 into the recording to 0:33 (transcription).

Catch Can," its knotty head ushering in a hard bop *tour de force*, with soloing from Farmer that would not be out of place in Art Blakey's Jazz Messengers (see Examples 4.6 and 4.7).

Between the first studio sessions for the album from December 18 to 23, and the final one on January 15, the band was busy, with a few days

EXAMPLE 4.6 Continued

at George Wein's Storyville Club in Boston in early January, plus a college concert in Milwaukee. In this, a pattern was being repeated, because there was a Jazz at the Philharmonic European tour coming up in May and June, and Mulligan was ensuring that the band was playing regularly and often before it set out. After appearing on the Steve Allen television show in February, there was a quick visit to the West Coast, before the last week of the month was spent in residence at the Ridge Crest Inn in Rochester, New York. Then there was a return for three weeks in April to the Black Hawk in San Francisco, before heading back East for another New York Town Hall concert.[49] The quartet set off for Sweden in mid-May.

Fortunately we do have at least one recording of the band during its pre-departure flurry of activity, because on its February visit to California, it starred in an episode of the public service broadcast *The Navy Swings*.[50] This jazz show, generally lasting around fifteen minutes, featured different guest musicians each week, and from 1957 to 1965 it

49 "Gerry Mulligan Who Originated the 'Ivy League' Haircut for Musicians Opens at the Blackhawk Next Tuesday," *Oakland Tribune*, April 1, 1959.

50 *Gerry Mulligan / Art Farmer Quartet in Stockholm and Hollywood, 1959*, Solar 4569871.

EXAMPLE 4.7 "As Catch Can," Farmer's solo (which makes an interesting comparison to Example 4.3) (transcription).

was heard on NPR stations across the country, the music always finishing in time for a naval recruitment message.

The seven brief numbers recorded for the broadcast start with a searing version of "Motel," the only surviving example of Farmer playing this with the quartet. His agile negotiation of the head, even at breakneck speed, is exemplary, and again his solo is free-blowing hard bop. Crow's bass lines urge the band on and Mulligan (straying off mike) adds some subtle additional harmonies. "My Funny Valentine" starts as a baritone feature, but when Farmer enters on the channel, he takes control in so confident and polished a way that it makes a fascinating contrast with Baker's fragile approach to the song. At just over half the duration of the version on *What Is There to Say?*, it benefits from concision, and not one note is wasted. There's a buoyant "Walkin' Shoes," and the rest of the material revisits the recent Columbia album. "Festive Minor" is somewhat rushed, possibly with an eye on the clock for this tightly timed broadcast. "As Catch Can" is every bit as frantic as the Newport performance, but it conveys the sense of a band having fun, and it is worth noting that a few weeks earlier, in his liner note for *What Is There to Say?*, Mulligan had made the point that:

> Jazz music is fun to me. All music can be fun for that matter, but what I mean is we usually have a hell of a good time playing and listening

to each other. But some of the people who do the most talking about jazz (that may even be the basic problem, right there!) don't seem to get any real fun out of listening to it. It seems to me that all the super intellectualizing on the technics of jazz and lack of response to the emotion and meaning of jazz is spoiling the fun for listeners and players alike.[51]

At almost the same time that he wrote those notes, the motion picture and soundtrack album of *I Want to Live!* were released, and in an interview with his namesake, Hugh Mulligan, for the Associated Press agency, he expanded a little on some of the same ideas:

> Jazzman Gerry Mulligan is the idol of the beat generation, but with his crew cut hair, neat business suit, and faultless grammar devoid of bop-talk, he neither looks, sounds, nor feels the part. "I have never identified myself with the beats," he insisted over a plate of scrambled eggs in a midtown restaurant. "They want to minimize all emotional response to life, which to me is the next thing to being dead. We went through all that in the '40s, the business of being cool and unemotional. I can't be one of the beats, because I have some enthusiasm for life."[52]

The article goes on to explore the movie in detail, expanding Johnny Mandel's point about it being perhaps the first time that jazz underscoring was used as an integral part of the plot of a drama. Mulligan uses his positive attitude toward life and toward music to draw a clear distinction between him, his musicians, and the unfortunate Miss Graham:

> "We had a pretty good idea of what was supposed to be happening at the time, as in the Frisco club sequence and Barbara's theme, but we had to employ imagination and fit ourselves into the mood, just like the actors, to recreate the erratic quality of jazz as it was played in the '40s," says Gerry in recalling the recording sessions.[53]

51 *What Is There to Say?*, Columbia CL 1307 (1959) [liner note].

52 Mulligan, Hugh: "Records: Gerry Mulligan Is Enthusiastic, Not Beat" [AP], *Corpus Christi Caller Times*, January 4, 1959.

53 Ibid.

The underlying reason for Mulligan's generally upbeat attitude at this time, aside from having one of the best quartets he ever led, was that by now his personal life was much more settled. As another reporter, Martin Abramson, wrote:

> One of Mulligan's old friends says Judy [Holliday] has helped change Gerry's temperament considerably. "He's much more congenial since he started to go with Judy, and he's much easier to get along with," the friend told me. "[She] just understands Gerry, his drive and his ambitions. She knows a great deal about jazz, too, so they've got that in common. Gerry's a great success as a jazz musician, but now he needs some success in the art of living."[54]

In the early months of 1959, Judy Holliday was coming in to the second year of her current Broadway run at the Shubert Theatre in *Bells Are Ringing*. On the nights when he was not playing with the quartet, Mulligan would often spend the evening as a listener at one of Manhattan's jazz clubs, before meeting up with Ms. Holliday in the small hours after she had finished at the theater.[55] On one occasion, a gossip columnist, aware that Mulligan had just released an album with Annie Ross, wrote:

> The most picturesque ringside at the Village Vanguard the other early morning was jazz genius Gerry Mulligan who sat with Annie Ross's pet kinkajou perched on his shoulder while Annie sang with Dave Lambert and Jon Hendricks. The kinkajou, name of Pierre, seemed far more at home in the nightclub atmosphere than several nervous customers at nearby tables who couldn't quite figure out the scene.[56]

Mention of the kinkajou (or "honey bear," a cousin of the raccoon) was a smart way of getting column inches, and keeping the names Mulligan and Ross linked in the newspapers. This was just the point when reviews (all more positive than that quoted earlier) of the *Sings a Song with Mulligan* record appeared, such as one that praises Ross's "smoky emotional quality [and] her groovy swinging."[57] Mulligan's press

54 Abramson, Martin: "Big Beat Comes Back," *Dover Daily Reporter* (OH), November 20, 1959.

55 "Judy Holliday's New Escort Is Jazz Star Gerry Mulligan, at the 'Bells' Stage Door Nightly," *Burlington Daily Times News*, January 6, 1959, p. 4.

56 *Onoenta Star*, February 2, 1959, p. 4.

57 "New Soloist, New Tunes and a Panorama of Jazz," *Oakland Tribune*, March 8, 1959.

coverage was also helped by yet another jazz poll success, this time topping the *Metronome* category for baritone saxophone with the largest number of votes cast for a single artist.[58] Norman Granz's publicity machine then went into full-scale action, informing US readers about the forthcoming seventh consecutive European tour of JATP, this time with Mulligan headlining along with Ella Fitzgerald and Gene Krupa.

If the *Navy Swings* broadcast gives us an aural picture of the Mulligan quartet immediately prior to its European tour, the critic Russ Wilson's review of the April Black Hawk residency adds a pen portrait. Describing Mulligan's "tall, spare figure" vibrating "like a reed" as he handles the unwieldy baritone, Wilson continues:

> Farmer, who is one of the bright young men on his horn, is in complete rapport with his fellows. Some of the ideas that he and Mulligan mull during their exchanges of fours are fantastic. Bailey and Crow provide faultless rhythmic support and the bassist additionally contributes some cogent solos. In passing it should be mentioned that the Mulligan quartet plays what has come to be termed "mainstream" jazz, which is one reason for the combo's widespread popularity.[59]

He then makes a direct comparison with Sonny Rollins's "hard bop" quartet, including trumpeter Freddie Hubbard, drummer Lennie McBrown, and Henry Grimes, who were appearing the same week at the San Francisco Jazz Workshop. Apart from a brief mention of the up-and-coming talent of Hubbard, he focuses on Rollins's "searing and ferocious" extended solos, with the implication that despite the leader's extraordinary gift for invention, this group did not enjoy the same popular appeal.

April was quite a complex month in Mulligan's personal life because, prior to shooting the movie of *Bells Are Ringing*, work on which was scheduled to begin in Hollywood later in 1959, Judy Holliday had just transferred from Broadway to the West Coast stage version of the show at the Los Angeles Civic Light Opera. Mulligan spent the one day a week when he was not playing at the Black Hawk shuttling down the coast to

58 Devine, Larry: "Off the Record," *Salt Lake Tribune*, February 8, 1959, p. 92.

59 Wilson, Russ: "Top Sax Men Thrill Jazz Fans," *Oakland Tribune*, April 9, 1959, p. 18.

be with Holliday.[60] Thereafter, following a short stop in New York, he would be away in Europe until early June.[61]

In his book *From Birdland to Broadway*, Bill Crow has given a detailed account of the convivial social life of this European JATP tour, which not only involved, as mentioned, Ella Fitzgerald and Gene Krupa, but brought in other stars for occasional concerts, including such American stars as bassist Oscar Pettiford, who happened to be in Europe at the time. However, in recording terms, the tour was to be the swan song for the Art Farmer edition of the Mulligan Quartet. The Stockholm evening from the start of the tour was captured on tape, as was the Rome event from June 4, shortly before the Norman Granz troupe finished its summer travels.

The Stockholm concert begins with a lively version of "As Catch Can," promoted from set-closer at Newport the previous year to become a rousing opener. Farmer sets things going after the head with a series of solo choruses—at one point running through a series of repeated short motifs reminiscent of the Paul Desmond collaboration described earlier. Then Mulligan turns in a nimble solo, the agility of which more than explains his consistent poll-winning. Sadly, his pianism is still short of the mark in a lumpy accompaniment to Farmer in "I Can't Get Started," but things are redeemed by "Just In Time," where the quartet recovers its natural extrovert swing, backing an exquisite solo from Farmer. By the time we get to exchanges of sixteen, eight, and four measures between the horns, we share the audience's excitement, which does not dim during the lengthy solo from Crow that follows. Hearing the band on this form, it is to be regretted that it did not cast the net wider for its recorded repertoire, because again the set largely revisits the music on *What Is There to Say?* The exception is a new piece called "Spring Is Sprung" that is built around a blues chord progression, and on which Mulligan plays a more fluent piano part than is his norm. But having at one point eschewed the blues, it seems odd for this band in particular to follow one twelve-measure sequence with another, as it then launches into an epic twelve-minute version of "Blueport." However, this track is easily the highlight of the set and admirably demonstrates Bailey's view that the Art Farmer version of the quartet was "hot!" The audience reaction is

60 Kilgallen, Dorothy: "Voice of Broadway," *Salt Lake Tribune*, April 26, 1959, p. B9.

61 Tour dates: May 19, Stockholm, Sweden; 20, Gothenburg; 21, Copenhagen, Denmark; 22, Paris, France; 23, The Hague, Netherlands (afternoon), Amsterdam (evening); 24, Basel, Switzerland; 29, Karlsruhe, West Germany; 31, Hamburg; June 2, Bologna, Italy; 3, Milan; 4, Rome; 5, Turin; 6, Padua; 7, Genoa.

tremendous after the dramatic exchanging of phrases between trumpet and baritone, and shows just how effective this edition of the band had become at playing to sizable audiences, after its season of festivals and prestigious concerts.

The Rome concert from one of the last four days of the tour has equally impressive playing from the quartet, this time with Crow featured more extensively than previously on the opening "As Catch Can," his solo followed by a chorus that highlights drum breaks from Bailey. From there the band heads into "Walkin' Shoes," and whereas the Chet Baker version always had an underlying sense of cool relaxation, there's an edge to this version that feels hotter. The quartet then revisits "Baubles, Bangles and Beads" from the Brookmeyer period, the reflective treatment of which makes one wish they had also looked at other repertoire from that time such as "That Old Feeling." Farmer's solo is a gem, especially as it melds seamlessly into Mulligan retaking the lead for the final chorus.

The rest of the repertoire from this lively and entertaining concert revisits earlier work by this version of the quartet, save for a look back at the sextet repertoire with a sensitive and beautiful rendition of "Moonlight in Vermont." The daringly slow tempo sounds completely natural, and the mutual support of Farmer, Mulligan, and Crow means that even at this speed the lack of a chordal instrument goes unnoticed. Crow's playing behind Mulligan's brilliantly inventive solo here is some of his best work with the various editions of the quartet with which he played. This chorus spurs Farmer into some dramatic soloing, behind which Crow and Mulligan combine to play supporting figures, which they sustain even when Bailey briefly slips into double time. The forensic exploration of this ballad is the highlight of the concert. With the band playing this well, it is to be regretted that this was its last recorded appearance.

Back in the United States, the quartet continued to appear sporadically in late July and August, first playing in Chicago, and then making a return visit to the New York Jazz Festival on Randall's Island. But by the beginning of September, Mulligan, Farmer, and Bailey were on the West Coast, starting what turned out to be five long months of intermittent work on another movie, based on Jack Kerouac's 1958 novel *The Subterraneans*, about the beat poet generation. With Judy Holliday still based in Los Angeles, this suited Mulligan very well, and when the band wasn't working, he made a couple of walk-on appearances as an acting extra in her film of *Bells Are Ringing*. Bill Crow remembered Holliday telling him: "Gerry doesn't realize how easy I made it for him when he did movies in Hollywood. He didn't have to go through any of the crap that most people go through, because I took him by the hand."[62]

Crow himself did not travel west with the other members of the quartet. When the producer Arthur Freed and director Vincente Minnelli first suggested the group might appear in *The Subterraneans*, they offered $300 a week per musician, for an estimated two weeks' work. In his role as the band's manager, Dave Bailey felt this was akin to saying they didn't really want them, so he and Farmer decided to ask for more. Not long afterward the producers raised the offer to $500. By this time Crow had found himself other work in New York, and he was also on the point of marrying his girlfriend Aileen. "I turned the movie down," he said. "And it was just as well I did, since the shooting of it ran far behind schedule. Dave and Art sat around Hollywood for three months waiting for their scenes to be finished."[63] (It was, in fact, almost double that time!)

In the event, the quartet as such did not appear in the movie, but Mulligan, Farmer, and Bailey did contribute to various elements of André Previn's jazz score for the picture, and made on-screen appearances as part of a larger group in which Mulligan also had an acting role as the Reverend Joshua Hoskins, a "street priest" who aims to convert listeners to the Lord through jazz. The first studio session for the soundtrack was on September 2. The final one was on February 3, 1960, and material cut on January 11 and 12 also made it into the soundtrack. Although (according to Bailey) he and Farmer were called to the set or soundstage for approximately two days a week, there was plenty of time, while they were on the movie's payroll, to sit in with other bands, principally at the Lamp nightclub, which soon afterward became drummer Shelly Manne's venue, the Manne-hole.[64] They worked there, among others, with the relatively unknown pianist Les McCann, whom Bailey later recommended to producer Alfred Lion at Blue Note.

Mulligan also used his down time from the movie to play in and around Los Angeles, and to record, making albums with Johnny Hodges and with Ben Webster. He appeared with Webster and blues singer Jimmy Witherspoon at the Renaissance Club for two weeks in December 1959. Along with bassist Leroy Vinnegar and pianist Jimmy Rowles, the drummer on these club dates was Mel Lewis, who was to play an important role in Mulligan's next big musical project, the Concert Jazz

62 Bill Crow interview, September 4, 2002.

63 Crow: *From Birdland to Broadway*, p. 176.

64 Jack: *Fifties Jazz Talk*, p. 19.

Band. But in late 1959, that was still in the future and would begin on the other side of the United States. We will come to the Hodges and Webster albums shortly, but first it is worth exploring *The Subterraneans* soundtrack.

The first session in September 1959 saw the most jazz-inflected pieces being recorded. There is an uptempo romp (riffing on the idea of the jazz priest) called "Bread and Wine," in which Mulligan is the principal soloist, given his on-screen role, but there are also strong solos from Art Farmer, altoist Art Pepper, tenorist Bill Perkins, and pianist Russ Freeman, who exchanges fours with Mulligan. This is the band seen on the cover photograph on the French issue of the soundtrack under the title *Les rats de cave* (Figure 4.3). The same group is featured on the blues "Things Are Looking Down," except that a second trumpeter, Jack Sheldon, is added to the lineup. In both cases bassist Buddy Clark shows himself to be a worthy successor to Red Mitchell and Bill Crow, and especially on "Things Are Looking Down" he provides a thoughtful underpinning to the rhythm, melding with Freeman's piano and Bailey's drumming.

It was not until January that the next batch of soundtrack recordings took place, by which time Mulligan had amused himself with another minor movie role, appearing as a bandleader and tenor saxophonist in a screen sequence of a cruise liner's big band in the Debbie Reynolds/Tony Curtis movie *The Rat Race*. His short dialogue scene with Curtis, who is (in a subtle on-screen joke) cast as a baritone player, involves Mulligan trying to dissuade Curtis from writing a love letter in order to come and mingle with the paying customers on the liner. Exasperated by Curtis's reluctance to leave the stand, Mulligan remarks that he'll only employ married musicians in future, as they never take time to write such letters!

Compared to the tight-knit jazz combo of the September recordings, the January and February 1960 *Subterraneans* sessions find Mulligan, Farmer, and Bailey, along with Red Mitchell, in the midst of a sizable Hollywood studio orchestra, albeit with Previn at the piano, plus some additional soloists: trumpeter Jack Sheldon, valve trombonist Bob Enevoldsen, and saxophonists Art Pepper and Bill Perkins. The main title sequence "Why Are We Afraid" is a somewhat stereotypical Hollywood soundtrack, with soaring strings and swelling French horns, but in one of the brief jazz-inflected moments, Mulligan and Pepper exchange phrases, and immediately grab the listener's attention. Pepper's beautiful alto sound sets the scene for "Two by Two," followed by Sheldon, over a bed of strings and an anonymous oboe soloist. As the piece moves into a slightly faster tempo, led by Previn, Mulligan takes a soulful six-measure

FIGURE 4.3 The French album cover for *The Subterraneans* showing a still in which (left to right) the musicians visible are Buddy Clark, Bob Enevoldsen (partially obscured), Mulligan, Art Farmer, and Dave Bailey.

solo. And this, apart from a single descending figure over the strings, is all we hear from him. "A Rose and the End" has a repetitive ostinato from Enevoldsen's trombone and there are brief outings for Pepper, an unidentified clarinetist and a violin solo, but Mulligan only appears momentarily in a vignette for the jazz front line. And for all those months in Hollywood, this is just about all there is of him on the original soundtrack album, though he can be heard on some of the additional cuts that made it to neither the movie nor the originally released record.

During the months that Mulligan was in Hollywood, he began meeting up quite regularly with the great ex-Ellingtonian tenor saxophonist Ben Webster, who was also temporarily on the West Coast. They had previously appeared together with Billie Holiday in the *Sound of Jazz* broadcast, but now they had the opportunity to get know one another better, particularly at several informal jams on weekends at the house where Judy Holliday was staying. Mulligan recalled:

> We did sessions for ourselves frequently on Sundays. I even went to his place many times and met his mother. They were very nice to me. I enjoyed those visits and, of course, I enjoyed the blowing with Ben [that] we did for ourselves at these little jams I would set up for us. We'd even try out some of our new tunes at these little pick-up sessions. This grew into a desire to do something together in public, which we did. . . . Ben and I were a focused, near functioning little band. That's why it worked.[65]

By 1959, Webster had established himself as one of the three great figures in the early development of the tenor saxophone in jazz, along with Coleman Hawkins and Lester Young. His distinctive playing had taken him from early days with Blanche Calloway and Andy Kirk to the orchestras of Cab Calloway and then Duke Ellington. Such was his commanding presence in the 1939–1941 Ellington Orchestra, along with bassist Jimmie Blanton, that this version of Duke's lineup has always been known as the "Blanton-Webster" band. After leaving and then rejoining Duke, Webster then freelanced extensively in the 1950s, prior to moving permanently to Europe in 1964. At the time of his recordings with Mulligan (the first session being on November 3, 1959), in the opinion of writer and producer Nat Hentoff, who had closely followed his career for years, Webster was at "the apex of his career, musically."[66] Hentoff also observed that by this point Mulligan was adept in playing jazz of all periods, so that he richly deserved composer and theorist George Russell's description of him as "Mr. Mainstream." Mulligan himself told the photographer William Claxton, who had documented his Californian career since the Chet Baker days: "I'm finally recording with one of my childhood heroes."[67]

Although the focus of this book is principally on Mulligan's own quartets, this quintet is worthy of attention because the album it

65 Mulligan interviewed by Phil Schaap in 1990, quoted in Marcus, Arnold: *Mulligan Meets Webster*, Masterworks 21349 (2014) [liner note].

66 Hentoff, Nat: *Gerry Mulligan Meets Ben Webster*, Verve MGV 8343 (1960) [liner note].

67 William Claxton quoted in Marcus, Arnold: *Mulligan Meets Webster*, Masterworks 21349 (2014) [liner note to reissue].

produced should be recognized as a masterpiece of small-group jazz. The six tracks that were originally released by Verve in 1960 each stand as exemplary mainstream jazz, but the five additional pieces that finally appeared in the CD era are equally exceptional. In his liner notes to the first release, Nat Hentoff wrote: "when everyone fits this well, the only problem is to have enough tape." Fortunately the tape kept running on both the November and December 1959 sessions.

The opening track of the 1960 LP is "Chelsea Bridge," and beneath Webster's delicate theme statement Mulligan creates the effect of waves or ripples moving on the river below. It is programmatic, but inspired, and sets a mood that runs through the entire track. The other two highlights of the album are an uptempo version of "Sunday" and Mulligan's "Who's Got Rhythm?" Of these, "Sunday" is brought in by pianist Jimmy Rowles in an almost stride style. Then, Mulligan's logical and hard-swinging solo is followed by Rowles, before Webster produces a solo that manages at the same time to be a somewhat abstract rumination on the theme, yet rhythmically compelling. "Who's Got Rhythm?" is a romp over the familiar "I Got Rhythm" chords, the head being a simple contrafact of Gershwin's original. But as well as some fine soloing, there's a moment when the two saxophones take the middle eight between Mel Lewis's drum interludes, and almost spontaneously recreate the brass riff from the last chorus of the 1940 Ellington recording of "Cottontail" in which Webster had been the star soloist. Here and there on the album are similar sly quotations that remind us that Mulligan had listened hard to Webster's prior output, and remembered it in detail.

The tracks that originally lay unreleased contain some gems as well. Webster's knotty original "Fajista" is one, the harmonic logic of Mulligan's opening solo contrasting with the wistful reflection in Webster's more melodic approach. "In a Mellow Tone" shows the entire quintet's familiarity with the original Ellington recording of this song, with Mulligan taking the theme on the head that was originally played by the reeds, while Webster takes the answering phrases of the brass section. But the whole piece sounds spacious whereas the full Ducal version sounds urgent. Webster's gentle, subtle solo takes a diametrically opposite course from Johnny Hodges on the big band recording, and while Hodges seemed then to be aiming to fit in as many notes as he could, Webster manages an equally powerful effect with very few.

There are two blues in this collection, a dramatically slow "For Bessie" credited to Webster, in which his tender, plaintive choruses live up to Hentoff's observation about this being a high point in his work. Mulligan keeps the mood going, and if Norman Granz (who produced the session) had previously complained about the lack of blues in Mulligan's "cerebral" quartet playing, he could have no such issues here. The December 2 recording date rounded off with a lengthy jam on a blues in B flat. Slightly disconcertingly, on the November recording Mulligan was on the left-hand stereo channel and Webster on the right, and their positions were reversed in December, so that on the issued album (which contains takes from both sessions) they appear to be swapping position between tracks. Nonetheless, this is a fine achievement, and markedly more consistent than the previous "Meets" session with Stan Getz, as well as displaying the kind of empathy between the players that only comes from regular playing together.

The record that survives from the quintet's live dates at the Renaissance has the band backing Jimmy Witherspoon on a repertoire that, with two exceptions, consists entirely of twelve-measure blues. It is a showcase for the singer, and his vocals draw out some energetic playing from Rowles and drummer Mel Lewis, as well as some fine backup playing behind his voice from the saxophonists, but it is to be regretted that the instrumental quintet did not get to make a live album of its own. Of its studio album, the eminent critic John S. Wilson summed it up perfectly in his *High Fidelity* review: "It is rare when a flawlessly finished performance of one selection comes out of a recording session. It is almost unheard of to have an entire session remain close to this level of perfection."[68]

Midway between the two studio dates with Webster, Norman Granz flew another Ellingtonian saxophonist out to California to record in what was becoming the *Gerry Mulligan Meets . . .* series. On November 17, Johnny Hodges joined Mulligan, pianist Claude Williamson, bassist Buddy Clark, and drummer Mel Lewis in the United Recorders studio in Hollywood. But whereas the collaboration with Webster was very much a meeting of equals (and that goes for the rhythm section as well), there's a slightly formal atmosphere about this record, and a very slight sense that Mulligan is in awe of Hodges. (Nat Hentoff quotes him in the liner note as saying Hodges had long been one of his idols, since he first picked up an alto saxophone.) This carries over to the rhythm section, although Lewis is at his dependable best and Clark plays as excellently as he does on *The Subterraneans* soundtrack. But Williamson, fine pianist that he is, lacks the easy, relaxed empathy and ability to surprise that Jimmy Rowles constantly displays.

68 Wilson, John S.: "Gerry Mulligan Meets Ben Webster," *High Fidelity*, quoted in Hentoff, Nat: *Gerry Mulligan Meets Johnny Hodges*, Verve MGV 8637 (1961) [liner note].

The result is a good, rather than a great, record. There is one uptempo piece, Mulligan's "18 Carrots for Rabbit," and the rest consists of medium to slow numbers. These include a first outing for Hodges's contrafact of "Sunny Side of the Street," which he called "Shady Side" and is perhaps the best-known piece from the album. But the highlight is a track on which the two principals play to their strengths. "What's the Rush" is a sumptuous ballad, written by Mulligan to lyrics by Judy Holliday (a collaboration that will be discussed further in the next chapter). He does not play on the piece, leaving Hodges to excel as the sole reed player, and the result is one of Hodges's most moving, elegiac solos. It is a reminder that, when he was not suffering from writer's block, Mulligan was still a first-rate composer.

Once filming of *The Subterraneans* was finished, in early February 1960, Mulligan headed back to New York, no longer with a regular quartet but with a new idea entirely.

CHAPTER 5

THE AFTERMATH AND LEGACY

ON HIS RETURN East, following the final February soundtrack recordings with André Previn, instead of reverting to the quartet format, Mulligan took the surprising step of deciding to form a big band. This was not least because he had managed to accrue quite a considerable amount of money during his stay in Los Angeles. While in the city he been on a weekly retainer for *The Subterraneans*, but there had also been session fees for the Webster and Hodges albums, revenue for the two weeks at the Renaissance with Ben Webster and Jimmy Witherspoon, and in particular, quite generous fees for his walk-on screen appearances in *Bells Are Ringing* and the *Rat Race*.

The Gerry Mulligan 1950s Quartets. Alyn Shipton, Oxford University Press. © Alyn Shipton 2023.
DOI: 10.1093/oso/9780197579756.003.0005

It is estimated that he sank around $30,000 of his own money in launching what became known as the Concert Jazz Band (CJB).[1] It would have slightly smaller brass and reed sections than the 1960 convention of four trumpets, four trombones, five reeds, and rhythm. Instead, it would have three trumpets, two trombones (one of them Brookmeyer's valve trombone), and a bass trombone, and in the five reeds (including Mulligan) there would be two baritones, plus two altos and a tenor. The most revolutionary idea in big band terms was not to have a chordal instrument, instead employing the trademark Mulligan rhythm section of just drums and bass. Although he stated that he didn't want the band to be beholden to a financial "angel," his growing association with Norman Granz meant that both through Verve Records and Jazz at the Philharmonic there would be significant monetary rewards available for recording and for concert appearances.

However, the first significant expense that he had to bear himself was to assemble the band, get together a book of arrangements, and organize rehearsals, prior to its first public engagement. The practice sessions took place at Lyn Oliver's studios on the Upper West Side. News of an imminent public debut first appeared in Dorothy Kilgallen's syndicated gossip column on March 26, 1960, when she announced: "Gerry Mulligan is putting together a big band—probably 15 men, plus Gerry's cool baritone sax."[2] The band was always conceived as a smaller unit than this suggests, and seldom grew beyond thirteen players (including Mulligan) but an early Granz press release, mentioning "15-pieces," led to several such mentions in papers and magazines.

The first booking for the group was to start in mid-April at the Basin Street East club in New York City. Mulligan needed arrangements and he needed them fast, so he buried the hatchet with Bob Brookmeyer and roped him in to write and to help organize both the "book" of charts and the rehearsals. Brookmeyer recalled:

> We were not speaking for a couple of years, owing to our domestic dispute, but he dropped by my apartment one day early in 1960 and he had a week at Basin Street for a big band. And he wanted me to write an arrangement of "Bweebida Bobbida." So we talked for a bit.

1 Jack, Gordon: "Gerry Mulligan's Concert Jazz Band: A History," *Jazz Journal*, September 7, 2021 [jazzjournal.co.uk/2021/09/07/gerry-mulligans-concert-jazz-band-a-history/]. $30,000 was equivalent to $280,000 in 2022.

2 Kilgallen, Dorothy: "Gary Crosby Has New Girl Friend," *Dover Daily Reporter*, March 26, 1960, p. 9.

> In the interim, he had tried to hire me away from Jimmy Giuffre, but I'd say, "You got Art Farmer, leave me alone." But this time we had a pretty civil conversation and we talked about what it would be like to work with a larger band and what size it should be, and then I remember him saying in one of our many conversations after that, that the CJB should be an outgrowth of the quartet. In other words we'd not develop from the sextet but the quartet. And that's what it became. It was Gerry and I, and then "them."[3]

While the rehearsals were in progress, Mulligan organized a warm-up gig before the club residency began, with a Sunday night at the Red Hill Inn, Pennsauken, near Camden, New Jersey, on April 3. Charts for the group were also being written by Al Cohn and Bill Holman, and some of these, along with Brookmeyer's, got their first public airing that weekend. Bass trombonist Alan Raph recalled that, more often than not, the band was able to make the transition very rapidly from first reading a chart to playing it at performance standard, owing to the exceptional talent of Brookmeyer. He said:

> Bob not only took the lead, but he had the very rare ability to sight read and come up with a definitive performance during the sight reading itself. Whatever he determined at the first reading of something usually became the way the tune was played. The lead trumpet players used to follow Bob. He just had that kind of insight.[4]

After the Red Hill Inn show, Mulligan brought the band into Basin Street East for two weeks on Thursday the 14th,[5] where, replacing the outgoing acts, singer Chris Connor and comedian Mort Sahl, the CJB shared the billing with another famous name. The press reported: "Sarah Vaughan divided the kudos with Gerry Mulligan, and all present trotted out the wildest adjectives—everything from 'marvelous' to 'sensational.'"[6]

Yet although Mulligan had been leading his quartet (and briefly sextet) since 1952, the added responsibility of fronting what had become a thirteen-piece group was quite different. Plus there was the additional

3 Interview with Bob Brookmeyer, September 2, 2002.

4 Interview with Alan Raph, September 5, 2002.

5 The club's acts were generally booked from Thursday to the following Wednesday. Date confirmed in Wilson, Earl: "The Midnight Earl," *Delaware County Daily Times*, April 20, 1960, p. 26.

6 Kilgallen, Dorothy: "Broadway," *Lowell Sun*, April 19, 1960, p. 18.

pressure of much greater celebrity than hitherto, not least as a consequence of his well-publicized activities in the movies. A typical gossip column account read: "Judy Holliday looked lovingly at her guy, saxophonist Gerry Mulligan, opening at jam-packed Basin Street East . . . and sighed: 'Isn't that the greatest looking music you ever heard?' "[7] And her attendance was not just for the opening night, but every evening of the run.[8]

During this initial Basin Street residency, as well as directing the group, his bandleader duties meant Mulligan had to arrange a swap of musicians, when, owing to prior commitments, tenorist Bill Holman could not see out the engagement, and Zoot Sims had to be brought in to take his place.[9] It seems that both trumpeter Blue Mitchell and tenor saxophonist Charlie Rouse were also briefly in the lineup, but left either just before (or during) the Basin Street gig, so they too had to be replaced.[10] Being both a bandleader and a celebrity meant—just as had been the case when he began seeing Judy Holliday and his social life burgeoned—that there was no time to write. In Bob Brookmeyer's view, this was, to say the least, regrettable. He said:

> To me the tragedy was that he was really a brilliant writer. He had many things that would have developed, that would have been completely new and moved things on, but he wrote one, maybe two pieces for the Concert Jazz Band. But when you are a bandleader, as Thad Jones found out, the first thing to go is your writing, if you are conducting every night, and the next thing to go is your playing, because you're busy conducting and that's a whole other field.[11]

It is to Mulligan's credit that he did not let his own playing suffer, but he was able to pace himself, because as the band was packed with fine soloists, he now played fewer solos across an evening than had been the case in the smaller groups. Mulligan himself regretted that he did not arrange more for this stellar lineup, which initially included trumpeters Don Ferrara and Phil Sunkel, trombonist Wayne Andre (alongside Brookmeyer), and saxophonists Dick Meldonian, Bill Holman, and Gene

7 Wilson: "The Midnight Earl," April 20, 1960, p. 26.

8 Wilson, Earl: "That's Earl Brother," *Decatur Daily*, April 27, 1960.

9 The online Mulligan discography by Gérard Dugelay and Kenneth Hallqvist [pdalbury.files.wordpress.com/2012/09/gm-discography-2011.pdf; accessed May 16, 2021].

10 Jack, Gordon: *Fifties Jazz Talk* (Lanham, MD, Scarecrow Press, 2004) p. 19.

11 Interview with Bob Brookmeyer, September 2, 2002.

Allen. At this point, apart from Gerry himself, drummer Dave Bailey was the sole survivor of the previous year's quartet. Mulligan recalled:

> I wrote very little for that band. Once I started the band it became much more than I ever intended, with a full-time job being a band-leader. It demanded a lot of me in terms of responsibility. Ultimately I had quite a lot of help from Norman Granz, because he made a lot of things possible with that band that I would never have been able to do without him. And that's aside from the fact that he recorded the band. Norman didn't care about bands, but he did that because he knew that I wanted a band.[12]

Despite press reports that ranged from the enthusiastic to the ecstatic, Mulligan himself was not happy with the Concert Jazz Band's opening residency. So despite "making a power play for the spring trade," as one reporter put it,[13] within three weeks of closing on April 27, he moved the band to a new residency at the club that would subsequently be forever identified with the CJB. Dorothy Kilgallen reported:

> He insists his May 17 opening at the Village Vanguard will be the true "debut" of his jazz band and the previous engagement was just a rehearsal. "We weren't ready for Basin St. East and they certainly weren't ready for us," says the candid Gerry.[14]

Opening on a Tuesday, as was customary at the Vanguard, and clearly happier about how things were sounding, Mulligan finally felt the band was ready to record, so on the afternoon of the Saturday of that first week at the club, they cut a double-sided 45 rpm single for Verve at Plaza Sound—the studio on the eighth floor of Radio City Music Hall in midtown Manhattan. The resulting version of Duke Ellington's "I'm Gonna Go Fishin'" (which the Duke had himself recast from his theme for the movie *Anatomy of a Murder*) is the first chance to hear the new band, in a fine arrangement by Bill Holman. By producing this single ahead of any subsequent album, Granz's strategy was that it would stir interest in the band from public and promoters alike.

12 Gerry Mulligan interviewed by Charles Fox, Glasgow Jazz Festival, July 1988.

13 Haimer, Mel: "Reports on . . .," *Las Cruces Sun News*, April 27, 1960, p 4.

14 *Hamilton Daily News Journal*, May 18, 1960, p. 6.

The tempo is faster than Ellington's on the *Feeling of Jazz* album, and in place of Ray Nance's growly introduction, the band launches straight into the piece as a full ensemble. Alan Raph's pedal notes on bass trombone give a distinctive timbre to the opening measures, and remind us of how Mulligan had previously used the tuba in his large band settings. Don Ferrara solos first on trumpet, with the band already doing what it was to do best, building ever more effective backup riffs behind him. A bridge passage alternating the tenor trombones with Raph's bass instrument continues into the first part of Jim Reider's tenor chorus, and then introduces a strong solo from Brookmeyer, before reappearing to launch the final climactic solo from Mulligan. Holman brings the whole band together for the final choruses, demonstrating Mulligan's maxim that "Our band shouts, but it doesn't scream."[15] The band swings in the Basie-ish manner of the Mulligan sextet, but its power, and the way it is used, is more reminiscent of Mulligan's Kenton charts from the time he arrived in California in 1952.

The band was back in the studio at the end of the Vanguard gig, between May 1 and June 3, but none of the tracks it recorded was issued at the time. Two weeks later it was due on the West Coast for the first of several festival appearances that arose as a result of Norman Granz's backing. The press announced:

> An array of jazz talent will appear during the second Annual Los Angeles Jazz Festival at the Hollywood Bowl on June 17 and 18. Among musical groups appearing are Duke Ellington and his orchestra, Steve Allen and his all stars . . . [and] Gerry Mulligan and his 15-piece orchestra.[16]

Going on the road meant that Dave Bailey took the decision at this point to leave the CJB. Playing with and managing Mulligan had been his main job since the birth of the sextet, but now he had begun to make good money playing studio sessions in a variety of styles, much of the management had been taken on by Granz's organization, so he saw no reason to go back on the road. As a result, at Brookmeyer's suggestion, Mulligan invited two musicians who had played on his Johnny Hodges album to join him when the band went to the West Coast—bassist Buddy Clark

15 Jack, Gordon: *Concert in the Rain*, Jazzband EBCD 2129-2 (1996) [liner note].
16 "Jazz Festival Stars Listed," *Oxnard Press Courier*, May 18, 1960, p. 28.

and drummer Mel Lewis. For Brookmeyer, this was a major turning point, and transformed the band. He said:

> It was a lot of fun with Mel. You could do anything with Mel. It was easy. Nick (Travis) and Mel and I ran the band. Gerry was the "Old Man," which is what you call the leader, and anything internal I handled, and then it went down to Nick or Mel but I was second in command in terms of hiring and firing and discipline. So it was very satisfying. I had all the joys of being a bandleader without being one. I'd have been scared to death to stand out in front of the band. I was the alternate bandleader, if Mulligan didn't show up, which happened a couple of times. I was petrified. But normally I had all the goodies without having to be the nervous wreck in front of the band.[17]

After the Hollywood Bowl, the band came back East, and there were more dates at the Red Hill Inn in New Jersey, before the band opened for a week at Pep's in Philadelphia. "General response to Mulligan's aggregation has been one of warm acceptance," wrote local Philly critic Bill Kagler.[18] More worrying was that after the first night of the gig, another member of the band caused a temporary panic by driving off to their hotel with cases containing both all the music and the group's money. This was soon resolved, but at the time it was reported that Mulligan's wayward band member took "everything but his gal, Judy Holliday!"[19]

The Philadelphia week was a warm-up for that year's Newport Jazz Festival, where the CJB was to appear on Friday, July 1. This was the Newport weekend that almost caused the organizers to close it down for good, with far too many people invading the small town for the number of tickets available for the open-air concerts in Freebody Park. It had been bad enough the year before, with critic George Hoefer reporting, "Drunkenness was common, rock 'n' roll blared from the radios of bumper to bumper convertibles, there were fights,"[20] but 1960 was to be far worse, and on the Saturday night there was a near riot.

What saved Mulligan's appearance on the Friday evening from similar rowdiness was the abysmal weather, which put off all but the most dedicated fans. And it is clear from this report that whereas some of the

17 Interview with Bob Brookmeyer, September 2, 2002.

18 Kagler, Bill: "Sounds and Sides," *Delaware County Daily Times*, June 24, 1960, p. 9.

19 Wilson, Earl, "It Happened Last Night," *Defiance News*, June 23, 1960, p. 7.

20 Hoefer quoted in Anderson, E. Wellington: "Jazz 60," *Fairfield Stag*, September 30, 1960.

world's top jazz musicians found the meteorological conditions unfavorable, the CJB remained undeterred:

> Friday Night's performance belonged exclusively to the Gerry Mulligan Big Band—or so it seemed. The Louis Armstrong and Dizzy Gillespie groups were listed on the program, but musically didn't quite make it. Although it poured rain (the beer came later) for the entire duration of the concert, the newly formed Mulligan band didn't sound at all disturbed. With some very good (probably Mulligan and Al Cohn) arrangements, "Sweet and Slow," "Blueport," and the ever-popular "Walkin' Shoes" proved excellent vehicles for the Mulligan baritone and the Bobby Brookmeyer valve trombone.[21]

Fortunately, the US Information Service recorded the concert (which was also broadcast live by Voice of America), and this gives us the chance to hear how the band played toward the close of its formative period, just over three weeks before it made its first full studio album. The opening number "Broadway" is not only a fine start to the set, but it reveals much of the way the band was to operate throughout its life.

Just as Mulligan and Brookmeyer had agreed, it developed the principles of the quartet, and this is clear from Mulligan's opening solo, where for the A sections of the first chorus he is accompanied by just Clark and Lewis, but in the middle eight B section (where normally the quartet's other horn would have added a backing riff or a counterpart to his solo line), the whole band falls in behind him, enriching the tonal palette. In his subsequent chorus, the horns play a simple riff backing. The variety of these riffs, some clearly displaying more arrangement than other more impromptu patterns, enhances all the solos, with the choruses for Gene Quill's mobile alto benefiting in particular. The fully scored segments of the piece are thrilling, exciting big band music, yet overall the effect is unlike any other large band of the time.

The CJB was also not afraid to play a slow, complex arrangement in the open-air setting of Newport, and against the constant sound of heavily falling rain, it makes a fine job of Brookmeyer's sensitive chart of Django Reinhardt's composition "Le manoir de mes rêves." Here the backing for Mulligan's extended solo is fully scored, and shows that, despite the pressures of band leading, his soloing remained acute. His own arrangement of "18 Carrots for Rabbit" that follows is primarily a vehicle

21 Ibid.

for the alto playing of Quill, but the full band sections show—as ever—that Mulligan's own writing could be effectively scaled up for larger forces, just as some his early work had been scaled down for quartet. Toward the end, Buddy Clark plays an excellent bass chorus that (with a few punctuations from Mulligan) immediately reminds us of the smaller lineup. The juxtaposition of the Reinhardt ballad and this uptempo romp also shows that plenty of thought had gone into the sequence of pieces in the band's one-hour set on the festival program. After a hard-swinging mid-tempo account of their recently recorded "I'm Gonna Go Fishin'," the set-closer is a dazzlingly played super-fast version of "Blueport" that leaves the audience yelling for more. (A perfunctory "Utter Chaos" sees the band off stage as the broadcast engineers fade down their mikes.)

While Newport audiences were experiencing riots and fights the following night, the CJB was appearing at that year's Jazz Jamboree at the Lewisohn Stadium in New York, and on Sunday it was a headliner at the Atlantic City Jazz Festival. The following week, it was back for a fortnight's residency at the Village Vanguard. This was to make final preparations for its return to the studio, where it would make a full-length album for Verve at the end of the month. Even if the press's attention toward the band largely concerned its festival appearances rather than its club sets, the Vanguard dates did keep Mulligan in the gossip columns (including a subtle sales pitch for an earlier album):

> Annie Ross may be trying to give Judy Holliday a little competition, real-life style, at any rate she's been turning up nightly to hear Gerry Mulligan perform at the Village Vanguard.[22]

The two weeks at the club, on the back of the festival gigs at the start of July, meant that when the band arrived at Plaza Sound on July 25, it was more than ready to record the album that critic Leonard Feather praised as being by "the best new jazz orchestra of the year."[23] Four tracks were remakes of material the band had first attempted to record at its May–June sessions, and clearly they had now played "Out of This World," "Manoir de mes rêves," "Bweebida Bobbida," and "Sweet and Slow" frequently enough to "own" the material.

22 Kilgallen, Dorothy: *Sarasota News*, July 19, 1960, p. 12.

23 Feather, Leonard: *Gerry Mulligan—The Concert Jazz Band*, Verve MGV V-8388 (1960) [liner note].

The whole album catches the band in fine form, but there's perhaps no better example of what Brookmeyer referred to as: "Gerry and I, and then 'them,'" than Bob's own arrangement of "You Took Advantage of Me." This is clearly a direct outgrowth from the quartet, with long passages of both Mulligan's and Brookmeyer's solos being accompanied by just bass and drums. But the full band moments make a dramatic contrast to these solos. Brookmeyer plays with time, adding solo breaks and (as shown in Example 5.1 from measure 57) including a section where he toys with a linear motif that is repeated over and over. He also produces a huge variety of tone, including growls and smears.

As can be seen in Example 5.2, Mulligan slightly displaces part of his subsequent solo, playing over the end of the eight measures leading into the channel (see measures 128–129) and then emphasizing the upward phrase in measures 137–138, as if that is the first rather than the second measure of the next "A" section, so as to give the impression of alternately stretching and compressing the chord sequence, although in fact he stays perfectly in place. It is a delight to hear the two principals having such fun with this well-known standard.

Granz hastened to release the album he simply called *The Concert Jazz Band*, so that it came out in mid-September, just in time for Mulligan's lengthy tour across the United States, to be followed by an extensive visit to Europe. After another preparatory booking at the Village Vanguard, the opening tour date was the 1960 Monterey Jazz Festival on September 23. Apparently Mulligan had injured an eye and during the last gigs before he set out for the West he was spotted wearing a somewhat piratical eye patch, but this did not inhibit his playing.[24] Reviewing Monterey, with a picture of Mulligan (now without his eye patch) and Quill "drawing record crowds" and looking forward to the next concert in the Bay Area, the *Oakland Tribune* confirmed that the touring personnel exactly corresponded with the band that had cut the album (save for the earlier "I'm Gonna Go Fishin'"):

> Gerry Mulligan's Concert Jazz Band . . . will be introduced to the Bay Area next Thursday night at the Longshore auditorium in San Francisco. The band played last Friday at the Monterey Jazz Festival, and its date in San Francisco is part of a 25-city transcontinental tour that will be followed by a trip to Europe. Like Mulligan's quartet,

24 *Associated Press* report, September 21, 1960, in various papers: Gerry Mulligan is "wearing a patch over an injured eye."

EXAMPLE 5.1 "You Took Advantage of Me" by Richard Rodgers and Lorenz Hart. Part of Brookmeyer's solo in a quartet setting within the Concert Jazz Band, from 1:11 to 1:42 (transcription).

EXAMPLE 5.2 Mulligan's solo with band accompaniment in "You Took Advantage of Me" (transcription).

EXAMPLE 5.2 Continued

which created a sensation in Northern California eight years ago when it played the Blackhawk, the band does not include a pianist. Members are saxophonists Mulligan and Gene Allen, baritones; Zoot Sims, tenor; Dick Meldonian, alto; and Gene Quill alto and clarinet; trumpeters Nick Travis, Don Ferrara and Conte Candoli; trombonists Bob Brookmeyer, Wayne Andre and Alan Raph; bassist Buddy Clark and drummer Mel Lewis. The band, which was organized in New York last spring, is sponsored by Norman Granz of Verve Records, which only this week released its first record, *Gerry Mulligan: The Concert Jazz Band*. The LP is an excellent showcase, the sides demonstrating the band's ability to operate in groovy ("Sweet and Slow"), tenor ("My Funny Valentine"), romantic ("Django's Castle"), and exciting ("Bweebida Bobbida") stylings. The album also discloses some fascinating arrangements and excellent soloists.[25]

25 *Oakland Tribune*, September 25, 1960, p. 116; photo in same edition, p. 26.

The tour (of twenty-five concerts rather than cities) was quite a feat of organization, but as it went on, the band grew ever further in cohesiveness and swing.[26] The publicity was helped by the release of the *Rat Race* and the *Subterraneans* movies in October, as well as a newly issued compilation album on Pacific Jazz of some of Mulligan's best previous work. This buzz of interest not only ensured good attendance, but also allowed him a moment of reflection in an interview published prior to the Tucson concert on October 3. Part of the piece ran:

> Gerry Mulligan . . . is shooting new life into what previously has been regarded as a dying field, that of big bands. . . . At 33 he is regarded as the world's top baritone saxophonist and is a winner of both *Down Beat* and *Metronome* polls. "As you get older, creativity improves," Gerry says. "Contrary to popular belief, jazz is not like athletics. It is not necessarily a young man's game." Mulligan himself is a good example of this, having matured slowly into his present status, in one critic's words, as "the world's most popular living saxophonist."[27]

The man who might well claim to have been "the world's most popular living clarinetist," Benny Goodman, was, by a quirk of fate, to be the next visiting musician to play at the Tucson Auditorium, a week after Mulligan, but his program was somewhat different, consisting of the Mozart and Weber clarinet concerti with the Tucson Symphony Orchestra!

While Mulligan was on the road for this Concert Jazz Band tour, he faced a new crisis on the domestic front. Walter Winchell's gossip column printed rumors of a rift between him and Judy Holliday, but the truth was that she had been unexpectedly hospitalized for an operation on a throat tumor (which turned out to be a harbinger of terminal cancer that set in the following year, eventually leading to her premature death, aged just forty-three, in 1965). Mulligan flew home briefly between the

26 Tour dates included: September 23, Monterey; 24, Empire Room, Hotel Senator, Sacramento; 25, Public Auditorium, Portland; 29, Longshore Auditorium, San Francisco; October 1, Civic Auditorium, Santa Monica; 2, Russ Auditorium, San Diego; 3, Tucson University Auditorium; 7, Music Hall, Kansas City; 9, Kiel Auditorium Opera House, St. Louis; 10, Memorial Auditorium, Louisville; 12, Taft Theatre, Cincinnati; 13, Syria Mosque, Pittsburgh; 14, Memorial Hall, Dayton; 15, Veterans Memorial Building, Columbus; 16, Masonic Hall, Cleveland; 19–23, Sutherland Hotel, Chicago; 29, Hunter College, New York. An additional performance was to be given at Denver, whereas an appearance planned for Seattle was canceled.

27 *Tucson Daily Citizen*, October 1, 1960, p. 15.

Pittsburgh and Chicago dates to spend time with her, before returning for five consecutive nights with the band at Chicago's Sutherland Hotel. The papers—telling of his swift visit to New York—reported: "She's OK after throat surgery."[28]

The Chicago residency stayed in Alan Raph's memory, because the hours and location at this South Side hotel were unusual. He recalled, "We used to start at ten and go until four. And we were on top of the bar in a squeezed-in space."[29]

Mulligan was briefly back home again toward the end of the month when the band played at New York's Hunter College, but twenty-four hours after that concert he was en route to Copenhagen, where the band's three-week European tour began on October 31.[30] Four days later, the band played a very well received show in West Berlin, although bass trombonist Alan Raph recalls the hall being heavily guarded by the German police. He remembers most of the tour's concerts would end with one, if not two encores, but on this occasion, "as soon as we finished the last note, half the audience got up and left. In fact they ran out, because—as we found out later—they were from East Berlin, and they had outstayed their curfew. If they all got back together in a large group, then they had a good chance of explaining themselves!" Yet their very presence in such numbers was strong evidence that Mulligan's reputation had already spread behind the iron curtain.[31]

Parts of the mid-November Milan concert were to appear on a Verve compilation—*Gerry Mulligan and the Concert Jazz Band on Tour*—which also included some tracks from the previous month's American shows. More instructive are the two virtually complete concerts, recorded a few days later than the Milan date, in Basel and Paris, that give us an opportunity to see how the mature band compared to its opening Newport appearance.

A track such as "Motel" from Basel shows, in particular, how fluent and deft the rhythm section had become. Lewis's playing drives the whole ensemble forward, and Clark walks his way through a hard-swinging couple of choruses. The ensemble work is also tight and disciplined, which is remarkable when one considers the somewhat random

28 Reports include *Chicago Tribune*, October 20, 1960, p. 18; *Decatur Daily*, October 31, 1960, p. 3.

29 Interview with Alan Raph, September 5, 2002.

30 Tour dates: October 31, Copenhagen; November 1, Stockholm; 2, Gothenburg; 4, West Berlin; 5, Amsterdam; 8, Düsseldorf; 11, Frankfurt; 12, Munich; 14, Milan; 17, Basel; 19, Paris.

31 Interview with Alan Raph, September 5, 2002.

appearance of the actual sheet music the band was working from. For example, having examined some of the arrangements, the introductory section of Gene Quill's part has the penciled note "mess around," but by now it is unlikely the bandmembers even looked at their music. The other highlight of this Swiss concert is Zoot Sims's extended solo on Bill Holman's chart for "Apple Core," his playing being uninhibited and technically excellent, and a brief stop-time section drawing applause from the crowd in mid-solo.

The Paris concert has its highlights, too. There's a thrill of recognition from the audience as the band launches into Johnny Mandel's "Black Nightgown," originally included in the *I Want to Live!* soundtrack. The band plays this with just the right jaunty swagger to bring it freshly to life. Mulligan himself is on good form on the ballads, "Body and Soul" and particularly "Come Rain or Come Shine," as well as one of the band's best recordings of "My Funny Valentine," where the backings (including glimpses of Gene Quill's clarinet amid the lower reeds and brass) produce a slightly sinister atmosphere that breaks completely free from the earlier influential quartet recording of the piece with Chet Baker. And from the uptempo pieces, "Bweebida Bobbida" comes into its own, with a fine authoritative performance and an extended solo from Mulligan, its history stretching right back to his earliest days as a writer and soloist.

Just ten days after returning from France, the band opened at the Village Vanguard for a two-week residency. If nothing else, the consistently excellent European concerts by the band (as evidenced by its broadcasts and recordings) had convinced Mulligan that the next Verve album ought to be in a live setting rather than a studio. At first glance, the cramped, almost triangular shape of the Village Vanguard on 7th Avenue in New York City might seem quite a challenging place to record so large a band. It had first been used for a live recording exactly three years before, with Sonny Rollins's trio. But whereas the club's intimate stage proved ideal to record a small group of tenor saxophone, bass, and drums, just as would be the case for Bill Evans's famous piano trio recordings in 1961, a thirteen-piece band, even though it had worked there several times, would be a challenge for the sound engineers. Alan Raph remembered: "The Village Vanguard was kinda crowded, although it later became a venue for even larger bands!"[32] Yet the very proximity of the musicians and their familiarity with the venue worked in their favor. Mulligan knew that Norman Granz would give him the option of taping

32 Alan Raph interview, September 5, 2002.

practically the entire duration of the residency, in order to pick the best moments, but ultimately this is not what he chose to release, as journalist Tony Winther reported:

> Although several nights of music were recorded, Mulligan decided to select the final takes from one Sunday afternoon, in order to maintain a consistency of mood. Mulligan's decision to record on location was taken with full realization of the hazards as well as the advantages of "in person" recording. "There are times," he explains, "when a few things may go wrong in such a performance, but when conditions are right, the band can achieve more vivid presence and can create more spontaneous excitement than in a studio. In that extended piano blues, for example, that closes the second side, we did many things on the spur of the moment that we'll never do again in quite that way. We fell into a romping, rocking 'head' arrangement that we all enjoyed enormously and that feeling is captured here."[33]

There was another reason why this residency became a special opportunity for the band to play at its best, and this was due to two changes of personnel. On the return from Europe, Conte Candoli left the trumpet section to be replaced by Clark Terry (who had quit Duke Ellington's band the previous year after almost a decade). At the same time, Buddy Clark opted to return to the West Coast to resume being a studio musician, and was replaced by Bill Crow, who probably understood Mulligan's music better than any other bassist. Crow himself recalled why several ingredients came together to make the Village Vanguard recordings exceptional:

> Bob was the musical straw boss. In a kind of an odd way, everybody played more for Bob than they did for Gerry. There was something about his sense of what was right, and his high ideals and his high standards, so that everybody used him as the sounding board to see if they were playing up to the level that they were hoping they were. And the band really benefited from the fact that there was a good riff-maker in each section: Clark and Brookmeyer and Gerry. And so our routine on most rhythm tunes was that once somebody was into their solo, you didn't go on to the next section until Gerry gave you the

33 Winther, Tony: "Record Review," *Nampa Free Press* (Idaho), June 10, 1961, p. 20 [quoting Mulligan from Nat Hentoff's liner note].

signal, because there were always possibilities. In the first place Gerry loves to play backgrounds, as he does with the quartet, so the rest of the saxophone section would harmonize with what he was playing as a background, and turn it into a riff. And right away, either Clark or Bob would think of something that was a good counterbalance to that in the brass, so we might end up with a whole new section that hadn't been written. It'd be the outgrowth of somebody's solo and it'd mean the solo could go on for two or three more choruses, before Gerry would give us the signal that would take us back to the next written section.[34]

A case in point is "Blueport," which opens the album and features a bebop-flavored trombone solo from Willie Dennis backed by a succession of spur-of-the moment riffs. The rhythm team of Crow and Lewis are, as Nat Hentoff says in his liner note, "firmly integrated and glowing,"[35] not just as they push the band forward from Dennis's solo into Jim Reider's tenor choruses (which also have plenty of spontaneous riffs), but also as they continue into Crow's solo and then back a series of exchanges between Mulligan and Clark Terry that include stop time as each soloist picks up from the other. In Terry, Mulligan had finally found the ideal trumpeter to counterbalance his and Brookmeyer's solo invention. The swapping between trumpet and baritone is utterly thrilling and some of the most exciting music Mulligan ever produced, a feeling intensified when the full ensemble returns and plays some knotty figures leading into the coda.

The arrangement of "Come Rain or Come Shine" from this record was by Mulligan himself. "Gerry didn't do a lot of arrangements for the band," recalled Raph, "but each one he did was really, really special and this was one of them. He was as close to genius as I will ever see. His playing was extraordinary, but his writing was incredibly good. It was beyond extraordinary."[36] The Vanguard version of this chart is even more sensitive and nuanced than the Paris recording of November 19. The intimate setting of the club allows Mulligan to play at a lower volume than usual throughout his extended solo, and the band comes down to meet

34 Interview with Bill Crow, September 4, 2002.

35 Hentoff, Nat: *Gerry Mulligan and the Concert Jazz Band at the Village Vanguard*, HMV CSO 1396 (1961) [liner note].

36 Interview with Alan Raph, September 5, 2002.

him, the voicings and the supporting lines creating a perfect cushion for his tender tone.

On the record this contrasts dramatically with the following track, Al Cohn's lively, irreverent "Lady Chatterley's Mother." It had originally been called "Mother's Day" but it was retitled by Mulligan, following the previous month's globally publicized trial in Britain at which, after six days of deliberation at London's Old Bailey, the jury decided that D. H. Lawrence's novel *Lady Chatterley's Lover* was not obscene.[37] Unusually for this normally sober and restrained criminal court, the public gallery burst into spontaneous applause when the judge, Mr. Justice Byrne, announced the decision, and Cohn's chart catches this joyous irreverent mood that was a bellwether for the decade that would become the "swinging sixties." The boisterous final shout chorus of this piece is a rare example of Mulligan adding to an arrangement, rather than trimming it back. According to Bill Crow, he felt something was missing when the band first ran down the chart, so Cohn gathered in the parts and at the next rehearsal, came in with a new final section. It is proof that Mulligan's rehearsals did not always require an eraser!

This LP's version of "Black Nightgown," in contrast to the Paris recording, includes a short cameo for Clark Terry (between solos for Mulligan and Brookmeyer that keep alive the idea of the quartet basis for the CJB) on which he plays flugelhorn. This was picked up by the press, which reported, regarding the club residency, that: "Carl [*sic*] Terry was playing beautiful notes on the flugelhorn, of all things." But we also learn that "Mr. Gerry Mulligan was wearing a tomato red shirt to match his new beard," an image that presaged his future appearance.[38] More significantly, despite his ravishing playing, this album was made at a very tough time for him personally, as we learn from another report that reads: "Those watching Gerry Mulligan's brilliant display of musicianship at the Village Vanguard wouldn't guess that he's quite a sad fellow off stage. He's mourning the death of his father, and plenty worried about Judy Holliday's illness."[39]

1961 began with Mulligan again topping the *Playboy* poll as the previous year's best baritone saxophonist.[40] Nonetheless, he took time out from bandleading in the early months of the year, to spend time with

37 "The Innocence of Lady Chatterley," *Evening Standard* (London), November 2, 1960, p. 1.

38 Sylvester, Robert: "Dream Street," *Sarasota News*, December 13, 1960, p. 8.

39 *Sarasota News*, December 16, 1960, p. 12.

40 UPI, "Frank, Ella Named Top Vocalists," *Columbus Daily Telegram*, January 12, 1961, p. 15.

Judy Holliday as she continued to convalesce. But this did not stop him from showing up for the occasional jam session around town, and she apparently "sat in the audience and beamed" when he joined the band on stage for a set at Birdland in February.[41] The same month he turned up at the Embers with Holliday, still sporting the beard that had been remarked upon during December's Vanguard sessions.[42]

In March, clean-shaven again (at Holliday's request), he reassembled the CJB, still with Clark Terry in its ranks, for a short residency at the Vanguard, prior to appearing at the first Fort Lauderdale Jazz Festival in Florida, which George Wein's organization had hurriedly put together when the City Council at Newport withheld permission for a permit allowing that year's festival there.[43] (It turned out that a truce was subsequently brokered, on the basis that henceforth the Newport festival would have a new and different production team.) Mulligan's band (reduced down to a sextet for some sets) was in Florida for a week, and it came back to the New York area at the end of March, returning to its old haunt of the Red Hill Inn for a weekend of concerts.

Most of April was spent on a vanity project in which members of Mulligan's CJB formed the basis of a studio orchestra to record an album backing up Judy Holliday's vocals. Bringing in a French horn section and adding a piano turned the band into something resembling a Broadway show orchestra or a Hollywood studio aggregation. Although Mulligan proved that he could write convincingly in that style—providing some rather lush settings for some of Holliday's own maudlin lyrics—it must have been a relief for the musicians when the band returned to its normal work, with a two-week residency at Birdland, starting on May 11.[44] By this time Clark Terry had left, and another distinctive trumpeter, Doc Severinsen, had taken his place. However, following the death of his father and Holliday's illness on the previous residency there, this time Mulligan was once again distracted from his bandleading duties by more bad news on the domestic front, when Holliday's mother was badly injured in an automobile accident. He spent time between sets at the club dashing to the Roosevelt Hospital to be with mother and daughter.[45] That

41 Wilson, Earl: "Broadway," *Lowell Sun*, February 14, 1961, p. 26.

42 Wilson, Earl: "Midnight Earl" *Delaware County Times*, February 24, 1961 p. 10.

43 "Annual Jazz Festival to Move to Florida," *Richmond Collegian*, February 24, 1961, p. 4.

44 "Gerry Mulligan and His Big Band Swing into Birdland on Thursday Night," *Uniontown Morning Herald*, May 3, 1961, p. 13.

45 Kilgallen, Dorothy: "Broadway," *Salt Lake Tribune*, May 8, 1961, p. 14.

same month, the first press reports signaled that the days of the Concert Jazz Band were numbered:

> Gerry Mulligan, whose "concert band" is packing Birdland with hipsters, gave out with some bluesy news at the jazz club last night. Gerry disclosed that he'll break up the big orchestra in mid-July, and devote most of his time to writing. There aren't enough cafés around the nation that can afford to pay the price for his "concert crew."[46]

And indeed that is what he did, although in a subsequent press interview with columnist Earl Wilson, despite being firm about his decision, he left the door open for re-forming the band at some future point. The key reason behind his decision was that at the end of 1960, Verve had changed hands.[47] Norman Granz had sold the label to MGM, and apart from honoring the contract to make one further LP, the record company's financial underpinning that the group's recordings had enjoyed would no longer be available.

Nonetheless, during June, the CJB kept busy, playing weekend sessions at Westbury, Long Island; at the Freedomland Park in the Bronx; and on the Harlem Jazz Festival. And on Sunday, July 2, the band headlined at a much scaled-down Newport Jazz Festival, under the new management of Sid Bernstein and John Drew. It shared a program with Art Blakey, George Shearing, and Sarah Vaughan. Shedding a little light on the make-up of the audience, one report (amid photographs of the tight security imposed to prevent the previous year's disturbances) mentioned that twenty-seven members of the Gerry Mulligan fan club of Scranton, Pennsylvania, had arrived together in five automobiles, to attend his concert. "They have been his followers for many years. Not one of the 27 is under 35 years old. All are women."[48]

A few days after that, following a television broadcast by the band on the *PM East* "Jazz for Squares" show, the group went into New York's

46 *Hamilton Daily News Journal*, May 25, 1961, p. 10.

47 The sale went through in the third week of November, and MGM paid $2.5 million, although Verve had amassed considerable loans, borrowing almost $75,000 from its distributors alone. Shortly after the deal, and at almost the moment that Mulligan finished the 1960 Vanguard residency that Verve recorded, Granz left for his new home in Switzerland, and (until he later founded Pablo) left the record business. More details in Havers, Richard: *Verve—the Sound of America* (London, Thames and Hudson, 2013) pp. 285–287.

48 *Newport Daily News*, July 3, 1961, p. 3.

Webster Hall studio to record the Verve album *A Concert in Jazz*, produced by Jim Davis. This would be the last time it was together until April the following year. Ironically, just days after it temporarily broke up, the CJB won "Big Band of the Year" in the *Downbeat* annual critics' poll.[49]

Earlier in the year, Mulligan had devoted himself to writing virtually the entire album for Judy Holliday, but for these new CJB sessions he found neither the time nor the inclination to produce more than one new chart, and that, "Summer's Over," had originally been written to Holliday's lyrics. Yet, as he told his friend Gene Lees, who was the editor of *Downbeat* at the time:

> If I haven't written much for the big band I've always been clear about what I wanted the writing to be like. I made my taste the criterion in my approach to the band, and usually if I made myself explicit to the arrangers, they were happier, because they knew the restrictions within which they could work. But I wanted to keep freedom in it too, to permit the guys to improvise patterns, riffs and the like in ensemble behind the soloist.[50]

The best example on the new album of this approach is the almost ten-minute version of George Russell's "All about Rosie," which the composer himself rearranged especially for the recording.

"I asked George to write something for the band," said Mulligan, "and when he turned in 'All About Rosie,' I almost died." Gerry felt that there could not have been a better reading than the CJB version (apart from the composer's own definitive 1957 record from Brandeis with Bill Evans as the featured piano soloist). Mulligan envisioned the three parts of the composition, developed from a children's ditty, as "Rosie's Early Life," "Rosie's Blues," and "Rosie Steps Out," and he mused: "The way George wrote it for us, Rosie's grown up."[51] Russell himself felt that in the American scene of the time there was a prevailing attitude that "jazz musicians could not write extended works," so he set out to prove that it was possible.[52] Having the opportunity to revisit "All about Rosie" was a very welcome development for him.

49 Winchell, Walter: *Burlington Daily Times*, July 25, 1961, p. 4.

50 Lees, Gene: *Meet Me at Jim and Andy's* (New York, Oxford, 1988) p. 224.

51 Cerulli, Dom: *Gerry Mulligan Presents a Concert in Jazz*, Verve 2304 424 (1961) [liner note].

52 Interview with George Russell, October 31, 2010.

The Concert Jazz Band re-formed sporadically, including a short club engagement in 1962 and recording an album in late 1963, but Bill Crow succinctly summed up the change, "We weren't the family we once were. We lost the continuity and the feeling of commitment . . . the band wasn't the center of our lives any more."[53]

Having made the decision that the CJB would fold in July 1961 (which involved pulling out of some contracted later dates), Mulligan stayed out of the limelight until early 1962, apart from a handful of freelance recordings and gigs as a soloist. When he did return to playing and bandleading, it was once again with a quartet, featuring Bob Brookmeyer, Bill Crow, and the former Count Basie drummer Gus Johnson. The first reports of this appeared in February:

> Gerry Mulligan who announced a few months ago that he was moving out of the nightclub field to concentrate on writing, goes back into the jazz scene February 13, when he opens at the Village Vanguard with his quartet.[54]

This new Mulligan quartet (with some occasional substitutions of bassist and drummer) would be his main band throughout 1962 and it is the summation of everything that he had achieved in his four-piece bands of the 1950s. We have a snapshot of the Vanguard date in a version of "I Know, Don't Know How" that was recorded there on February 25, which is the only surviving track from two nights at the club captured on tape for a new Verve album *The Gerry Mulligan Quartet*.[55] The ever-swinging Gus Johnson, showing off his Basie credentials, provides excellent support, his brushwork backing Mulligan and a move to sticks (emphasizing the offbeat) prompts Brookmeyer into some highly effective playing—both in the sense that it connects with the audience but also that it contains smears, growls, and a huge dynamic range. Both horns back Crow's eloquent bass solo, but the highlight in the track is the final part of Mulligan's solo (see Example 5.3), in which his chiseled phrases and Brookmeyer's underpinning seem more composed than improvised.

Following the Vanguard dates, the quartet spent a week at the Showboat in Philadelphia and another at Baker's Keyboard Lounge in Detroit. But perhaps its most interesting work was to improvise the background

53 Crow, Bill: *From Birdland to Broadway* (New York, Oxford, 1992) p. 183.

54 Kilgallen, Dorothy: "Broadway," *Lowell Sun*, Jan 24, 1962, p. 34.

55 Verve LP MG V-6 8466.

EXAMPLE 5.3 Part of Mulligan's solo on "I Know, Don't Know How" (transcription from 2:13 to 2:54).

music in real time for the soundtrack of a live television play. This was the *DuPont Show of the Week*, "The Action in New Orleans," which went out on network television on April 4, and was billed as a comedy romance set in the Crescent City in 1928. It starred Bob Cummings as a confidence man and Audrey Meadows as "a lively Ohio widow."[56] One advantage of the long experience of this Mulligan-Brookmeyer quartet and its capacity for building collective improvisations out of very little was that it was ideally suited to the spontaneous addition of music to a drama. The press reports ran:

> Mulligan and his quartet, which consists of himself on baritone saxophone, Bob Brookmeyre [*sic*] on trombone, Bill Crow on bass and Gus Johnson on drums, located themselves in a sound studio with a clear view of the actors and sets of "The Action In New Orleans," and improvised the entire score from themes that Mulligan had earlier composed. The Mulligan improvisation is sustained for nearly all of the program's entire 54 minutes of running time (excluding commercials). Said Mulligan: "We started playing around 1:30 in the afternoon for the run-through and dress rehearsal, and didn't stop until close to midnight, when taping concluded." Producer Lewis Freedman added: "This was frankly an experiment, but we think a good one."[57]

By the time this television recording had been aired, rumors were rife that the Concert Jazz Band was to be re-formed. One report ran "Gerry Mulligan on tour with his quartet is in a mood to organize a big band again next month. Pals say Gerry is in love with that big band sound, and just can't seem to be happy without it."[58] But in the event, the band (slightly enlarged to include both Clark Terry and Doc Severinsen in the trumpet section) played just a couple of weeks at Birdland in New York in late April, and a half dozen tracks were eventually issued by the indefatigable bootlegger Boris Rose on his Alto label, with material recorded off air during a broadcast from the club.[59] More problematic for Mulligan, as soon as the Birdland reunion ended, was that his quartet was contracted to complete the recording for Verve that had begun at the Vanguard in

56 Pat Hinton: "Highlights," *Altoona Mirror*, April 14, 1962, p. 9.

57 "Gerry Mulligan Provides Jazz Background in Show," *Gastonia Gazette*, April 14, 1962, p. 13.

58 *Oswego Palladium Times*, March 12, 1962, p. 7.

59 *Gerry Mulligan Provocative Tones* (Alto ALP 717).

FIGURE 5.1 The album cover (Verve V-8466) that triggered the recording session.

February. (See Figure 5.1.) However, a purely practical issue threatened its timely completion. His difficulty was summed up in this report:

> Gerry Mulligan called his quartet into a rush recording session to salvage a record cover. His bassist, Bill Crow, decided to join Benny Goodman's Russian tour, and they had to make the disc before he took off, because his picture was on the album cover.[60]

The recording sessions took place on May 14 and 15, by which time Crow was dividing his time between Goodman and Mulligan. The reassembled Goodman big band had begun to rehearse in New York on April 14, and then made a national TV broadcast in *The Bell Telephone*

60 "Rush Recording," *Salt Lake Tribune*, May 21, 1962, p. 22.

Hour on April 25, just as Crow began his two weeks at Birdland with Mulligan's Concert Jazz Band. (Mel Lewis was also dividing his time between the two bands.) Then came a series of more intensive rehearsals with Benny in New York, so the Mulligan Quartet record date had to be squeezed in just before Goodman left to play preparatory gigs in Chicago, St. Louis, and San Francisco, prior to opening for six nights at the Seattle World's Fair on May 20.[61] His band was then scheduled to fly "out of Seattle and over the Pole to Moscow, May 27."[62]

Crow's short-term contract with Goodman was only for the six-week Russian visit, plus the warm-up gigs and World's Fair. It was agreed that he would rejoin Mulligan soon after his return, not least because Norman Granz had booked the Mulligan Quartet for a fall tour of Europe under the JATP umbrella, and, even though Granz had sold the Verve label, it made sense to travel with the same lineup as the one featured on the new album.

The May recording session produced five usable tracks, although several more were recorded. Interestingly Mulligan's sole new composition for the album was "Love in New Orleans," developed from one of the thematic elements he had written for the *DuPont Show of the Week* television broadcast in April. The melody has an air of familiarity, but the structure is slightly unusual in that it runs AABBA plus a two-measure tag. The other "new" piece credited to Mulligan, "Piano Train," is simply a twelve-measure blues, played at the keyboard by Brookmeyer, who proves that he remained a more adept pianist than Mulligan, whose "Piano Blues" had been a frequent item on CJB programs and can be heard (mistitled "Spring Is Sprung") in a twenty-one-minute version on the larger band's record from the Olympia in Paris. In particular, Brookmeyer's lightness of touch works well with the rhythm team of Crow and Johnson. The piano choruses that follow Mulligan's first baritone solo are reminiscent of the minimal style of Johnson's former boss Count Basie, and the drumming makes quite a contrast from that of Bailey or Lewis. On more than one occasion, piano phrases are echoed in passing on the snare, giving a constant percussion commentary on the piece, yet proving that overall Johnson is a masterly swing and mainstream drummer.

61 Dates from Smith, Chris: *View from the Back of the Band: The Life and Music of Mel Lewis* (Denton, University of North Texas Press, 2014) p. 92; and Firestone, Ross: *Swing Swing Swing: The Life and Times of Benny Goodman* (London, Hodder and Stoughton, 1993), p. 410.

62 *Kingsport News*, April 24, 1962, p. 4.

The album introduced some fresh quartet repertoire alongside "Love in New Orleans," of which Kurt Weill's "Lost in the Stars" is the standout, its theme stated by Brookmeyer and showing just why the CJB members thought so highly of his instinct for phrasing. The song was the title number of a show that had a short Broadway run in 1949, but must have been in the minds of the quartet in 1962, because the conductor Julius Rudel had just released a recording of the full score with the New York–based Orchestra of St. Luke's. This understated performance is a perfect example of Mulligan's final quartet from the period covered by this book (see Example 5.4). Both horns solo, but the closing choruses with phrases passing between them, sometimes spontaneously playing in unison, their complex rhythmic ideas frequently almost telepathically echoed by Crow, before leading to a tranquil coda, show a level of maturity and depth greater than any of the band's previous work. The mood continues into Brookmeyer's rhapsodic statement of Frank Loesser's song "I Believe in You" from the show *How to Succeed in Business without Really Trying*, which was about a quarter way through its 1,417-night run on Broadway when the album was cut.

Once the record was finished, Mulligan had to find a temporary replacement for Bill Crow, and the choice was Wyatt Ruther, an old colleague of Bob Brookmeyer's, who had most recently been with the George Shearing Quintet and the Buddy Rich Orchestra. He joined Mulligan in Washington for both a concert and Voice of America broadcast in early June, and later in the month they played at the 3rd Festival of New York City. Between quartet gigs, Mulligan had started work both on a sequel to his earlier album with Paul Desmond, and on a specially assembled studio quintet session for Columbia, with Tommy Flanagan on piano, and his old colleague Dave Bailey on drums.

In early July, the Quartet with Ruther, Brookmeyer, and Johnson played at Newport, and for one set, the group was joined by Coleman Hawkins. (This proved sufficiently successful that they repeated the partnership at a festival in Cincinnati in late August.) Newport audiences also saw Mulligan appearing in a quartet with Paul Desmond, and sitting in with Dave Brubeck (maybe a harbinger of his later association with Dave in the late 1960s from the time of their *Compadres* album).

Immediately after Newport, the Mulligan Quartet set off for the West Coast via Las Vegas and in late July appeared both on Ralph Gleason's television show and another *Navy Swings* broadcast. Back in the East, they spent early August at Basin Street West in New York, also appearing the same month at the city's Museum of Modern Art, by which time Bill

EXAMPLE 5.4 "Lost in the Stars," part of the final chorus (transcription).

Crow had rejoined, after his eventful stay with Goodman.[63] Then it was off to California for the Monterey Festival in September, where Mulligan again appeared with Paul Desmond as well as with his own quartet.

63 Summarized in Crow, Bill: *From Birdland to Broadway* (New York, Oxford, 1992) p. 195ff.

EXAMPLE 5.4 Continued

At the beginning of October, the band set off for its European tour, sharing the bill with Horace Silver's quintet, and starting on October 6 in Paris.[64] (See Figure 5.2.) The evening house of this first concert at

64 The tour dates were: October 6, Paris; 7, Berlin (according to Bill Crow this did not happen owing to Russian aircraft preventing Western flights into the city); 8, Copenhagen; 10, Gothenburg; 11, Stockholm; 12, Düsseldorf; 17, Munich; 18, Zurich; 20, The Hague (matinee) and Amsterdam (evening).

FIGURE 5.2 Publicity photo for the 1962 European Tour. © Bill Crow. Used by permission.

L'Olympia was recorded by Norman Granz, and subsequently released on his Pablo label. It would be hard to disagree with jazz historian Robert Gordon, who wrote that by this point "Mulligan and Brookmeyer . . . had developed an almost superhuman ability to read each other's mind."[65] This is apparent at the start of their set, as they ease from a simple repeated introductory phrase into the main theme of "Open Country," their swapping of the melodic lines more relaxed and spontaneous sounding than on earlier versions. Johnson's drumming here is ideally suited to the band and his brushwork is urgent and propulsive, knitting perfectly with

65 Gordon, Robert: *The Gerry Mulligan Quartets in Concert*, Pablo PACD 5309-2 (2001) [liner note].

Crow's flowing bass lines. Johnson's transition to sticks is almost unnoticeable, and his hi-hat work behind Brookmeyer's tonally wide-ranging solo again recalls his Basie experience. "Love in New Orleans" from the quartet's then current album gets a fine, confident outing, after which comes a recently composed jazz waltz by Mulligan, "Four for Three," that the quartet had been playing on live concerts since around the time of Newport. The set closes with a lengthy "Subterranean Blues," adapted by Mulligan from André Previn's "Things Are Looking Down," written for *The Subterraneans*. This has Brookmeyer on piano, and as well as providing a thoughtful and inventive backing for Mulligan, the pianist draws creatively on ideas of dissonance in his solo.

Although several of the European concerts were broadcast, the only other one to have been issued at the time of writing is the Zurich evening from close to the end of the tour. Here "Open Country" benefits from a fine solo by Bill Crow that his fellow bassist Jimmy Woode compared favorably to the work of the masterly Milt Hinton.[66] The Swiss Radio engineers did a splendid job of capturing the sound of the quartet and particularly on this piece, and in the version of "Love in New Orleans" that follows we hear every nuance of the performance in studio quality. Again, on the latter, alongside fine solos from the horns, Crow produces a show-stopping solo.

The following number "17 Mile Drive" was another recent Mulligan composition that the band had been developing while on the road, and it moves at a brisk tempo, with Mulligan producing some of his most exciting baritone playing of the night. Then Mulligan and Brookmeyer take turns at the piano on back-to-back twelve-measure pieces, "Subterranean Blues" and "Spring Is Sprung," before Mulligan produces one of his best pieces of pianism to date on a measured version of "Darn That Dream." The set closer is a very speedy rendition of "Blueport" that stands as perhaps the finest example of this particular quartet, not least because of Johnson's uninhibited drumming. Every member of the band solos with dazzling accomplishment, and the rapport between Mulligan and Brookmeyer is so close and telepathic that they barely sound like the same musicians as on their Parisian Salle Pleyel recordings from eight years before. This flamboyant recording could not be a greater contrast to the comparative restraint of the 1952–1953 Chet Baker edition of the quartet, with the whole band here playing with extrovert flair, and displaying no notion whatsoever of "West Coast cool." It is, as Jimmy

66 Woode, Jimmy: *Gerry Mulligan Quartet: Zurich 1962*, TCB 02092 (1997) [liner note].

Woode commented, "a don't-hold-me-back blues," propelled by "one of the most heralded straightahead swingers of all time" on drums.[67]

After a couple of weeks' break, the band went into the Village Vanguard for a fortnight in November, before reassembling at New York's A and R Studios in mid-December to make their final recording of 1962. *The Gerry Mulligan Quartet—Spring Is Sprung* was cut for the Dutch Philips label, and largely consists of studio versions of the repertoire the group had recently been playing in Europe. An exception is the opening track—an arrangement of the Sweets Edison/Count Basie piece "Jive at Five." It is a fine example of mainstream swing, which harks back to the style of the first California concerts by the Sextet. The rest of the repertoire is well played and polished, but it lacks the spark of the Zurich concert. "17 Mile Drive," for instance, has a strong Brookmeyer solo, but this time around, Mulligan sounds more considered than spontaneous. Yet when this album was released it was the only available example of the band's mature late 1962 work, and was praised at the time for its "Joie de vivre and vivacity" and being "live wire entertainment."[68] Another review observed that in his "more traditional approach to jazz," Mulligan's "style, that was once challenging, is the accepted norm."[69]

This was no mean achievement. The band retained what *Time* had called, in 1953, its mix of the "rich and orderly" with "tumbling with bell-over-mouthpiece impromptu,"[70] yet now there was also a combination of experience and sophistication about the quartet that had grown steadily with the passing years. The ups and downs of Mulligan's and Brookmeyer's personal relationship had not prevented their professional association from maturing and deepening with the years, and it is clear from comments recorded earlier in this book that both saw the Sextet and the Concert Jazz Band as outgrowths from the Quartet, which remained at the core of their musical partnership.

The quartet with Brookmeyer, Crow, and Johnson would continue into early 1963, including a tour to the UK (for which Dave Bailey rejoined). There would be further sporadic reunions in the years that followed. The Concert Jazz Band (with a few changes in personnel) was also reassembled in the studio in December 1962 to make a further album. But in recording terms, the "1950s Quartet" finished its output

67 Ibid.

68 Levy, Dick: "Records in Review," *Westport Town Crier*, May 9, 1963, p. 54.

69 "Jazz Approach Varies Widely," *Lake Charles American Press*, June 4, 1963, p. 33.

70 "Counterpoint Jazz," *Time*, February 2, 1953.

with the *Spring Is Sprung* album, and reached its high point with the 1962 Zurich concert. In its ten-year life, Mulligan's "pianoless" quartet created a new genre of music, and settled into a style that is now best thought of as "mainstream," drawing on the new developments in jazz of the late 1940s and early 1950s to be sure, but never losing straight-ahead rhythmic energy and swing. From the outset, the band was racially mixed, and for the greater part of its life, this remained the case. Even if some of his decisions were somewhat last-minute, Mulligan always selected the musicians he believed to be the best for the group at the time, irrespective of social or ethnic background.

Much of this book has explored the contrapuntal musical relationship between Mulligan and his frontline quartet partners, Chet Baker, Bob Brookmeyer, Jon Eardley, and Art Farmer (as well as Lee Konitz and Paul Desmond, on occasion). There is no doubt that each of these partners saw their responsibility as being to create melodic lines that integrated and intertwined with those of one of jazz's most inventive soloists, arrangers, and composers. And there is no better conclusion to this book than a passage that Jimmy Woode quoted from a letter to Mulligan from Brookmeyer, written shortly before Mulligan's death in 1996. He said:

> I often get asked by interviewers what it was like to play in the quartet with you, and the answer has not changed in the last 42 years. "It felt like playing with Bach." And indeed it did.[71]

71 Woode: *Gerry Mulligan Quartet: Zurich 1962.*

ACKNOWLEDGMENTS

Firstly, thanks are due to all those fellow musicians or musical associates of Gerry Mulligan who were kind enough to spend time talking to me about his life and work: Dave Bailey, Bob Brookmeyer, Dave Brubeck, Bill Crow, Henry Grimes, Jim Hall, Chico Hamilton, Peter Ind, Lee Konitz, John Lewis, Alan Raph, Shorty Rogers, Annie Ross, Bobby Short, Clark Terry, and Jimmy Woode. Equally, the following record producers were generous with their time and comments: George Avakian, Ira Gitler, Orrin Keepnews, and Bob Weinstock. I would also like to thank the British trumpeter, arranger, and conductor Guy Barker for sharing with me his interview with Johnny Mandel, from a project we worked on together exploring jazz in the movies. As mentioned in the Preface, I should particularly single out Bill Crow for his help at every stage of this book, and for the photographs he has kindly supplied. Although I was not able to discuss their work with Mulligan with Bill's fellow bassists Peck Morrison and Red Mitchell, I am grateful to both for spending time with me in the 1980s, and discussing aspects of their playing style and technique.

I owe a debt of gratitude to those who have written at length about musicians whose careers intersected with Mulligan's, and with whom I have discussed aspects of this book, namely Stephanie Stein Crease (on Gil Evans), James Gavin (on Chet Baker), and Dave Gelly (on Stan Getz). I have consulted many of the standard discographies, but I am most grateful to the published work of Gérard Dugelay and Kenneth Hallqvist, which has dovetailed with my own extensive research in the

American press to create the most accurate chronology of Mulligan's 1950s career so far assembled.

My colleagues at BBC Radio enabled me to meet and interview several of the musicians named above, and my thanks go to Felix Carey, Terry Carter, Derek Drescher, Sam Hickling, and Oliver Jones for allowing me to ask many of my own questions to supplement those needed for broadcast. I am also grateful to Lisa Knorr and all those at Telarc in the 1990s, who made it possible for me to write about the final period of Mulligan's work and to meet many of his later associates as well as to have a most fruitful conversation with Franca Mulligan.

The world of Mulligan research would be the poorer were it not for the lifelong endeavors of Gordon Jack, and this book has largely been made possible by his generosity and kindness in reading and commenting on drafts, and in providing access to much of his own writing, photographs, and interviews, as well as some of the rarest items listed in the bibliography. My friend and musical colleague Robert Fowler shared scores with me of music for the Mulligan Concert Jazz Band, a group that he brilliantly recreated for a series of UK concerts in 2015, and this was invaluable in exploring the music of this great ensemble.

Every book in this series includes detailed music examples, and in this case I am more than grateful to my colleague Adrian Fry for turning my rough transcriptions and notes into the elegantly typeset examples that grace these pages. We have discussed every aspect of these, explored the harmonic and melodic territory they cover, and tried to present material that will elucidate the development of the Mulligan quartets, sextets, and larger ensembles. Another good friend and colleague (and fine baritone saxophonist) Alan Barnes has also kindly spent time reading early drafts of the book and the examples therein, and many of his helpful comments are incorporated in the final text.

Archival material in the book comes from the Elliot Lawrence Collection at the American Heritage Center in the University of Wyoming at Laramie. I would like to thank the archivist John R. Waggener and his staff for their help and assistance. I would also like to thank Rachael Beale (of Bath Spa University) for helping to obtain some of the books consulted at a time when Covid-19 made the normal process of inter-library loans impossible. That said, Kathryn Adamson, my colleague at the library of the Royal Academy of Music in London, was very helpful in tracing hard-to-find material. Tom Tierney and Toby Silver at Sony Music Entertainment in New York tracked down Don Hunstein's photograph of the 1959 quartet, while Luca Balbo at Hal Leonard Europe

Ltd and Charlotte Mortimer of Faber Music Licensing have been most helpful in clearing music copyrights.

As ever, Professor Tim Jones and the research department of the Royal Academy of Music have supported my work, and I am most grateful to them.

Finally, my thanks go to Jeremy Barham, the series editor, with whom—in the process of discussing the genesis of this book—I had a most entertaining time tracking down a necktie in Oxford, UK. And I am grateful to my editor at Oxford University Press, Lauralee Yeary, for commissioning the book, and for some penetrating and helpful reviews. Equally Timothy DeWerff has been a most careful and attentive copy editor, with whom it has been a pleasure to work.

DISCOGRAPHY 1952–1962

This is a chronology of the sessions discussed in this book, mainly limited to the quartet, but where applicable including quintet, sextet, tentet(te), and Concert Jazz Band recordings. Issue details are generally the tracks' earliest appearance on LP, though some were not released until the CD era.

GERRY MULLIGAN QUARTET

August 16, 1952 (Los Angeles): Chet Baker, t; Gerry Mulligan, bars; Bob Whitlock, b; Chico Hamilton, d. *Bernie's Tune / Mullenium / Utter Chaos / Lullaby of the Leaves* Pacific Jazz LP-1.

September 2, 1952 (San Francisco): Chet Baker, t; Gerry Mulligan, bars; Carson Smith, b; Chico Hamilton, d. *Line for Lyons / Carioca / My Funny Valentine / Bark for Barksdale* Fantasy LP 3-6.

October 15/16, 1952 (Los Angeles): Chet Baker, t; Gerry Mulligan, bars; Bob Whitlock, b; Chico Hamilton, d. *Nights at the Turntable / Frenesi / Freeway / Soft Shoe / Walkin' Shoes / Aren't You Glad You're You* Pacific Jazz LP-1.

January 9, 1953 (Hollywood): Chet Baker, t; Gerry Mulligan, bars; Carson Smith, b; Chico Hamilton, d. *Limelight / The Lady Is a Tramp / Turnstile / Moonlight in Vermont* Fantasy LP 3-6.

(Early) January 1953 (Haig Club, Los Angeles) Chet Baker, t; Gerry Mulligan, bars; Carson Smith, b; Chico Hamilton, d. *Aren't You Glad You're You / Get Happy / Ponciana / Godchild* Pacific Jazz CDP 7243 8 38263 2.

GERRY MULLIGAN QUARTET WITH LEE KONITZ

January 23, 1953 (Haig Club, Los Angeles) Chet Baker, t; Lee Konitz, as; Gerry Mulligan, bars; Carson Smith, b; Larry Bunker, d. *Too Marvelous for Words / Lover Man / I'll Remember April / These Foolish Things / All the Things You Are / Bernie's Tune* Pacific PJ LP-10.

GERRY MULLIGAN TENTETTE

January 29, 1953 (Hollywood) Chet Baker, Pete Candoli, t; Bob Enevoldsen, vtb; John Graas, frh; Ray Siegel, tu; Bud Shank, as; Gerry Mulligan, Don Davidson, bars; Joe Mondragon, b; Chico Hamilton, d. *A Ballad / Westwood Walk / Walkin' Shoes / Rocker* Capitol LP T-691.

GERRY MULLIGAN QUARTET WITH LEE KONITZ

January 30, 1953 (Los Angeles) Chet Baker, t; Lee Konitz, as; Gerry Mulligan, bars; Carson Smith, b; Larry Bunker, d. *Almost Like Being in Love / Sextet / Broadway* Pacific LP-2.

GERRY MULLIGAN TENTETTE

January 31, 1953 (Hollywood) Chet Baker, Pete Candoli, t; Bob Enevoldsen, vtb; John Graas, frh; Ray Siegel, tu; Bud Shank, as; Gerry Mulligan, bars, p; Don Davidson, bars; Joe Mondragon, b; Larry Bunker, d. *Takin' a Chance on Love/ Flash / Simbah / Ontet* Capitol LP T-691.

GERRY MULLIGAN QUARTET WITH LEE KONITZ

February 1, 1953 (Los Angeles) Chet Baker, t; Lee Konitz, as; Gerry Mulligan, bars; Joe Mondragon, b; Larry Bunker, d. *I Can't Believe That You're in Love with Me / Lady Be Good* Pacific LP-2.

GERRY MULLIGAN QUARTET

February 24, 1953 (Los Angeles) Chet Baker, t; Gerry Mulligan, bars; Carson Smith, b; Larry Bunker, d. *Carson City Stage / Cherry / Motel / Makin' Whoopee* Pacific LP-2.

April 27, 1953 (Los Angeles). Chet Baker, t; Gerry Mulligan, bars; Carson Smith, b; Larry Bunker, d. *Love Me or Leave Me / Swing House / Jeru* Pacific LP-5; *My Old Flame* Pacific LP-10.

April 29/30, 1953 (Hollywood) Chet Baker, t; Gerry Mulligan, bars; Carson Smith, b; Larry Bunker, d. *Darn That Dream / I May Be Wrong / I'm Beginning to See the Light / The Nearness of You / Tea for Two* Pacific LP-5.

May 7, 1953 (Los Angeles) Chet Baker, t; Gerry Mulligan, bars; Carson Smith, b; Larry Bunker, d. *Half Nelson / Lady Bird / Speak Low / Varsity Drag / Love Me or Leave Me / Swing House* Gene Norman Presents LP 3.

May 20, 1953 (The Haig, Los Angeles) Chet Baker, t; Gerry Mulligan, bars; Carson Smith, b; Larry Bunker, d. *Five Brothers / I Can't Get Started / Ide's Side / Fun House (Haig and Haig) / My Funny Valentine* Pacific PJ-8.

June 1, 1954 (Paris) Bob Brookmeyer, vtb; Gerry Mulligan, bars; Red Mitchell, b; Frank Isola, d. *Bernie's Tune / Walkin' Shoes / The Nearness of You / Love Me or Leave Me / Soft Shoe / Bark for Barksdale* Vogue DP07; *My Funny Valentine / Motel / Utter Chaos / Turnstile / Utter Chaos* Vogue LP 494-30.

June 3, 1954 (Paris) Bob Brookmeyer, vtb; Gerry Mulligan, bars; Red Mitchell, b; Frank Isola, d. *I May Be Wrong / Five Brothers / Gold Rush / Makin' Whoopee / The Lady Is a Tramp / Laura* Vogue DP07; *Motel / Utter Chaos* Vogue LP 494-30.

June 5, 1954 (Paris) Bob Brookmeyer, vtb; Gerry Mulligan, bars; Red Mitchell, b; Frank Isola, d. *Five Brothers* Vogue CD 851; *Lullaby of the Leaves / Limelight* Vogue DP07; *The Nearness of You* Vogue LP 494-30.

June 7, 1954 (Paris) Bob Brookmeyer, vtb; Gerry Mulligan, bars; Red Mitchell, b; Frank Isola, d. *Come Out Wherever You Are / Moonlight in Vermont* Vogue DP07; *Love Me or Leave Me / Laura / Line for Lyons* Vogue LAE 12015.

July 17, 1954 (Newport, RI) Tony Fruscella, t; Gerry Mulligan, bars; Red Mitchell, b; Frank Isola, d. *Bernie's Tune / The Lady Is a Tramp/ Lullaby of the Leaves* Sounds of Yesteryear CD DSOY 2237.

November 12, 1954 (Stockton, CA) Jon Eardley, t; Gerry Mulligan, bars, p; Red Mitchell, b; Chico Hamilton, d. *Blues Going Up / Little Girl Blue / Piano Blues / Yardbird Suite / Utter Chaos* Pacific 1201; *Bark for Barksdale* World Pacific 1247; *Soft Shoe* Pacific JWC 500; *Blues for Tiny* Pacific PJ-8; *Makin' Whoopee / Darn That Dream / Ontet* Pacific CDP 7 46860-2.

December 14, 1954 (San Diego, CA) Jon Eardley, t; Gerry Mulligan, bars, p; Red Mitchell, b; Chico Hamilton, d. *Makin' Whoopee / Nights at the Turntable / Blues for Tiny / Frenesi / Limelight* Pacific CDP 7 46864-2.

GERRY MULLIGAN SEXTET

December 14, 1954 (San Diego, CA) Jon Eardley, t; Bob Brookmeyer, vtb; Zoot Sims, ts; Gerry Mulligan, bars, p; Red Mitchell, b; Larry Bunker, d. *I'll Remember April / Western Reunion / I Know, Don't Know How / Red Door* Pacific ST 20145; *It Don't Mean a Thing / In a Sentimental Mood / Moon Mist / Flamingo / There Will Never Be Another You* Pacific CDP 7 46864-2.

September 21, 1955 (New York) Jon Eardley, t; Bob Brookmeyer, vtb; Zoot Sims, ts; Gerry Mulligan, bars, p; Peck Morrison, b; Dave Bailey, d. *Bernie's Tune / Mud Bug* EmArcy MG 36056; *Blues / The Lady Is a Tramp / Demanton* EmArcy 195J-35; *Ellington Medley (Moon Mist / In a Sentimental Mood)* EmArcy 135J-35.

September 22, 1955 (New York) Jon Eardley, t; Bob Brookmeyer, vtb; Zoot Sims, ts; Gerry Mulligan, bars, p; Peck Morrison, b; Dave Bailey, d. *Apple Core / Sweet and Lovely* EmArcy MG 36056; *Broadway / Bernie's Tune* EmArcy 195J-35; *Westwood Walk / Blue at the Roots* EmArcy 135J-35.

October 31, 1955 (New York) Jon Eardley, t; Bob Brookmeyer, vtb; Zoot Sims, ts; Gerry Mulligan, bars, p; Peck Morrison, b; Dave Bailey, d. *Broadway / Nights at the Turntable / Everything Happens to Me / The Lady Is a Tramp* EmArcy MG 36056; *Demanton* EmArcy 135J-35.

October 1955 (Basin Street, New York) Jon Eardley, t; Bob Brookmeyer, vtb; Zoot Sims, ts; Gerry Mulligan, bars, p; Peck Morrison, b; Dave Bailey, d. *Apple Core / Moonlight in Vermont / Nights at the Turntable / Broadway* Rare Live RLR 88660.

December 3, 1955 (Basin Street, New York) Jon Eardley, t; Bob Brookmeyer, vtb; Zoot Sims, ts; Gerry Mulligan, bars, p; Peck Morrison, b; Dave Bailey, d. *Utter Chaos / The Red Door / Soft Shoe / Makin' Whoopee / Bernie's Tune* Rare Live RLR 88660.

January 25, 1956 (New York) Jon Eardley, t; Bob Brookmeyer, vtb; Zoot Sims, ts; Gerry Mulligan, bars, p; Bill Crow, b; Dave Bailey, d. *Ain't It the Truth* EmArcy MG 36088; *Mainstream* EmArcy MG 36101; *Westwood Walk / La plus que lente* EmArcy 195J-36.

February 25, 1956 (Milan, Italy) Jon Eardley, t; Bob Brookmeyer, vtb; Zoot Sims, ts; Gerry Mulligan, bars, p; Bill Crow, b; Dave Bailey, d. *Bernie's Tune / Walkin' Shoes / Ontet* Rare Live RLR 88660.

April 7, 1956 (Concertgebouw, Amsterdam) Jon Eardley, t; Bob Brookmeyer, vtb; Zoot Sims, ts; Gerry Mulligan, bars, p; Bill Crow, b; Dave Bailey, d. *Mud Bug / Nights at the Turntable / Ain't It the Truth / Line for Lyons / Demanton / Utter Chaos / Broadway / Sweet and Lovely / The Red Door / I May Be Wrong / My Funny Valentine / Westwood Walk / I'm Beginning to See the Light / Stars and Stripes / Western Reunion* Music Center Netherlands MCN 0801.

GERRY MULLIGAN QUARTET

July 29, 1956 (TV show, New York) Bob Brookmeyer, vtb, p; Gerry Mulligan, bars, p; Bill Crow, b; Dave Bailey d. *Line for Lyons / My Funny Valentine / Five Brothers* Rare Live RLR 88660.

August 1956 (TV Show, New York) Bob Brookmeyer, vtb, p; Gerry Mulligan, bars, p; Bill Crow, b; Dave Bailey d. *Line for Lyons* Rare Live RLR 88660.

GERRY MULLIGAN SEXTET

September 26, 1956 (New York) Don Ferrara, t; Bob Brookmeyer, vtb; Zoot Sims, ts; Gerry Mulligan, bars, p; Bill Crow, b; Dave Bailey, d. *Igloo / Elevation / Lollypop / Blue at the Roots* EmArcy MG 36101; *La plus que lente / Makin' Whoopee* EmArcy 135J-35.

GERRY MULLIGAN QUARTET

December 1–6, 1956 (Storyville, Boston) Bob Brookmeyer, vtb, p; Gerry Mulligan, bars, p; Bill Crow, b; Dave Bailey d. *That Old Feeling / Birth of the Blues / Baubles, Bangles and Beads / Rustic Hop / Open Country / Bike Up the Strand / Utter Chaos / Bweebida Bobbida / Storyville Story* Pacific Jazz 1228; *Utter Chaos (2) / Blues at the Roots / Ide's Side / I Can't Get Started / Frenesi / Flash / Honeysuckle Rose / Limelight* Pacific CDP 7 944722-2.

May 17, 1957 (Stockholm, Sweden) Bob Brookmeyer, vtb; Gerry Mulligan, bars, p; Joe Benjamin, b; Dave Bailey d. *Come Out, Come Out, Wherever You Are / Birth of the Blues / Moonlight in Vermont / Lullaby of the Leaves / Open Country / I Can't Get Started / Frenesi / Baubles, Bangles and Beads / Yardbird Suite / Walkin' Shoes / My*

Funny Valentine / Blues at the Roots / Bernie's Tune Editions Atlas/ Charly WIS CD 633.

July 6, 1957 (Newport, RI) Bob Brookmeyer, vtb; Gerry Mulligan, bars; Joe Benjamin, b; Dave Bailey d. *My Funny Valentine / Utter Chaos* Verve MGV 8235.

GERRY MULLIGAN / PAUL DESMOND QUARTET

August 2, 1957 (Hollywood) Paul Desmond, as; Gerry Mulligan, bars, p; Joe Benjamin, b; Dave Bailey d. *Blues in Time / Body and Soul / Wintersong* Verve MGV 8246.

GERRY MULLIGAN QUARTET

August 2, 1957 (Hollywood Bowl) Bob Brookmeyer, vtb, p; Gerry Mulligan, bars, p; Bill Crow, b; Dave Bailey d. *Come Out Wherever You Are / Baubles, Bangles and Beads / Laura / Bweebida Bobbida / Utter Chaos* Pablo PACD 5309-2.

GERRY MULLIGAN / THELONIOUS MONK QUARTET

August 12/13, 1957 (New York) Gerry Mulligan, bars; Thelonious Monk, p; Wilbur Ware, b; Shadow Wilson, d. *Round Midnight / Rhythm-a-ning / Sweet and Lovely / Decidedly / Straight No Chaser / I Mean You* Milestone M47067.

GERRY MULLIGAN / PAUL DESMOND QUARTET

August 27, 1957 (New York) Paul Desmond, as; Gerry Mulligan, bars, p; Joe Benjamin, b; Dave Bailey d. *Fallout / Line for Lyons / Battle Hymn of the Republican / Stand Still* Verve MGV 8246.

GERRY MULLIGAN / STAN GETZ QUINTET

October 12, 1957 (Los Angeles) Stan Getz, ts, bars*; Gerry Mulligan, bars, ts*; Lou Levy, p; Ray Brown, b; Stan Levey, d. *That Old Feeling / This Can't Be Love/ A Ballad / Let's Fall in Love* / Too Close for Comfort* / Anything Goes** Verve MGV 8249; *Scrapple from the Apple / I Didn't Know What Time It Was* Verve MGV 8348.

GERRY MULLIGAN OCTET

December 4/5, 1957 (New York) Lee Konitz, as; Allen Eager, Zoot Sims, as, ts; Al Cohn, ts, bars; Gerry Mulligan, bars; Freddie Green, g; Henry Grimes, b; Dave Bailey, d. *Four and One Moore / Crazy Day / Turnstile / Sextet / Disc Jockey Jump / Venue De Milo / Revelation* Pacific WP 1237.

GERRY MULLIGAN QUARTET

December 3/11/17, 1957 (New York) Chet Baker, t; Gerry Mulligan, bars; Henry Grimes, b; Dave Bailey d. *Ornithology / Reunion / When Your Lover Has Gone / Trav'lin' Light / My Heart Belongs to Daddy / Stardust / Surrey with the Fringe on Top / Jersey Bounce* Pacific WP 1241; *Gee Baby, Ain't I Good to You / People Will Say We're in Love / The Song Is You / I Got Rhythm / All the Things You Are* Pacific CD B2 46857.

GERRY MULLIGAN TRIO WITH ANNIE ROSS

December 11, 1957 (New York) Annie Ross, v; Gerry Mulligan, bars; Henry Grimes, b; Dave Bailey d. *The Lady's in Love with You* Pacific WP 1253.

GERRY MULLIGAN QUARTET WITH ANNIE ROSS

December 17, 1957 (New York) Annie Ross, v; Chet Baker, t; Gerry Mulligan, bars; Henry Grimes, b; Dave Bailey d. *It Don't Mean a Thing* WP 1253; *You Turned the Tables on Me / I've Grown Accustomed to Your Face* Pacific B21K 46852.

February 11, 1958 (Los Angeles) Annie Ross, v; Chet Baker, t; Gerry Mulligan, bars; Henry Grimes, b; Dave Bailey d. *This Time the Dream's on Me / Let There Be Love / Between the Devil and the Deep Blue Sea / How about You* Pacific WP 1253.

GERRY MULLIGAN QUARTET

April 30, 1958 (Timex TV show, New York) Art Farmer, t; Gerry Mulligan, bars; Henry Grimes, b; Dave Bailey d. *Utter Chaos / Night Walk* Radiola MR 1095; *Utter Chaos / Bernie's Tune* Rare Live RLR 88660.

GERRY MULLIGAN SEPTET

May 24, 1958 (Los Angeles studio session for *I Want to Live*) Art Farmer, t; Frank Rosolino, tb; Bud Shank, as; Gerry Mulligan, bars; Pete Jolly, p; Red Mitchell, b; Shelly Manne, d; Johnny Mandel, arr, dir. *Black Nightgown / Theme "I Want to Live" / Night Watch / Frisco Club / Barbara's Theme / Life's a Funny Thing* United Artists UAL 4006.

GERRY MULLIGAN QUARTET

July 6, 1958 (Newport, RI) Art Farmer, t; Gerry Mulligan, bars; Bill Crow, b; Dave Bailey d. *Festive Minor / Bernie's Tune / Baubles, Bangles and Beads / Blueport / Moonlight in Vermont / News from Blueport / Line for Lyons / As Catch Can* Rare Live RLR 88639.

GERRY MULLIGAN QUARTET WITH ANNIE ROSS

September 25, 1958 (Los Angeles) Annie Ross, v; Art Farmer, t; Gerry Mulligan, bars; Bill Crow, b; Dave Bailey d. *I Feel Pretty / All of You/ Give Me the Simple Life / I've Grown Accustomed to Your Face* Pacific WP 1253; *This Is Always / My Old Flame* Pacific B21K 46852.

GERRY MULLIGAN QUARTET

December 17, 1958 (New York) Art Farmer, t; Gerry Mulligan, bars; Bill Crow, b; Dave Bailey d. *Blueport* Columbia CL 1307.

December 23, 1958 (New York) Art Farmer, t; Gerry Mulligan, bars; Bill Crow, b; Dave Bailey d. *As Catch Can / My Funny Valentine / Utter Chaos* Columbia CL 1307.

January 15, 1959 (New York) Art Farmer, t; Gerry Mulligan, bars; Bill Crow, b; Dave Bailey d. *What Is There to Say? / Just in Time / News from Blueport / Festive Minor* Columbia CL 1307.

February 1959 (Hollywood, *Navy Swings* broadcast) Art Farmer, t; Gerry Mulligan, bars; Bill Crow, b; Dave Bailey d. *Motel / My Funny Valentine / Walkin' Shoes / Festive Minor / As Catch Can / News from Blueport / Just in Time* Solar 4569871.

May 19, 1959 (Stockholm, Sweden) Art Farmer, t; Gerry Mulligan, bars; Bill Crow, b; Dave Bailey d. *As Catch Can / I Can't Get Started / Just in Time / What Is There to Say? / Spring Is Sprung / Blueport / Utter Chaos* Solar 4569871.

June 19, 1959 (Rome, Italy) Art Farmer, t; Gerry Mulligan, bars; Bill Crow, b; Dave Bailey d. *As Catch Can / Walkin' Shoes / Baubles, Bangles and Beads / Just in Time / I Can't Get Started / News from Blueport / Moonlight in Vermont / Spring Is Sprung / Blueport* Lonehill LHJ 10103.

ANDRÉ PREVIN AND HIS ORCHESTRA

September 2, 1959 (Hollywood, from *The Subterraneans*) Art Farmer, t; Bob Enevoldsen, vtb; Art Pepper, as; Bill Perkins, ts; Gerry Mulligan, bars; Russ Freeman, p; Buddy Clark, b; Dave Bailey, d; André Previn, dir. *Bread and Wine / Things Are Looking Down* Banda Sonora BGSZ 103; *Red Drum Blues* Rhino R2 79805.

GERRY MULLIGAN / BEN WEBSTER QUINTET

November 3, 1959 (Hollywood) Ben Webster, ts; Gerry Mulligan, bars; Jimmy Rowles, p; Leroy Vinnegar, b; Mel Lewis, d. *Chelsea Bridge / Go Home / Who's Got Rhythm* Verve MGV 8343; *In a Mellow Tone / What Is This Thing Called Love / For Bessie* Verve CD 841 661-2.

GERRY MULLIGAN / JOHNNY HODGES QUINTET

November 17, 1959 (Hollywood) Johnny Hodges, as; Gerry Mulligan, bars; Claude Williamson, p; Buddy Clark, b; Mel Lewis, d. *Bunny / 18 Carrots for Rabbit / Shady Side / What's It All About? / What's the Rush? / Backbeat* Verve MGV 8637.

GERRY MULLIGAN / BEN WEBSTER QUINTET

December 2, 1959 (Hollywood) Ben Webster, ts; Gerry Mulligan, bars; Jimmy Rowles, p; Leroy Vinnegar, b; Mel Lewis, d. *Tell Me When / The Cat Walk / Sunday* Verve MGV 8343; *Fajista / Blues in B Flat* Verve CD 539 055-2.

GERRY MULLIGAN / BEN WEBSTER QUINTET WITH JIMMY WITHERSPOON

December 2/9, 1959 (Renaissance Club, Hollywood) Ben Webster, ts; Gerry Mulligan, bars; Jimmy Rowles, p; Leroy Vinnegar, b; Mel Lewis, d; Jimmy Witherspoon, v. *Times Gettin' Tougher Than Tough*

/ How Long Blues / Corinne Corrina / C. C. Rider / Roll 'Em Pete / Every Day I Have the Blues / Goin' to Kansas City / Outskirts of Town / Trouble in Mind / St. Louis Blues HiFi Jazz J246.

ANDRÉ PREVIN AND HIS ORCHESTRA

January 11, 1960 (Hollywood, from *The Subterraneans*) Art Farmer, t; Bob Enevoldsen, vtb; Art Pepper, as; Bill Perkins, ts; Gerry Mulligan, bars; André Previn, p, dir; Red Mitchell, b; Shelly Manne, d; plus studio orchestra. *Why Are We Afraid / Two by Two / Look Ma, No Clothes / Analyst* Banda Sonora BGSZ 103.

January 12, 1959 (Hollywood, from *The Subterraneans*) Art Farmer, t; Bob Enevoldsen, vtb; Art Pepper, as; Bill Perkins, ts; Gerry Mulligan, bars; Russ Freeman, p; Buddy Clark, b; Dave Bailey, d; André Previn, dir. *Spaghetti Fantasy* Rhino R2 79805.

February 3, 1959 (Hollywood, from *The Subterraneans*) Art Farmer, t; Bob Enevoldsen, vtb; Art Pepper, as; Bill Perkins, ts; Gerry Mulligan, bars; Russ Freeman, p; Buddy Clark, b; Dave Bailey, d; André Previn, dir; plus studio orchestra. *Main Title / Togetherness* FSM CD V7 No. 19.

GERRY MULLIGAN AND THE CONCERT JAZZ BAND

May 21, 1960 (New York) Danny Stiles, Don Ferrara, Phil Sunkel, t; Bob Brookmeyer, vtb; Wayne Andre, tb; Alan Raph, btb; Gene Quill, cl, as; Dick Meldonian, as; Jim Reider, ts; Gene Allen, bars, cl; Gerry Mulligan, bars; Bill Takas, b; Dave Bailey, d. *I'm Gonna Go Fishin'* Verve 10216.

July 1, 1960 (Newport, RI) Conte Candoli, Don Ferrara, Phil Sunkel, t; Bob Brookmeyer, vtb; Wayne Andre, tb; Alan Raph, btb; Gene Quill, cl, as; Dick Meldonian, Jim Reider, ts; Gene Allen, bars, cl; Gerry Mulligan, bars, p; Buddy Clark, b; Mel Lewis, d. *Utter Chaos / Broadway / Theme: "I Want to Live" / You're Clear out of This World / Manoir de mes rêves / 18 Carrots for Rabbit / Walkin' Shoes / I'm Gonna Go Fishin' / Blueport / The Anthill* Jazz Band EBCD 2129-2.

July 25–27 (New York) Conte Candoli, Don Ferrara, Nick Travis, t; Bob Brookmeyer, vtb; Wayne Andre, tb; Alan Raph, btb; Gene Quill, cl, as; Dick Meldonian, as; Zoot Sims, ts; Gene Allen, bars, cl; Gerry Mulligan, bars, p; Buddy Clark, b; Mel Lewis, d. *Out of This World / Manoir de mes rêves / Bweebida Bobbida / Sweet and Slow /*

You Took Advantage of Me / My Funny Valentine / Broadway Verve MGV 8388.

October 1, 1960 (Santa Monica, CA) Conte Candoli, Don Ferrara, Nick Travis, t; Bob Brookmeyer, vtb, p; Willie Dennis, tb; Alan Raph, btb; Gene Quill, cl, as; Bob Donovan, as; Zoot Sims, Jim Reider, ts; Gene Allen, bars, cl; Gerry Mulligan, bars, p; Buddy Clark, b; Mel Lewis, d. *Come Rain or Come Shine / Go Home / The Red Door* Verve MGV 8438.

November 4, 1960 (West Berlin, Germany) Conte Candoli, Don Ferrara, Nick Travis, t; Bob Brookmeyer, vtb; Willie Dennis, tb; Alan Raph, btb; Gene Quill, cl, as; Bob Donovan, as; Zoot Sims, Jim Reider, ts; Gene Allen, bars, cl; Gerry Mulligan, bars; Buddy Clark, b; Mel Lewis, d. *Theme: "I Want to Live"* Verve MGV 8438.

November 14, 1960 (Milan, Italy) Conte Candoli, Don Ferrara, Nick Travis, t; Bob Brookmeyer, vtb; Willie Dennis, tb; Alan Raph, btb; Gene Quill, cl, as; Bob Donovan, as; Zoot Sims, Jim Reider, ts; Gene Allen, bars, cl; Gerry Mulligan, bars; Buddy Clark, b; Mel Lewis, d. *Go Home / Apple Core / Barbara's Theme* Verve MGV 8438.

November 17, 1960 (Basel, Switzerland) Conte Candoli, Don Ferrara, Nick Travis, t; Bob Brookmeyer, vtb; Willie Dennis, tb; Alan Raph, btb; Gene Quill, cl, as; Bob Donovan, as; Zoot Sims, Jim Reider, ts; Gene Allen, bars, cl; Gerry Mulligan, bars, p; Buddy Clark, b; Mel Lewis, d. *Utter Chaos / You Took Advantage of Me / Black Nightgown / Motel / Walkin' Shoes / Body and Soul / Apple Core / Go Home / I'm Gonna Go Fishin' / Piano Blues / Come Rain or Come Shine / Barbara's Theme / Blueport* TCB CD 02122.

November 19, 1960 (Paris, France) Conte Candoli, Don Ferrara, Nick Travis, t; Bob Brookmeyer, vtb; Willie Dennis, tb; Alan Raph, btb; Gene Quill, cl, as; Bob Donovan, as; Zoot Sims, Jim Reider, ts; Gene Allen, bars, cl; Gerry Mulligan, bars. p; Buddy Clark, b; Mel Lewis, d. *You Took Advantage of Me / Black Nightgown / Body and Soul / Barbara's Theme / Apple Core / Come Rain or Come Shine / Piano Blues / My Funny Valentine / I'm Gonna Go Fishin' / Broadway / Bweebida Bobbida / Go Home / Blueport* Gambit CD 64249.

December 11, 1960 (Village Vanguard, New York) Clark Terry, Don Ferrara, Nick Travis, t; Bob Brookmeyer, vtb; Willie Dennis, tb; Alan Raph, btb; Gene Quill, cl, as; Bob Donovan, as; Jim Reider, ts; Gene Allen, bars, cl; Gerry Mulligan, bars. p; Bill Crow, b; Mel Lewis, d. *Lady Chatterley's Mother / Body and Soul / Let My People Be / Come Rain or Come Shine / Blueport / Black Nightgown* Verve MGV 6-8396.

May 13, 1961 (Birdland, New York) Doc Severinsen, Don Ferrara, Nick Travis, t; Bob Brookmeyer, vtb; Willie Dennis, tb; Alan Raph, btb; Gene Quill, cl, as; Bob Donovan, as; Al Cohn, Jim Reider, ts; Gene Allen, bars, cl; Gerry Mulligan, bars; Bill Crow, b; Mel Lewis, d. *Bweebida Bobbida / My Funny Valentine / Out of This World / Lady Chatterley's Mother* Alto AL717.

July 10–11, 1961 (New York) Doc Severinsen, Don Ferrara, Nick Travis, t; Bob Brookmeyer, vtb; Willie Dennis, tb; Alan Raph, btb; Gene Quill, cl, as; Bob Donovan, as; Jim Reider, ts; Gene Allen, bars, cl; Gerry Mulligan, bars, p; Bill Crow, b; Mel Lewis, d. *All about Rosie / Weep / Chuggin' / Israel / Summer's Over / I Know, Don't Know How* Verve MGV 6-8415.

GERRY MULLIGAN QUARTET

February 25, 1962 (Village Vanguard, New York) Bob Brookmeyer, vtb; Gerry Mulligan, bars; Bill Crow, b; Gus Johnson, d. *I Know, Don't Know How* Verve MGV 8455.

GERRY MULLIGAN AND THE CONCERT JAZZ BAND

April 26, 1962 (Birdland, New York) Doc Severinsen, Don Ferrara, Nick Travis, Clark Terry t; Bob Brookmeyer, vtb; Willie Dennis, Tony Studd, tb; Alan Raph, btb; Gene Quill, cl, as; Bob Donovan, as; Jim Reider, ts; Gene Allen, bars, cl; Gerry Mulligan, bars, p; Bill Crow, b; Mel Lewis, d. *Theme: "I Want to Live" / Chuggin' / Manoir de mes rêves / I'm Gonna Go Fishin' / Summer Is Over / You Took Advantage of Me* Alto AL 717.

GERRY MULLIGAN QUARTET

May 14–15, 1962 (New York) Bob Brookmeyer, vtb, p; Gerry Mulligan, bars; Bill Crow, b; Gus Johnson, d. *Piano Train / Lost in the Stars / I'm Getting Sentimental over You / Love in New Orleans / I Believe in You* Verve MGV 6-8466.

July 18, 1962 (Ralph Gleason TV show, Los Angeles) Bob Brookmeyer, vtb, p; Gerry Mulligan, bars; Wyatt Ruther, b; Gus Johnson, d. *Four for Three / Darn That Dream / Open Country / Utter Chaos* Koch Jazz CD 8559.

October 6, 1962 (Paris, France) Bob Brookmeyer, vtb, p; Gerry Mulligan, bars, p; Bill Crow, b; Gus Johnson, d. *Spring Is Sprung / Subterranean Blues / Darn That Dream / Blueport / Utter Chaos*

Gambit CD 64249; *Open Country / Love in New Orleans / Four for Three / Subterranean Blues* (2) Pablo PACD 5309-2.

October 18, 1962 (Zurich, Switzerland) Bob Brookmeyer, vtb, p; Gerry Mulligan, bars, p; Bill Crow, b; Gus Johnson, d. *Utter Chaos / Open Country / Love in New Orleans / 17 Mile Drive / Subterranean Blues / Spring Is Sprung / Darn That Dream / Blueport* TCB CD 02092.

December 11–12, 1962 (New York) Bob Brookmeyer, vtb, p; Gerry Mulligan, bars, p; Bill Crow, b; Gus Johnson, d. *Spring Is Sprung / Open Country / Four for Three / Jive at Five / 17 Mile Drive / Subterranean Blues* Philips PHS 600-077.

GERRY MULLIGAN AND THE CONCERT JAZZ BAND

December 18, 1962 (New York) Clark Terry, flh; Doc Severinsen, Don Ferrara, Nick Travis, Clark Terry t; Bob Brookmeyer, vtb; Willie Dennis, tb; Tony Studd, btb; Gene Quill, cl, as; Eddie Caine, as; Jim Reider, ts; Gene Allen, bars, cl; Gerry Mulligan, bars, p; Jim Hall, g; Bill Crow, b; Gus Johnson, d. *Big City Blues / Pretty Little Gipsy / Little Rock Getaway / A Ballad / Big City Life / Bridgehampton South / My Kinda Love / Bridgehampton Strut* Verve MGV 8515.

BIBLIOGRAPHY

Balliett, Whitney: *Collected Works: A Journal of Jazz 1954–2000* (London, Granta, 2000).

Baraka, Amiri: *Blues People: The Negro Experience in White America and the Music That Developed from It* (New York, William Morrow, 1963).

Bartlett, Simon: "An Exploration of the Origin and Expressions of Implied Harmony in the Gerry Mulligan Quartet with Chet Baker (1952–53)" (M.Mus. thesis, Sydney Conservatorium of Music, University of Sydney, 2015).

Crow, Bill: *From Birdland to Broadway* (New York and Oxford, Oxford University Press, 1992).

Crowther, Bruce: *Gene Krupa, His Life and Times* (Tunbridge Wells, UK, Spellmount, 1987).

Davis, Miles (with Troupe, Quincy): *Miles: The Autobiography* (London, Macmillan, 1990).

Fine, Richard Samuel: *The Birth of Jeru* (PhD thesis, University of Maryland, 2010).

Firestone, Ross: *Swing Swing Swing: The Life and Times of Benny Goodman* (London, Hodder and Stoughton, 1993).

Gavin, James: *Deep in a Dream, The Long Night of Chet Baker* (London, Chatto and Windus, 2002).

Gelly, Dave: *Stan Getz, Nobody Else but Me* (San Francisco, Backbeat Books, 2002).

Gioia, Ted: *West Coast Jazz* (New York, Oxford University Press, 1992).

Gordon, Robert: *Jazz West Coast* (London, Quartet, 1986).

Hamilton, Andy: *Lee Konitz—Conversations on the Improviser's Art* (Ann Arbor, University of Michigan Press, 2007).

Havers, Richard: *Verve—the Sound of America* (London, Thames and Hudson, 2013).

Hershorn, Tad: *Norman Granz: The Man Who Used Jazz for Justice* (Berkeley, University of California Press, 2011).

Ind, Peter: *Jazz Visions* (London, Equinox, 2006).

Jack, Gordon: *Fifties Jazz Talk* (Lanham, MD, Scarecrow Press, 2004).

Josephson, Sanford: *Jeru's Journey* (Milwaukee, Hal Leonard, 2015).

Klinkowitz, Jerome: *Listen: Gerry Mulligan* (New York, Schirmer, 1991).

Kofsky, Frank: *Black Nationalism and the Revolution in Music* (New York, Pathfinder Press, 1970).
Krenshaw, Kimberley; Gotanda, Neil; and Peller, Gary: *Critical Race Theory* (New York, New Press, 1995).
Lees, Gene: *Meet Me at Jim and Andy's* (New York, Oxford, 1988).
Perchard, Tom: *After Django, Making Jazz in Postwar France* (Ann Arbor, University of Michigan Press, 2013).
Pullman, Peter: *Wail: The Life of Bud Powell* (New York, Peter Pullman, LLC, 2012).
Shipton, Alyn: *A New History of Jazz* (London, Continuum, 2007, 2nd ed.).
Smith, Chris: *View from the Back of the Band: The Life and Music of Mel Lewis* (Denton, University of North Texas Press, 2014).
Stein Crease, Stephanie: *Gil Evans, Out of the Cool* (Chicago, Chicago Review Press, 2002).
Stratemann, Klaus: *Ellington Day by Day and Film by Film* (Copenhagen, JazzMedia, 1992).
Tirro, Frank: *The Birth of the Cool of Miles Davis and His Associates* (Hillsdale, NY, Pendragon Press, 2009).
Tournès, Ludovic: *New Orleans sur Seine: Histoire du Jazz en France* (Paris, Fayard, 1999).
Ulanov, Barry: *A History of Jazz in America* (London, Hutchinson, 1950).

INDEX

For the benefit of digital users, indexed terms that span two pages (e.g., 52–53) may, on occasion, appear on only one of those pages.

Figures and Music examples are indicated by *f*, following the page number

"17 Mile Drive," 218–19
"18 Carrots for Rabbit," 186, 194–95

Action in New Orleans, The (TV show and score), 211, 213
AFM (American Federation of Musicians), 19, 26, 33, 52, 77
"Ain't It the Truth," 124–26, 129
Albam, Manny, 139
"All About Rosie," 208
"All of You," 158
"All The things You Are," 75
Allen, Gene, 190–91, 199
Amsterdam, Concertgebouw, 125–26
Andre, Wayne, 190–91, 199
Annie Ross Sings a Song with Mulligan, (album), 155–59, 176–77
Anthony, Bill, 89–90, 103
"Anthropology," 16–17
"Apple Core," 202
"Aren't You Glad You're You," 71, 72
"As Catch Can," 171–72, 172*f*, 174*f*, 174, 178–79
Auld, Georgie, 34, 84, 130
Avakian, George, 94, 117

Bailey, Dave, 118–19, 124, 125*f*, 126, 128–29, 131–34, 139, 141, 146, 149, 152, 153–54, 156–57, 158, 160, 161–62, 164–65, 169, 171*f*, 171–72, 177–79, 181, 182*f*, 214, 219–20
  as band manager, 141, 161, 180, 192–93
  and Concert Jazz Band, 190–91, 192–93
Baker, Chet (Chesney Henry), 22, 23, 25, 41, 46, 59–61, 68, 93, 96, 100, 108, 137, 158, 171, 202, 218
  and Mulligan, 46, 47–50, 51, 52, 54*f*, 55*f*, 56, 57*f*, 60*f*, 62*f*, 63*f*, 70–72, 75, 78, 82–83, 84, 87, 96–97, 102, 114–15, 116–17, 154–57
  and narcotics, 67, 83
  and Parker, 46–47, 48*f*, 49–50
  Quartet, 87, 90, 114–15, 116–17
"Ballad, A," 150
Balliett, Whitney, 146, 153
Baltimore, 102, 103
  Club Tijuana, 101–2

Bandstand USA (radio program), 131
Barber, Bill, 16–17, 19, 31
"Bark For Barksdale," 55, 59, 96, 107
Barnet, Charlie, 49, 50
Basel, 95, 201–2
Basie, Count, 17, 85, 106, 124, 129, 131, 153, 218
"Battle Hymn of the Republican," 147
"Baubles, Bangles, and Beads," 134, 140, 141, 179
Beat the Band (movie), 12–13
Bells Are Ringing, 170–71, 176, 177–78, 179–80, 187
Benjamin, Joe, 138, 139–40, 146–47, 149, 152
Bennett, John, 44–45, 47–48
Berkeley Community Theatre, 103, 141
"Bernie's Tune," 50, 51, 52–53, 54*f*, 55*f*, 58–61, 96, 100*f*, 100, 101*f*, 119–20, 120*f*, 121*f*, 123, 124, 139, 160, 165, 168
"Between the Devil and the Deep Blue Sea," 157
"Bike Up the Strand," 136
"Birdhouse," 11–12, 15
"Birth of the Blues," 134, 139–40
"Black Nightgown," 163, 202, 205
"Blueport," 165–66, 166*f*, 168, 169, 171, 178–79, 194–95, 204, 218–19
"Blues For Tiny," 107, 109*f*
"Blues Going Up," 106, 106*f*
"Blues in Time," 147
Bock, Richard, 45, 47, 51, 61, 66, 71–73, 74, 81, 83–84, 85, 87, 91, 94, 105, 153–54, 155
"Body and Soul," 147, 202
Boston, 102–3, 167
  Storyville Club, 91, 117, 134, 137–38, 139, 168, 173
  Symphony Hall, 122
Boyd, Jeffie Lee, 64, 83, 85
"Bread and Wine," 181
"Broadway," 30, 75, 119, 126, 194
Brookmeyer, Bob, 39, 42, 89–91, 93, 95, 96, 102, 103, 104, 123, 129, 134, 138, 139–41, 150, 165, 168, 170, 209, 211, 212*f*, 217*f*
  and Concert Jazz Band, 136–37, 188–89, 190–91, 192–93, 194, 196–99, 197*f*, 198*f*, 203–4
  interaction with Mulligan, 96–97, 99*f*, 126, 127*f*, 134–36, 136*f*, 137*f*, 141, 209, 214, 216–19, 220
  Leaves Quartet, 97, 141, 153–54
  Mulligan Sextet, 105, 108–14, 117, 120–22, 124–25, 125*f*, 128–29, 131–33
  on piano, 213, 216–19
Brown, Clifford, 117, 118
Brown, Ray, 150
Brubeck, Dave, 53–56, 59, 89–90, 94, 102–4, 115, 116–17, 122, 129, 141, 146–47, 165–66, 214
"Budo," 26, 27
Bunker, Larry, 73–75, 81–83, 105, 108, 110, 117
"Bweebida Bobbida," 35–36, 37*f*, 38*f*, 134, 135*f*, 136*f*, 141, 188–89, 195, 199, 202

Candoli, Conte, 199, 203
Capitol (record company), 18, 22–23, 26–27, 30–31, 77, 82, 86
"Carioca," 58–60, 72
Carisi, Johnny, 17, 19–20
"Carson City Stage," 82
Castiac, CA, Wayside Honor Rancho (prison), 86
"Catch as Catch Can," 164, 165*f*, 168
CBS
  Camera 3 (TV show), 128–29
  (Radio network), 4, 5, 6, 129
  Timex All Star Jazz Festival, 160
"Chelsea Bridge," 184
"Cherry," 82
Chicago, 1, 3, 33, 103, 131, 149, 151, 179
  Modern Jazz Room, 126
  Orchestra Hall, 122
  Sutherland Hotel, 200–1
Clark, Buddy, 181, 182*f*, 185, 192–93, 195, 199, 203
Clarke, Kenny, 32, 156
Claxton, William, 183
Cleveland, 103, 151
  Loop Lounge, 117–18
Cohn, Al, 33, 34, 36, 153, 189, 194, 205
Collins, Dick, 89
Collins, Herb, 7

Collins, Junior, 17, 19
Coltrane, John, 132–33, 144
Columbia (record company), 6, 14, 94, 117, 139, 165, 169–70, 171*f*, 214
Comden, Betty, 170
"Come Out, Come Out, Wherever You Are," 97, 141
"Come Rain or Come Shine," 202, 204
Concert in Jazz, A (album), 207–8
Concert Jazz Band, The (album), 199
Condon, Eddie, 34, 99, 168
Connor, Chris, 131, 138, 143, 161, 168, 189
Copenhagen, 201
"Cottontail," 184
"Crazy Day," 153
Criss, Sonny, 47
Crow, Bill, 35, 36*f*, 120, 123–25, 125*f*, 126, 127*f*, 128–29, 131–32, 133–34, 138, 139, 158, 159-60, 161–62, 163–65, 167*f*, 169, 170, 171*f*, 174, 177, 178–80, 209, 211, 212*f*, 213, 214–215, 216–18, 217*f*
  and Benny Goodman, 212–13, 216–18
  and Concert Jazz Band, 203–4, 205, 209
Curtis, Tony, 181

"Darn That Dream," 218
Davis, Miles, 13, 17–19, 20, 22–25, 26, 27–28, 30–31, 46, 58, 84, 117, 144, 151, 169
  Birth of the Cool, 18, 22–23, 145
  Nonet, 18, 19–20, 22, 23–25, 24*f*, 26, 27–28, 30–31, 32, 34, 36, 42, 59, 73, 78, 153
"Decidedly," 146
Delauney, Charles, 61, 94–96
"Demanton," 126
Desmond, Paul, 104, 122, 141, 146–50, 148*f*, 178, 214–15
Detroit, Baker's Keyboard Lounge, 209
"Disc Jockey Jump," 13, 14*f*, 15, 33, 78, 150, 153
Discovery Records (record label), 45, 73
"Donna Lee," 16
Down Beat, 56, 69–70, 71, 115, 200, 208

Eager, Allen, 32–33, 34–35, 153
Eardley, Jon, 101–2, 105–8, 106*f*, 108*f*, 110, 114, 117–18, 125*f*, 126, 128, 130, 132–33
"Elevation," 17, 131
Ellington, Duke, 6, 28, 34, 83, 85, 99, 102, 104, 111, 119, 126, 146, 165–67, 183-84, 191–92
"Ellington Medley," 111
EmArcy (record company), 117, 119, 123–24, 126, 130–131
Embassy (record company, Denmark), 60
Enevoldsen, Bob, 78, 181–82, 182*f*
Evans, Gil, 16–19, 23, 116

"Fajista," 184
Fantasy (record company), 53–54, 56, 59–61, 65, 67, 69, 70–71, 84, 102, 103, 117, 147
Farmer, Art, 93, 146, 154, 158, 160–64, 164*f*, 165*f*, 165–66, 166*f*, 168–69, 171*f*, 171–72, 172*f*, 174*f*, 174, 177, 178–79, 180, 181, 182*f*, 189
Ferrara, Don, 31, 130, 131, 132, 190, 192, 199
"Festive Minor," 165, 171, 174
"Fine and Mellow," 153
Fitzgerald, Ella, 58, 177, 178
"Five Brothers," 33, 84, 96, 129
"Flash," 81
Follow That Music (movie), 12
"For Bessie," 184
Fort Lauderdale Jazz Festival, 206
"Four and One Moore," 33, 153
"Four Brothers," 13, 33
"Four for Three," 218
Freeman, Russ, 115, 181
"Freeway," 61–62, 63*f*
French Lick Jazz Festival (IN), 168–69
"Frenesi," 107
Fruscella, Tony, 100–1, 100*f*, 101*f*

Garner, Erroll, 45, 47, 115, 129, 131, 168
Gerry Mulligan and the Concert Jazz Band on Tour, (album), 201
Gerry Mulligan Meets Stan Getz (album), 149
Gerry Mulligan Quartet, The (album), 209, 212*f*, 213–14
Gerry Mulligan Songbook, The (album), 153
Gerry Mulligan The Arranger (album), 139

"Get Happy," 71, 72
Getz, Stan, 23, 31, 33, 71, 74, 89, 102–4, 123, 132, 141, 149–50, 165
Gillespie, Dizzy, 16, 26, 45, 46, 78, 85, 156, 169, 194
Gitler, Ira, 26, 34–35, 161
Giuffre, Jimmy, 13, 33, 130, 169–70, 189
"Give Me the Simple Life," 158
Glaser, Joe, 122
Gleason, Ralph J., 56, 69, 84–85, 214
"Godchild," 22–25, 24*f*, 29, 35, 71, 73, 81
Goodman, Benny, 4, 6, 99, 200, 212–13, 215
Gordon, Dexter, 32, 50
Graas, John, 45
Graettinger, Bob, 30, 42
Graham, Barbara, 161–62, 175
Granz, Norman, 10, 102, 103–4, 107, 115, 147, 149, 150, 165, 177, 178, 184–85, 188, 191, 192, 196, 199, 202–3, 213, 217
  Sells Verve, 207, 213
Gray, Wardell, 32, 50, 74
Great South Bay Jazz Festival, 168–69
Green, Adolph, 170
Green, Freddie, 152, 153
Grimes, Henry, 152, 153, 154–55, 157, 158, 160-61, 171–72, 177

"Half Nelson," 84
Hamilton, Chico (Foreststorn), 41, 46, 47–49, 56, 58–59, 71, 72–73, 74, 78, 81, 96, 105–7, 126, 131, 151
  Drum kit, 50–51
Hampton, Lionel, 50, 115, 157, 160–61
Harte, Richard, 51
Hawkins, Coleman, 153, 156, 161, 214
Heath, Percy, 117, 130
Hendricks, Jon, 157, 160, 176
Hentoff, Nat, 146, 153, 183, 184–85
Herman, Woody, 11, 33, 85, 130
Hermosa Beach, Lighthouse Club, 43, 45
Hodeir, André, 94, 96
Hodges, Johnny, 119, 180–81, 184, 185–86, 187, 192
Holiday, Billie, 50, 101, 129, 153, 182
Holliday, Judy, 170, 176, 177–78, 179–80, 183, 186, 190, 193, 195, 206
  illness, 200–1, 205–6
  vocal album, 206, 208
Holman, Bill, 43, 153, 189, 190–92, 202
Horne, Lena, 50, 73, 78
"How About You," 157
"How High The Moon," 6–8, 7*f*, 8*f*, 12

"I Can't Believe That You're in Love with Me," 75
"I Can't Get Started," 84, 178
"Ide's Side," 35, 84
"Igloo," 131
"I Know, Don't Know How," 110, 114, 112*f*, 209, 210*f*
"I'll Remember April," 75
"I May Be Wrong," 33, 84
"I'm Beginning to See the Light," 84
"I Mean You," 145, 146
"I'm Gonna Go Fishin'," 191, 195, 196
"In a Mellow Tone," 184
Ind, Peter, 31
"Indiana," 6, 8, 11, 12*f*
"Irresistible You," 47
Isola, Frank, 89, 91, 96, 97, 100, 103, 105, 119
"Israel," 19
"It Don't Mean a Thing, if it Ain't Got That Swing," 111, 155–57
I Want To Live! (movie), 161–63, 164*f*, 175, 202

Jackson, Chubby, 33
Jackson, Milt, 130
Jazz at the Philharmonic (JATP), 10, 52, 92–93, 102, 103–4, 140, 173, 177, 188, 213
  European tour, 1959, 178–79
Jazz Concerto Grosso (album), 150–51
Jazz on a Summer's Day (movie), 164, 169
"Jeru," 22, 23–24, 27, 35, 61–62, 84
"Jive at Five," 219
Johnson, Gus, 209, 211, 212*f*, 213, 217–18, 217*f*
Johnson, J. J., 31, 119
Jolly, Pete, 163
Jones, Eddie, 124, 153
Jones, Jo, 106, 124, 153

Jones, Quincy, 161
"Just in Time," 170, 178

Kalamazoo, Michigan, 1–2
St. Augustine's School, 2
Karusell (record company, Sweden), 60
Kay, Connie, 117, 130
Keepnews, Orrin, 143–44, 145, 146
Kennedy, Charles, 12, 34
Kenton, Stan, 42–43, 62, 74, 84, 86
Kerouac, Jack, 179
Kilgallen, Dorothy, 116, 126–27, 129, 130–31, 188, 191
Konitz, Lee, 16–17, 19, 20, 22–23, 28, 30–31, 32, 34, 43, 78, 82, 87, 129–30, 140, 149, 151–52, 153–54
recording with Mulligan, 74–75, 90, 149, 153
Krupa, Gene, 3, 8–9, 10, 11–12, 12*f*, 13, 14*f*, 14–15, 77, 78, 91–92, 94, 118, 129, 160, 168, 177, 178
album of Mulligan arrangements, 15
on film, 12–13
interest in classical music, 10–11, 13

"Lady Be Good," 75, 76*f*
"Lady Chatterley's Mother," 205
"Lady is a Tramp, The," 69, 100, 119–20
Lambert, Dave, 157, 159–60
Lambert, Hendricks and Ross, 157, 160, 176
"Laura," 96–97, 98*f*, 99*f*, 141
Lawrence, Elliot, 3–7, 7*f*, 8*f*, 8–11, 15, 18, 31, 35–36, 39, 42, 86, 115, 131, 139
archive (University of Wyoming), 6–7, 37*f*
Orchestra, 6–9, 29
recording of Mulligan arrangements, 9, 11
use of French horn, 5
Lesser, Leo, Jr., 104, 107
"Let There Be Love," 157
Levey, Stan, 150
Levitt, Al, 31
Levy, Lou, 150
Lewis, John, 19–20, 21*f*, 31, 130
Lewis, Mel, 180–81, 184, 185, 193, 194, 199, 201, 204, 213
"Limelight" ("Limelite"), 69, 107
"Line for Lyons," 54, 59–60, 60*f*, 126, 127*f*, 128, 129, 147, 148*f*
"Little Girl Blue," 106
"Lollypop," 131
London, Royal Festival Hall, 139
Los Angeles, 39, 41, 65–66, 102–3, 158
331 (club), 74
L.A.P.D., 83
Ambassador Hotel (Cocoanut Grove), 44
Civic Light Opera, 177–78
Cottage Italia, 46
Crescendo (club), 77–78
Embassy Theatre, 90
Gold Star Studios, 56, 61, 62, 82
Haig Club, 44–45, 46, 47–48, 51, 54–56, 67, 70, 71, 72–73, 74–75, 82, 83–84, 85, 91, 104, 141
Hollywood Bowl, 140, 141, 192, 193
Palladium, 74
Radio Recorders (studio), 68–69
Renaissance Club, 180, 185, 187
Shrine Auditorium, 103
Surf Club, 73
Tiffany Club, 46, 89
Trade Winds Club, 47
United Recorders (studio), 185
"Lost in the Stars," 214, 215*f*
"Love in New Orleans," 213–14, 218
"Love Me or Leave Me," 96
"Lover Man," 75
"Lullaby of the Leaves," 51, 100–1, 140
Lyons, Jimmy, 59, 169

Madden, Gail, 30, 31, 32, 36*f*, 39, 41–43, 62–64, 85, 92, 114, 123
"Mainstream," 124
"Making Whoopee," 82, 96, 107, 123
Mandel, Johnny, 162–63, 175, 202
Manne, Shelly, 43, 105, 141, 163
"Manoir de mes rêves, Le," 194–95
Marion, Ohio, 1

McKibbon, Al, 31
McPartland, Marian, 123, 138
Meldonian, Dick, 190, 199
Metronome, 4, 23, 70, 177, 200
MGM (record label), 207
Milan, 124, 201
Miller, Bernie, 52
Miller, Bill, 77
Miller, Glenn, 10
Mitchell, Red, 46, 47, 81, 90, 96, 97, 100, 105–6, 107–9, 114, 117, 119, 123–24, 130, 139, 163, 166, 181
  bass solos, 106–7, 106*f*, 109*f*, 110–11, 111*f*
Modern Jazz Quartet (MJQ), 130
Mondragon, Joe, 46, 47, 75, 78
Monk, Thelonious, 32, 93, 117, 143–46, 153, 161, 169
Monterey Jazz Festival, 59, 169, 196, 215
"Moonlight in Vermont," 69, 121, 179
Moore, Brew, 29, 33, 34, 35, 85
Morgan, Alun, 97
Morrison, Peck, 118, 119, 122, 123–24, 133
"Motel," 82–83, 96, 139, 174, 201–2
"Move," 20–22, 21*f*, 26, 27
"Mud Bug," 119, 126
"Mullennium," 139
Mulligan, Arlyne Brown, 30, 85–86, 90, 91–92, 92*f*, 94, 97, 101–2, 114, 116, 117, 122, 130, 138, 140–41
Mulligan, George, 1–2
Mulligan, Gerry, 36*f*, 92*f*, 138, 140–41, 171*f*, 182*f*, 212*f*, 217*f*
  alto saxophone, 10, 12–13, 14
  arranging for Kenton, 42–43, 62
  arranging for Krupa, 9–10, 11–12, 12*f*, 13– 15, 14*f*, 15
  arranging for Lawrence, 6–9, 7*f*, 8*f*, 11, 17, 35–36
  arranging for Thornhill, 16, 17, 18, 22–23, 29, 93
  and Bob Weinstock, 32–34
  baritone saxophone, 2, 6–7, 10, 13, 22–23, 34, 41–42, 78, 140, 194, 200, 205
  and Chet Baker, 46, 47–48, 51, 52–53, 53*f*, 54*f*, 55*f*, 71–72, 87, 102, 114–15, 116–17
  Concert Jazz Band, 13, 34, 121–22, 180–81, 188–209, 197*f*, 198*f*, 211, 219
  Early life, 1–3
  on film, 12–13, 161–62, 163–64, 164*f*, 175, 179–80, 181, 182*f*
  First Quartet, 22, 23, 28, 31–32, 41, 47–48, 49–50, 51, 57–58, 62*f*, 68*f*, 69–70, 71, 82, 87
  heroin addiction, 29, 39, 46, 64, 73, 83
  interaction with Brookmeyer, 96–97, 126, 127*f*, 134–36, 136*f*, 137*f*, 141, 209, 210*f*, 214, 217–19, 220
  jail, 86
  and Miles Davis, 19–20, 22–25, 29
  piano playing, 81–82, 125, 125*f*, 132, 136, 178, 218
  Second Quartet, 39, 89–91, 95–96, 101–2, 104, 105, 128–29, 131
  sextet, 105, 107–8, 110, 110*f*, 117–18, 121*f*, 125*f*, 126–28, 130, 131–32
  and Stan Getz, 33, 71, 102–4, 149–50
  tentet(te), 35–39, 38*f*, 42, 75, 77, 78, 79*f*, 81–82, 86–87, 90
  use of French horn, 7–8, 36
Mulligan, Louise, 1–2
Mulligan, Reed Brown, 130–31, 141
Mulligan Meets Monk (album), 143, 145–46
"Mulligan's Too," 32, 34–35
"My Funny Valentine," 55–58, 57*f*, 84, 96, 128, 139–40, 170, 174, 199, 202

Navy Swings, The (radio program), 173–74, 177, 214
"Nearness of You, The," 96
Newark, Mosque Theatre, 103
Newport Jazz Festival, 98, 100–101, 105, 116–17, 126–28, 140, 144, 146, 161, 163–68, 193–95, 206, 207, 214
"News From Blueport," 165–67, 167*f*, 171
New York, 16, 150
  52nd Street, 16, 18
  A and R Studios, 219
  Apex Studios, 33
  Apollo Theatre, 31

Basin Street (club), 91–93, 116, 118–19, 121–23, 124, 126
Basin Street East (club), 188, 189–90, 191
Basin Street West (club), 214
Birdland (club), 30–31, 206–7, 211, 213
Carnegie Hall, 103, 115, 122, 144, 146
Central Park, 35, 36*f*, 77, 130, 140, 143
Cinemart Studio, 33
Club 43 (Queens), 31
Columbia University, 169
Composer (club), 138
Don José's (rehearsal hall), 34
Five Spot, 144
Freedomland (Bronx), 207
Harlem Jazz Festival, 207
Hickory House, 123
Hunter College, 201
Lewisohn Stadium, 167, 195
Lyn Oliver's studio, 188
Museum of Modern Art, 214
Nola Studios, 117–18
Open Door (club), 101
Paramount Hotel, 39
Plaza Sound, 191, 195
Randall's Island, 129, 179
Roseland Theater, 92
Royal Roost (club), 17, 19, 20, 22–23, 25, 30, 32, 33, 92
Shubert Theatre, 176
Town Hall, 169, 173
Village Vanguard, 176, 191, 192, 195, 202–5, 209, 211, 219
Webster Hall, 208
"Nights at the Turntable," 107, 119
"Night Watch," 163
Norgran (record company), 103
Norman, Gene, 77, 83–84, 85, 86, 91

O'Day, Anita, 126, 129, 152
O'Grady, John Edward, 83
"Ontet," 81, 124–26
"Open Country," 136, 137*f*, 139, 217–18
"Ornithology," 12
Ottison, Ted, 46
"Out of this World," 195

Pablo (Record company), 217
Pacific Jazz (record company), 41, 50, 51, 53, 56, 61, 62*f*, 65, 68*f*, 69–70, 74, 82, 84, 86, 90, 94, 105, 111, 117, 134, 149, 153–54, 200
Page, Walter, 124
Paris, 144, 156–57, 165, 201, 202, 204–5, 216–18
L'Olympia, 124, 213, 216–18
Salle Pleyel, 94–95, 96–97, 129, 218
Salon Du Jazz, 94, 96
Parker, Charlie, 11–12, 17, 18, 19, 26, 34, 45, 85, 107, 108, 156
and Chet Baker, 46–47, 48*f*
"Parker's Mood," 19
Pasadena, Civic Auditorium, 83
Payne, Sonny, 124
Pell, Dave, 46, 65
Pennsauken (NJ), Red Hill Inn, 139, 152, 189, 193, 206
Pepper, Art, 43, 73, 181–82
Perkins, Bill, 181
Peterson, Oscar, 149
Pettiford, Oscar, 109, 118, 178
Philadelphia, 2, 3–4, 18, 29, 91, 103, 122
Academy of Music, 94, 122
Blue Note (club), 94
Pep's (club), 193
Philadelphia Orchestra, 5
Showboat (club), 209
WCAU Radio, 2, 4, 5
West Philadelphia Catholic High School, 2
Philips (record company), 126, 219
"Piano Blues," 107, 213
Playboy, 205
"Polka Dots and Moonbeams," 111
"Ponciana," 71, 72
Powell, Bud, 16, 30, 58
Prestige (record company), 32, 33–34, 35, 41, 77, 84, 153, 161
Previn, André, 105, 180, 181, 187, 218

Quill, Gene, 195, 196, 199, 202

Raph, Alan, 189, 192, 199, 201, 202–3, 204
Rat Race, The (movie), 181, 187, 200

"Red Door, The" 110, 119, 122
Reider, Jim, 192, 204
Renaud, Henri, 94
"Reunion," 154–55
Reunion With Chet Baker (album), 154–55
Rhythm (record company, France), 96
Rich, Buddy, 143, 214
Riverside (record company), 143, 145
Roach, Max, 17, 19, 22, 29, 31, 117, 118, 131
"Rocker," 78, 82
Rodney, Red, 6, 9, 12, 17
Rogers, Shorty, 35, 43–44, 84, 105, 124
Rollins, Sonny, 161, 169, 177, 202
Rome, 178, 179
Rosolino, Frank, 162–63, 164*f*
Ross, Annie, 153–54, 155–60, 169, 176, 195
"Round Midnight," 117
Rowles, Jimmy, 46, 47, 82, 180, 184, 185
Rugolo, Pete, 43
Rumsey, Howard, 43
Rundell, Tommy, 46
Russell, Curley, 20
Russell, George, 183, 208
"Rustic Hop," 137
Ruther, Wyatt, 214

San Diego, 105, 107
San Francisco, 53, 58–59, 67, 69, 90–91, 149
  Black Hawk (club), 53, 56, 61, 68, 71, 91, 172–73, 177, 196, 199
  Downbeat (club), 90
  Jazz Workshop, 177
  Longshore Auditorium, 196
  Municipal Auditorium, 103
Sauter-Finegan Orchestra, 122
Savoy (record company), 19
Schuller, Gunther, 31
Seattle World's Fair, 213
Severinsen, Doc, 206, 211
"Sextet," 75
Shad, Bob, 117
"Shady Side," 186
Shank, Bud, 162–63, 164*f*
Shearing, George, 82, 94, 126, 129, 151, 160, 207, 214
Sheldon, Jack, 181
Short, Bobby, 44–45, 47
Siegelstein, Sandy, 31
Silver, Horace, 160, 216
"Simbah," 82
Simon, George T., 4, 35
Sims, Zoot, 33–35, 105, 108, 110–11, 114, 117, 121–22, 124–25, 125*f*, 126, 128, 132–33, 153
  in Concert Jazz Band, 190, 199, 202
Smith, Carson, 56–58, 57*f*, 67–68, 71–72, 73, 75, 82, 85, 91
Smith, Paul, 46
Smith, Vern, 46
"Soft Shoe," 107, 122
Sound of Jazz (TV program), 153, 182
Souplet, Jacques, 95
"So What (Hoo Hah)" 34
Spanier, Muggsy, 46, 85
"Spring is Sprung," 178, 213, 218–19
Spring is Sprung (album), 219
"Stand Still," 148
"Stardust," 155, 156*f*
State College (PA), 138
Stockholm, 139, 178
Stockton, CA, 105
"Storyville Story," 134
Strictly From Dixie (radio program), 100
Styne, Jule, 170
Subterraneans, The (movie), 179–82, 182*f*, 185, 186, 187, 200, 218
Sulieman, Idrees, 117–18
Sullivan, Maxine, 168
"Summer's Over," 208
"Sunday," 184
Sunkel, Phil, 150, 190
"Sweet and Lovely," 120, 146
"Sweet and Slow," 194, 195, 199
Swing (record company, France), 60–61, 62*f*
"Swing House," 43, 84

"Taking a Chance on Love," 81
Tatum, Art, 46, 51, 99, 131
Taylor, Billy, 101, 139
"Tea For Two," 84, 117, 146
Terry, Clark, 132, 136, 203–4, 205, 206, 211
"That Old Feeling," 134, 150, 179
"Things Are Looking Down," 181, 218

"This Can't Be Love," 150
"This is Always," 158
"This Time The Dream's On Me," 157
Thompson, Lucky, 119
Thornhill, Claude, 5, 7, 15, 16–17, 18–19, 22–24, 29, 72–73, 93, 110–11, 123
  Use of French horn, 5, 7, 15
Time (magazine), 70, 73, 75
Tirro, Frank, 22–23
"Too Marvelous For Words," 74
Torin, "Symphony Sid," 33
Toronto, Massey Hall, 131, 134
Travis, Nick, 193, 199
Trenner, Donn, 46, 47
Tristano, Lennie, 26, 30–31, 130
Tucker, Tommy, 2–3, 86
Turetsky, Phil, 47, 50, 51, 55, 61, 74, 75, 81, 90
"Turnstile," 69, 153
"Twisted," 157
"Two By Two," 181
Two of a Mind (album), 147

Ulanov, Barry, 22–23
University of Pennsylvania, 3–4
Urso, Phil, 29, 31, 81, 115
"Utter Chaos," 54, 141, 160, 195

Van Gelder, Rudy, 61, 71
"Varsity Drag," 84
Vaughan, Sarah, 94, 189, 207
"Venus De Milo," 23, 153
Verve (record company), 146, 149, 184, 188, 191, 195, 199, 201–2, 207–8, 209, 211–12, 212*f*
Vinnegar, Leroy, 180
Vogue (record company, France), 61, 95
Vogue (record company, UK), 60–61
Voice of America (radio program), 138, 194, 214

Waldron, Mal, 153
"Walkin' Shoes," 62, 64–65, 66*f*, 78, 79*f*, 82, 96, 125, 139, 174, 179, 194
Wallington, George, 22, 24*f*, 29, 34, 71, 73, 81
Ware, Wilbur, 143, 144, 146
Warren, Earl, 153
Warrington, Johnny, 2–3, 4, 5–6
Washington, D.C., 214
  Library of Congress, 8, 24–25, 41
  National Guard Armory, 122
  Patio Lounge, 121
Washington, Dinah, 17
Wasserman, Herb, 116
Watkins, Ralph, 17, 92
Webster, Ben, 153, 161, 180–81, 182–85, 187
Wein, George, 117, 128, 134, 168, 173, 206
Weinstock, Bob, 32, 33–35, 161
West Berlin, 201
"Western Reunion," 107, 110*f*, 111, 111*f*, 114, 119, 126
"What Is There to Say?," 170, 171, 174, 178
"What's The Rush?," 186
"When Your Lover Has Gone," 154
White, Bobby, 56
Whitlock, Bob, 30, 41, 46, 48, 50, 51, 52, 56, 63, 67, 96
"Who's Got Rhythm," 184
"Why Are We Afraid," 181
Wiggins, Gerry, 131
Williamson, Claude, 185
Wilson, Billy, 46
Wilson, Russ, 15
Wilson, Shadow, 143, 144, 145
Wilson, Teddy, 101
Winchell, Walter, 200
Winding, Kai, 29, 73, 85, 117, 119, 131, 138
"Wintersong," 147
Winther, Tony, 203
Witherspoon, Jimmy, 180, 185, 187
Woode, Jimmy, 218–19, 220
Woods, Phil, 15

"Yardbird Suite," 16, 107, 108*f*, 114, 140
Young, Lester, 29, 129, 153
"Young Blood," 42
"You Took Advantage of Me," 196, 197*f*, 198*f*

Zandy, Ed, 16
Zurich, 218, 219–20
Zwerin, Mike, 22, 29